Resource-Constrained Economies:
The North American Dilemma

Resource-Constrained Economies: The North American Dilemma

Based on material presented at the
34th annual meeting of the
Soil Conservation Society of America,
July 29-August 1, 1979, Chateau
Laurier, Ottawa, Ontario

Published by the
Soil Conservation Society of America
Ankeny, Iowa

Library of Congress Catalog Card Number 80-16502

ISBN 0-935734-05-8

$8.50

Library of Congress Cataloging in Publication Data

Resource-constrained economies.

  Includes index.
    1. Natural resources—North America—Congresses.
2. Conservation of natural resources—North America—
Congresses. 3. Land use—North America—Congresses.
4. Environmental policy—North America—Congresses.
I. Soil Conservation Society of America.
HC95.R47   333.7'097   80-16502
ISBN 0-935734-05-8

Soil Conservation Society of America
7515 N.E. Ankeny Road
Ankeny, Iowa 50021

President: Gerald R. Calhoun

President Elect: Jesse L. Hicks

Vice President: Robert C. Baum

Second Vice President: Chris J. Johannsen

Treasurer: H. Lynn Horak

Council: Elmer E. Offerman, R. Larry Sandifer, Carl V. Thompson, Jerry V. Mannering, Howard M. Hughes, Allen L. Fisk, Earl Burnett, Richard F. Sanders, David R. Cressman, William C. Moldenhauer

Staff: William H. Greiner, Executive Vice President; Larry D. Davis, Administrative Assistant; Tim Kautza, Program Assistant; Max Schnepf, Editor; James L. Sanders, Assistant Editor

The Soil Conservation Society of America, founded in 1945, is a nonprofit scientific and educational association dedicated to advancing the science and art of good land use. Its 15,000 members worldwide include researchers, administrators, educators, planners, technicians, legislators, farmers and ranchers, and others with a profound interest in the wise use of land and related natural resources. Most academic disciplines concerned with the management of land and related natural resources are represented.

Opinions, interpretations, and conclusions expressed in this book are those of the authors.

This book is based on material presented at the 34th annual meeting of the Soil Conservation Society of America, held July 29-August 1, 1979, at the Chateau Laurier, Ottawa, Ontario. The following members of the Society served on the annual meeting program core committee: David R. Cressman (chairman), Kitchener, Ontario; Neil Sampson (vice-chairman), Washington, D.C.; Ira C. Brown, Ottawa, Ontario; J. P. Bruce, Ottawa, Ontario; Julian Dumanski, Ottawa, Ontario; and Max Peterson, Washington, D.C. Other members of the full program committee included chairpersons of the Society's resource conservation divisions: Frederick L. Gilbert (Soil Resources), Syracuse, New York; Eugene J. Pope (Water Resources), Lincoln, Nebraska; L. Duane Bartee (Air Resources), Lincoln, Nebraska; W. Curtis Sharp (Plant Resources), West Chester, Pennsylvania; Chester A. McConnell (Fish and Wildlife Resources), Lawrenceburg, Tennessee; Beverly J. Miller (Environmental Conservation Education), Salt Lake City, Utah; Robert E. Craft (Land Use Planning), Champaign, Illinois; Donn DeCoursey (Erosion and Sedimentation), Oxford, Mississippi; William L. Powers (Waste Management), Manhattan, Kansas; Clarence M. Maesner (Outdoor Recreation), Portland, Oregon; and Gerald E. Schuman (Surface Mine Reclamation), Cheyenne, Wyoming.

Contents

Foreword

At the core of the resource scarcity issue currently is oil. The modern world has become enormously dependent upon the petroleum industry, not only for liquid fuel, but for a wide range of uses, from drugs to diapers, from fertilizers to fashions. Oil is a marvelously flexible resource, and we have used it lavishly. Years from now, people will look back and see the oil consumption pattern as a big roller coaster. We used a little at the end of the last century, then built demand with the ubiquitous automobile, oil furnaces in our houses, oil-fired thermal generating plants, diesel trains, jet planes, and all those special uses, like petrochemicals and even charcoal briquettes. Except for its basic use as a portable liquid fuel for cars and planes, all the increase has been from substitutions: for coal and wood in space heating, for natural nutrient cycles in soil, for coal in railway engines, for water in electrical generating and even in water mills, for natural fibers in clothing, and so on.

Now we are on the dizzy descent from the top of the roller coaster; and just as we substituted all the way up, we will substitute all the way down.

There are two somewhat different forms of substitution here. First, we can substitute for energy. We can drive smaller cars, turn the heat down, give the air conditioner a rest, use manual can openers, walk, bicycle, insulate our houses and ourselves, sweat a little in summer and shiver a bit in winter, and we can use such products as wood instead of steel or aluminum, thus reducing energy needs in production.

Second, we can substitute for oil. We can return to natural fibers for textiles; shift to coal and wood-based feedstocks for the chemical industries; make gaseous and liquid fuels from coal, wood, and straw; burn municipal wastes to generate electricity; and tap the potential of low-head hydro power.

It is evident that this substitution process will depend to a much greater extent than before on renewable resources, notably forests, soil, and water.

This substitution for oil, coming madly down from the heights of consumption, is a warning to us of what can happen in the case of other resources. In theory, all nonrenewable resources must suffer the same fate of eventual depletion, with soaring price increases and forced substitution. It may take 50 years to run out of copper, 100 years to run out of uranium, and 200 years to run out of coal, but the time will come. We can do two things about this. First, we can stretch their useful life by increasing the efficiency of extraction and processing; we can recycle wastes. Second, we can substitute renewables.

But we have to recognize that renewables can get caught up in this too. A resource may be renewable, but that does not mean it is automatically renewing. In the past, we have not done our part to assist nature in renewal. Fisheries and forests in particular have been exploited as mines, as stocks rather than as flows. Indeed, we will not renew the giant redwoods and sequoias of California or the magnificent coastal forest of British Columbia with its 300-year-old firs and cedars. And the ship-mast pines of Nova Scotia and Maine are gone forever also. But we can restore these forests to sustained production.

It is crucial to the national interests of Canada and the United States that we act to restore sustainability to all our renewable resources. At the same time, we must husband our nonrenewable resources through conservation, substitution, and recycling of wastes. The resources are not only our inheritance, which we must pass on to future generations, they are also a major foundation of our prosperity.

With natural resources increasing in value in the future, our economic growth depends on using our resources wisely and on conserving them. In the future, they can be used both as the basis for highly processed products and as substitutes for those nonrenewables that will be increasingly costly and in short supply. But if this is to happen, the resources must be husbanded and managed to ensure continuing supply. We must become good stewards.

As a member of Canada's federal government, I strongly urge a national economic strategy that reflects this conservation of resources, the need to sustain their productivity, and to apply technological innovation to their production and processing.

Of course, the basis for this long-term strategic approach must be the basic productivity of soil and water. If we lose this, our future is grim indeed. I know that we can work together to use our resources less wastefully, more imaginatively, and in a fully sustained fashion so that we can hand our rich resource inheritance—intact and hopefully enhanced—to future generations.

The Honorable John Fraser
Minister of the Environment
Environment Canada

Preface

The mixed economies of North America developed in a climate of ample, even surplus resources. Unrestrained growth and technological advances based on these resources have long been the cornerstones of our economic systems. The public has been conditioned to expect that more—or different—resources will always be available to support any foreseeable level of economic growth. Waste, despoilation, and accelerated consumption have been unpleasant byproducts of this attitude toward unlimited resources.

Frustrated and angered by the lineups at gasoline pumps, the chill of underheated homes in winter, escalating petroleum prices, and ceaseless inflation, the public is beginning to recognize that its resource base can no longer be taken for granted. Limits have suddenly become a reality. As we approach these limits, pressures on our economies intensify and life becomes a little less comfortable.

What adjustments, if any, are needed in our North American economies to cope with this emerging climate of resource constraints? Strongly divergent positions are common among responses to such a question. At one extreme are those who argue that technological innovation and substitution are the key to solving the problem of resource constraints. At the other extreme are those promoting conservation and no-growth economies, people who see innovative technology leading toward greater resource waste, environmental degradation, and fossil fuel dependency. Despite these divergent viewpoints, it seems clear that society cannot ultimately escape the need to make choices among some potentially disagreeable futures. Clearly, we face a dilemma of significant proportions.

The right direction for North American societies probably lies somewhere between these extremes. While growth and technology have in the past spawned undesirable consequences, technology has the potential to improve the quality of life and some growth is needed to maintain jobs and living standards. The challenge is to achieve selective and orderly growth and to channel technological innovation in areas that do not stimulate extensive use of resources or needlessly degrade the environment.

Recognizing that the cumulative influence of these constraints would inevitably necessitate a shift in natural resource management philosophies, the Soil Conservation Society of America adopted the theme "Resource-Constrained Economies: The North American Dilemma" for its 34th annual meeting in Ottawa, Ontario. The goal of the program committee was to confront registrants with the reality of resource constraints, to stimulate a rethinking of traditional resource management policies, and to encourage exploration of a broader range of policy options.

To focus the theme, the program committee identified a number of questions for consideraton by the invited speakers. What are the most significant constraints that resource managers are likely to face in the foreseeable future? Which resources will introduce initially felt constraints, and how will they affect market economy functions? Can public policies in land use, soil and water conservation, water resource policy, energy policy, agricultural programs, or environmental quality improvement help ease the impact of a transition to the resource-constrained economy? How will North America respond to the needs of the people in underdeveloped or resource-poor nations of the world? Will pressures from the developed world continue to restrict the access of poor nations to scarce resources?

This book contains a selection of papers on various dimensions of the problem of resource-constrained economies. The presentations by Jane Yarn and Kenneth Hare develop an overview by identifying the range of emerging constraints. John Livingston uses an analogy of species adaptation to changing environmental conditions to warn us about the necessity of modifying our dependencies on finite resources to enable society to better adjust to a perpetually changing global environment.

Yves Cathelinaud then examines current responses to constraints in the land use arena in Japan and Western European countries. Robert Sugarman and David Unger review two current institutional approaches for responding to constraints in the management of land, water, and air resources.

The papers presented in two sets of concurrent sessions examine specific constraints affecting the management of water, food and fiber, public education, land, energy, and environmental quality. They identify the range of constraints facing managers and offer some innovative suggestions for more effective management strategies.

The conference was planned as a learning experience, but much of what was learned and experienced is not captured in the following papers. Some of the best learning experiences came during a meet-the-press session with the keynote speakers, in a round-table discussion luncheon, in the questions of individual speakers, and in hallway conversations.

Resource management professionals have a major leadership responsibility in helping North American societies find acceptable resolutions to the problems and issues emerging in resource-constrained economies. The Soil Conservation Society of America hopes that publication of these papers can help better equip resource professionals to carry out this responsibility and contribute to better public understanding and constructive dialogue on the issues.

D. R. Cressman
Program Chairman
1979   *Thirty-fourth Annual Meeting*

I. RESOURCE CONSTRAINTS: AN OVERVIEW

1
Resource-constrained economies: A U.S. perspective

Jane Yarn

There was a time, not all that long ago in terms of human history, when this continent's natural resources seemed either inexhaustible or infinitely renewable. This was the basic assumption underlying the European settlement of North America—that the continent's living resources would restore themselves through natural regenerative processes, even when repeatedly depleted. When explorers and colonists first arrived on our shores, they were astonished at the richness and variety of the plant and animal life. John Cabot, exploring Newfoundland in 1497, noted the mast-sized trees that came to the water's edge, and his son, Sebastian, reported that salmon, sole, and codfish were "so abundant as to slow up the advance of the ship" (*3*).

Unlike the native Indian tribes, most of which appear to have had a fairly sophisticated understanding of their relationship with nature, the European settlers arrived in this country with the view that land was a commodity and nature was something to be subdued. And, in fact, the vastness of the continent's natural resources made it possible for nature to absorb this misguided notion for more than a century.

Two views of natural resources

By the middle and late nineteenth century, when our first national forests and national parks were set aside, the wholesale raid on some natural re-

Jane Yarn is a member of the Council on Environmental Quality, Washington, D.C.

sources had become obvious. Land had been overgrazed, overfarmed, overmined, and overtimbered. Out of these excesses, the first national concern over our relationship with nature began to develop, and it seems to have followed two basic lines of thought.

George Perkins Marsh, a great naturalist, published his classic book, *Man and Nature*, in 1864, examining the relationship between man and the earth. The book influenced Carl Schurz, secretary of the interior in the 1870s, and Gifford Pinchot, who founded the U.S. Forest Service in 1898. These men and others who followed them held the view that the wholesale assault on our natural heritage had to end and that nature should be carefully managed, protected, and used.

The other view, meanwhile, began to flow from the thoughts of John Muir, a naturalist and scholar who helped found the Sierra Club in 1864. This view held that natural assets should be preserved and protected, not for their practical value, but for their beauty—for aesthetic reasons.

The conservation and environmental movements in the United States have been guided by these two views: one, that nature should be carefully managed and used, and the other, that nature should be protected and preserved. Even today it is possible to provoke a heated argument between two good environmentalist friends simply by raising the question of use versus preservation.

Concern about the natural environment, whether directed at wise use or preservation, began to make itself felt in the United States during the late nineteenth century and early twentieth century, especially during the presidential terms of Theodore and Franklin Delano Roosevelt. The National Park Service was created; national parks, forests, and waterfowl refuges were set aside; and the Soil Conservation Service was founded to deal with the problems of soil erosion and the abandonment of cropland.

With the publication of *Silent Spring* in 1962, the environmental movement became a potent force for change in the way America and the world at large looks at its natural resources, its environment, and the relationships between land, air, water, and living things. Many of the destructive trends and practices of the past have been halted; much progress has been made in reducing air and water pollution; wetlands, once regarded as useless and fit only for drainage and development, are now protected by federal legislation; water resources, once dammed or channelized indiscriminately, are now recognized as vital and delicate aspects of the human life-support system, which must be protected and prudently managed. The comprehensive water resources policy adopted by the Carter Administration puts the nation's emphasis on such areas as water conservation, improved state-federal cooperation, and improved state planning.

Some alarming trends

Despite successes in some areas, however, a number of alarming trends are continuing and, in some cases, accelerating.

The most urgent and obvious problem is energy. The world's reservoir of petroleum is being depleted by our profligate driving, heating, and air-conditioning habits. The petroleum crisis is real, and it is going to continue as long as the economy of the free world depends so heavily on fossil fuels. The free world simply cannot continue to consume fossil fuels at a growth rate of 3.5 to 5 percent a year; instead, we must learn to make better, more productive use of the fuel that is available until we can make the transition into a society based on renewable energy sources—wind, falling water, ocean temperature gradients, plant material or biomass, and other direct and indirect products of our world's ultimate and virtually inexhaustible energy source, the sun.

President Carter has committed the nation to a goal of obtaining one-fifth of our energy from solar and other renewable sources by the year 2000. But as we move aggressively toward a solar society, we must also begin to use existing energy sources effectively. If we do, it will be possible to cut our energy growth rate substantially without in any way slowing economic growth or progress. In fact, the United States can prosper on much less energy than has been commonly supposed (1). The technology is at hand to wring far more consumer goods and services out of each unit of fuel than we use, whether it be a ton of coal or a barrel of oil. With only a moderate effort to improve energy productivity, our energy consumption in the year 2000 need not exceed current use by more than about 25 percent; with a more determined effort it need not increase by more than 10 to 15 percent.

The achievement of a low energy growth future would largely avoid the very serious environmental and economic difficulties posed by high energy growth:

• Instead of building more than 500 new coal and nuclear power plants by the year 2000, the United States can get by with the 150 or so plants now ordered or under construction—greatly reducing projected pollution, radiation hazards, and land disruption caused by mining and transmission lines.

• Instead of deepening our dependence on unreliable foreign sources of fuel, we can substantially cut oil and gas imports, helping not only our energy security, but our balance of payments as well.

• Instead of investing more and more money in new mines, oil wells, and power plants, we can get the energy we need through conservation and make capital available for investments that generate more jobs and create more benefits for society.

In general, then, despite the short-term annoyances of gas lines, lowered thermostats, and constantly-rising fuel prices, there is reason for optimism about our long-term energy prospects. Solar energy, which, unlike conventional hard technologies, poses little risk to the climate and creates little direct air pollution, no radiation hazards, and no risk of nuclear weapons proliferations is already a serious option with some applications at or near commercial feasibility. Because rapid progress in solar economics is expected to rise, a variety of solar technologies for the production of heat, electricity, and liquid fuels can be made competitive during the coming decade.

And for the period beyond the year 2000, we can now speak of an energy future supported by safe, clean, and renewable sources of energy, efficiently utilized.

But there are other trends that, if left unchecked, could develop into serious threats to our very way of life.

Probably the simplest and perhaps the smartest advice on land was given to us by the American Humorist Will Rogers several decades ago: "Buy it," he said, "They ain't makin' it anymore."

Not only is nobody making land anymore, but we are losing a substantial portion of the land we have, year after year. Between 1960 and 1970, an average of 2,000 acres of land each day was shifted from rural to urban use. Since then, the pace of this shift has increased to the point that recent information from the Soil Conservation Service reveals that the United States is losing its productive agricultural lands at the rate of one-half square mile, or 320 acres, per hour.

Of the three million acres of agricultural land now being lost to other uses each year, one million acres is prime farmland—the most efficient, energy-conserving, environmentally stable land available to us for meeting domestic and international food needs. The pressure to convert prime farmland to other uses is particularly intense because the very factors that make such land ideal for agriculture also make it desirable for residential construction, shopping centers, artificial lakes, and other development.

As our prime agricultural land is lost to other uses, the pressure grows to produce more food and fiber on the land still available for farming. The United States is the major supplier of food for a world whose population will increase by nearly 2.3 billion by the year 2000. The increased food production to feed that population must come from an amount of agricultural land that can only be increased about 5 percent; and most of that increase would have to come from wetlands and forests that have essential biological functions of their own to perform. Wetlands, for example, are the breeding ground and habitat of 80 percent of all commercial fish. Destruction of forests can contribute to an increase in carbon dioxide in the atmosphere, potentially altering the earth's climate.

Our efforts to get more food from the given amount of land available can cause other problems. In the United States, we are beginning to see evidence that the so-called "green revolution" techniques—the application of increased amounts of fertilizer, increased irrigation, multiple croppings, and so forth—are reaching a point of diminishing returns. There are areas in the United States in which crop yields diminish as more and more fertilizer and water are applied. Monocultural techniques are also becoming a matter of concern. Land is not being allowed to lie fallow in order to recover its fertility. Crops are not being rotated. Farms are being plowed from fence row to fence row.

The result of these practices is the continuing degradation of soils due to water and wind erosion. Since 1935, wind and water erosion have effectively destroyed 100 million acres of potential cropland and removed half the topsoil on an additional 100 million acres. The 1977 U.S. Department of Agriculture erosion inventory found that 4.2 billion tons of soil was eroding from agricultural lands each year. Studies throughout the country have found annual soil losses of more than 50 tons an acre in many places.

Increased irrigation also adds salts to our soil faster than we or nature can remove them. The San Joaquin Valley in California, one of the world's most productive agricultural areas, is starting to take on the appearance of a desert. A perched and salt-laden water table is creeping upwards towards the root zone on about 400,000 acres of land.[1] Once it reaches the roots, it will inhibit the ability of plants to absorb moisture and oxygen, and they will die. So far, only about 2,000 to 4,000 acres of cropland in the valley have been affected, but by the year 2020, unless an economical way is found to wash the salt out of the soil, some 1.1 million acres of the San Joaquin's 1.8 million acres of cropland will become unproductive.

The consequences of soil erosion and excessive salinity are well-known. Billions of dollars worth of plant nutrients are lost every year; crop yields are drastically reduced; agricultural runoff pollutes the nation's waters. Pesticides, dissolved solids, nutrients, sediment, organic material, and pathogens from agriculture adversely affect about two-thirds of the river basins in the United States. Neil Sampson, executive vice president of the National Association of Conservation Districts, has stated the seriousness of the problem well: "The strength of the nation comes from the land, and the land is in trouble" (4).

What can our nation do to solve these mutually reinforcing problems of soil erosion and agricultural land conversion before we find ourselves without enough productive land to feed our own country, let alone the rest of the world? We at the President's Council on Environmental Quality (CEQ), as well as other officials throughout the federal government, are seriously concerned about these and other agricultural problems—the need for integrated pest management to replace the indiscriminate use of organic pesticides, the protection of wetlands and forests, the preservation of wildlife— and we are conducting a number of interagency studies in an effort to define the problems and reach some conclusions on how to deal with them.

Some global issues

There are not just national or continental issues but global issues as well that should concern North Americans. CEQ and the State Department are now in the midst of preparing a comprehensive study of projected changes in the world's population, natural resources, and environment between now and the end of this century. This "Global 2000" study, which should be completed by the end of this year, has identified several trends or conditions, which, if allowed to continue, could seriously threaten the ecological,

[1]Sheridan, David. "U.S. Arid Land Problems," an unpublished memorandum dated April 27, 1979.

economic, and political stability of the world. Projections show that the resolute growth of world population, expected to increase by 50 percent to 6.35 billion by the year 2000, and the rising expectations of peoples on all continents are exerting intolerable pressures on a number of ecological systems. Grazing lands are being overgrazed. Crop lands are being over-farmed, mismanaged, and lost by millions of acres annually to desertification. There are indications that we may be taking protein out of the sea at such a rate that established fisheries will be unable to replenish themselves. Even fresh water could become scarce in some parts of the world.

The finding causing the most immediate concern, however, is the head-long destruction of the world's tropical forests. Although hard information on deforestation rates is hard to come by, the Global 2000 study estimates that 20 million hectares of closed forest (forestland with a complete cover of trees) are being lost each year out of a worldwide total of 2.6 billion hectares. If that rate of loss continues—an area roughly half the size of California disappearing each year—the world's closed forests would decline to about 2.1 billion hectares in 2000, causing extensive suffering for tens of millions of people and severe damage to the environment as well.

According to the Global 2000 estimates, almost all of the loss of closed forest is occurring in the tropical and near-tropical regions of Latin America, Africa, South Asia, Southeast Asia, and the Pacific Islands. In temperate forests, on the other hand, cuts are roughly in balance with new growth.

There are several reasons for this disturbing loss of the world's forests: the search for farmland or wood for fuel by growing populations; world demands for timber products; and the increasing demand for beef raised in pastures carved out of the forest. Shifting "slash and burn" cultivation of forests is also responsible for some of the loss.

The environmental consequences of deforestation at this rate are potentially enormous. Trees and other plants help tropical soil hold its nutrients; when the forest cover is lost, exposure to strong sunlight and high temperatures modifies the soil structure and heavy rainfall leaches the nutrients, leaving the soil unsuitable for cultivation within a few years. In some areas where the soil is poor and the cutting extensive, the loss of forest may be permanent. Deforestation also removes natural protection against flooding and destroys habitat for millions of plant and animal species, including many species that directly benefit mankind.

A more speculative but equally serious consequence of forest loss is its possible impact on the world's climate. Removal of the light-absorbing forests could change weather patterns by altering the reflection of light and heat from the earth's surface. Loss of forests, which store half of the carbon in the earth's biomass, could also increase the carbon dioxide concentration in the atmosphere. Some scientists believe that rising carbon dioxide concentrations will cause a warming of the earth toward the poles, possibly resulting in partial melting of the polar ice caps. The consequences of this possibility for world agriculture and coastal communities are not difficult to imagine.

The United States, other nations, and international organizations have taken a number of steps to try to protect and restore world forests, but much more needs to be done. One of the more obvious needs is for better information on global environmental conditions and trends so that, for example, we could have a much firmer hold on the true extent of deforestation and the areas that are most adversely affected.

One of the main goals at the Council on Environmental Quality over the next few years will be to build on the Global 2000 study by encouraging public officials, both in the United States and throughout the world, to broaden their perspectives—not just spatially, so they can think in terms that transcend national boundaries, but temporally, so they think of the world in terms of how it will look 20 or 50 or 100 years from now, not just how it will look at the end of their congressional terms. One of the main reasons for the Global 2000 study was to establish a systematic base for government decision-making over the next 20 years.

The study will show that a number of current policies and programs must be modified, or serious and perhaps unacceptable environmental effects will result. In many ways, the prospects outlined in the study are bleak, but by presenting a bleak case we can dramatize the need for change while there is still time to make changes.

None of the problems I have outlined are insoluble. What is required is the concerted action of professionals, public officials, and concerned citizens throughout the world. Doom is inevitable only if we fail to use our collective wisdom to meet the challenges before us. And if we choose to face these problems and deal with them, the years ahead could be the most exciting and fulfilling of our lives. As the eminent French naturalist, Rene Dubos, has written: "Crises are practially always a source of enrichment and of renewal because they encourage the search for new solutions" (2).

REFERENCES

1. Council on Environmental Quality. 1979. *The good news about energy.* U.S. Government Printing Office, Washington, D.C.
2. Dubos, Rene. 1974. *The humanizing of humans.* Saturday Review: December 13.
3. Kimball, Thomas L., and Raymond E. Johnson. 1978. *The richness of American wildlife.* In H. P. Brokaw [ed.] *Wildlife and America.* U.S. Government Printing Office, Washington, D.C.
4. Sampson, Neil. 1979. *Protecting farmland: The ethical dimension.* National Association of Conservation Districts, Washington, D.C.

2
Climate, soil and agriculture:
The uncertain future

F. Kenneth Hare

Climate is a resource. The major energy source for man is not oil, not coal, not hydro, but solar energy, which enters the human economy through photosynthesis. Food, natural fibers, and timber depend on this remarkable feat of catalytic chemistry that can hardly be duplicated in the laboratory. Carbon comes from the atmosphere, water from rain via the soil, and energy from sunlight. The heat of the atmosphere and oceans permits plants of all kinds to grow. These things are part of the climatic system that, with the global ecosystem, is the first resource of mankind.

Climate is a resource in two senses. If we adopt the economist's restrictive meaning of the word—that a resource is something scarce that needs to be allocated—the climate that is good for recreation, food production, and other purposes will command a high price. It costs more to buy a farm in the Corn Belt than on the Canadian prairies. Part of that higher price pays for the superior climate. In a more general sense, climate and its elements are a set of resources that we learn to exploit. They are also hazards that we must learn to avoid. Whichever usage one follows, climate has value; and that value may change.

Nature and stability of climate

Climate denotes the habitual state and behavior of the atmosphere. The ocean and the soil also have a climate in the same sense, as does the living

---

F. Kenneth Hare is provost of Trinity College, Toronto, Ontario.

cover of the earth (the bioclimate). Climate varies from place to place, but is fairly stable in time. In layman's terms, it is the expectation of weather. We know from experience that one decade is much like the next as long as we remain in one place. Even successive centuries are much alike. Weather comes and goes, but climate goes on all the time. The general view is that climate can be taken for granted. It is predictable enough for us to disregard it once we have adapted our technology accordingly.

To define climate professionally, we choose an arbitrary reference period, usually 30 years. Within this period we compute mean values for the chief parameters, such as temperature and rainfall. We also compute measures of the variability within the reference period. The package of mean values and variability statistics makes up the climate that is characteristic of the past few decades rather than the present time. We use this package with the confidence that things will continue as they were.

But this may not be so. The past record shows that climatic variation is a reality on many time scales. Climate clearly depends on where we choose to put the reference period and on how long we make it. Past climatic variation includes:

• A sequence of glacial and interglacial epochs over the past two million years in which prolonged glacial epochs tended to occur about 100,000 years apart. We currently are about 10,000 years into a warm interglacial period. Some past interglacial periods have only lasted this long.

• Striking changes within the past 15,000 years. From 15,000 to 8,000 B.P. (before present), there was rapid melting of the colossal continental glaciers that covered Europe and northern North America, though Antarctica and Greenland remained ice-covered. Since then conditions have been much warmer. After about 5,000 B.P., conditions became slightly cooler and in some areas drier than before. Civilization is a creature of the past 10,000 years. Our technological history has been colored by adaptation to this relatively benign post-glacial climate.

• Within the past millennium there was a warm medieval phase, a harshly colder episode between the fifteenth and eighteenth centuries (the Little Ice Age), and a slow recovery to mildness in our own century.

• Within our own century, northern hemisphere temperatures rose slowly to a peak in 1938; since then the climate has slowly cooled by about 0.5 degrees Celsius on a hemispheric average. Since 1965 the cooling has been less marked, and some observers claim to detect a reversal. The southern hemisphere may have been getting warmer for some decades.

A large body of empirical research lies behind these statements, which is adequately summarized elsewhere (2, 4, 10). They are no longer seriously in dispute. What they show is that climate is indeed a fairly stable system. Changes in the past 10,000 years have been quite small and even smaller in our own century. The change in mean air temperature for the northern hemisphere since 1938 has been less than the usual local warming between 10 and 11 in the morning. What, then, is all the fuss about?

The answer lies in variability, rather than variation. In the 1970s a series of major shocks was administered to the world's economy by large anomalies in climate. Price changes accompanied these impacts, and nothing impresses people more than a sharp rise in the price of food or energy. Part of the inflation since 1972 has been due to climate-related crop and fishing failures on a scale unknown since the 1930s. The events of 1972 alone, such as drought in Africa, India, the Soviet Union, and Australia and failure of the Peruvian anchovy harvest due to ocean circulation changes, pushed climatologists from obscurity into the front line.

Climate always has varied, and there is little clear evidence that overall variability has increased. Even the most extreme anomalies of the 1970s have parallels in earlier events. The Sahelian drought in Africa, for example, had several predecessors over the previous 500 years. What has changed is the vulnerability of the human economy. Pastoral nomads, like the Tuareg and Fulani, had for centuries ridden out each drought by changes in migration, in numbers of livestock, and by endurance (3). Indian peasant cultivators somehow survived countless failures of the monsoon also. We in North America adapted easily to the ferocious winters of the late nineteenth century. But modern man is, in some ways, more vulnerable. Human numbers have increased in areas where food supply is marginal. Old social and economic customs, notably nomadism, have decayed, as have elaborate irrigation works. And in advanced Western societies the rising price of energy, the huge increase in per capita consumption of water, and the demand for indoor comfort have greatly increased our sensitivity to climatic anomalies.

The World Climate Conference of 1979, convened in Geneva by the World Meteorological Organization (WMO), threw much light on this increased sensitivity (14). It was the direct outgrowth of world alarm about food and energy supply and about destructive processes like desertification (itself the subject of a United Nations political Conference in 1977). The World Climate Conference was a conference of experts, mainly on the impact of climate, rather than its physical characteristics. This change of emphasis will also affect the World Climate Program to be launched shortly by WMO and the International Council of Scientific Unions. Several countries, notably the United States, have initiated comparable national programs. The coming decade will see large-scale research into the nature, identification, and mitigation of climatic impact.

The next century

Can we foresee changes in the climatic systems that will constrain the human economy in the next century? Will there be constraints even if there is no basic change? Can we avoid such constraints by political and economic devices?

Among professional climatologists there is now wide, but not universal, agreement that significant changes in climate will occur in the next century. Indeed, they are already in progress. These changes will be due to progressive alterations in atmospheric composition that are already quite striking.

The rise in atmospheric carbon dioxide content is well established. Since detailed monitoring began in 1957, the rise has been continuous and worldwide, though variable in rate. The atmospheric carbon reservoir stands at 700 billion metric tons, or about 335 parts per million by volume. It is increasing at about 1 part per million by volume per year, equivalent to 3 percent per decade in carbon content. The net annual gain is about 2 billion metric tons. Annual fossil fuel consumption is 5 billion metric tons. So about 40 percent of the carbon in consumed oil, gas, and coal is staying in the atmosphere. We are not sure what is happening to the rest (8).

The usual guess has been that the oceans are dissolving the remaining 60 percent. Recent calculations (12), however, cast doubt on the ability of the oceans to absorb nearly so much. An alternative guess is that increased photosynthesis is transferring carbon into plant tissues and the soil. But this too poses difficulties. Recent studies suggest that deforestation, especially in the tropical rainforest of Amazonia, and decreasing organic content in soils have led to a net transfer of carbon to the atmosphere (1, 13). So we are unsure about the sources and sinks for atmospheric carbon. What we are sure about is the spectacular rise in carbon dioxide load. If this continues, and it probaby will, we can expect a doubling of carbon dioxide content by the middle or late twenty-first century.

A doubling of carbon dioxide content may raise the earth's surface temperature 2 to 3 degrees Celsius (6, 7). The effect is likely to be most marked in high latitudes due to partial melting of the pack-ice in the polar oceans. A rise of over 10 degrees Celsius is likely in these latitudes. The rise of carbon dioxide should soon override the slow cooling that has been going on since 1938. The effect is due to the optical properties of carbon dioxide, which is transparent to sunlight, but opaque to some wavelengths of the earth's emitted radiation.

Other gases now being added to the atmosphere have similar properties and will contribute to further heating. The list includes many synthetics, like the halocarbons, and nitrous oxide from increased fertilizer use. One estimate puts the combined heating effect by 2050 A.D. at 1.5 to 6 degrees Celsius with the most likely rise in the 3 to 4 degree range. This is a heating like nothing the world has experienced in the past 10,000 years (5).

This carbon dioxide and related heating effect is undoubtedly the central climatological research problem of the day. We do not understand the overall carbon cycle well and cannot adequately predict whether the build-up of carbon dioxide will continue. If it does, however, we face a probable climatic revolution in the next century.

What kind of revolution?

A rise in temperature on the scale just mentioned must certainly have a dramatic effect on natural ecosystems and on food sources. Unfortunately the precise nature of the impact cannot be foretold. It is likely to be unequal in distribution. Some countries may gain; others may lose. Drastic economic readjustments will be necessary.

The direct impact of such a temperature rise is easy to predict. It would tend to benefit frost-prone areas near the poleward limits of cultivation, such as Canada's fertile areas and much of the Soviet Union and Scandinavia. On the other hand, a rise in temperature would be a hindrance or even a hazard to cultivation and pastoralism along the warm, dry margin of the settled world. The desert fringe would suffer to the detriment of Africa, inner Asia, and the dry belt of northwest India and Pakistan. Dense populations occupy some of these areas. Everywhere a rise in temperature would tend to accelerate the oxidation of soil carbon. At sea, moreover, the solubility of carbon dioxide would be reduced. The complex carbon chemistry of the surface layer of the oceans would also change.

The impact would, however, be largely indirect, through altered distribution of rainfall. The drastic change in poleward temperature gradient implied by the calculated warming would alter the world's system of winds and storms. This in turn would affect the distribution of rainfall over the continents, hence crop yields. We cannot yet predict the nature and size of such changes. To do so must involve the use of coupled atmosphere-ocean circulation models with a degree of sophistication not yet achieved. It will be some time before we can make any kind of quantitative statement about the nature of the change in rainfall.

The present situation is thus highly unsettling. We think we can see a major change in world climate coming that is bound to upset the world's soils, forests, oceans, fisheries, croplands, and pastures. The food supply that will be put under stress by rising population levels and dietary sophistication may also be imperiled by changing rainfall patterns and possibly by temperature changes. But we cannot yet predict the changes in enough detail to be precise about the impacts on man.

As pressure on food, energy, land, and water increases, however, so will the impact of climate's other attribute: its variability. We are unable to say whether variability will increase. But even if it is maintained at present levels, the economies of fringe areas will be increasingly vulnerable. Large populations live near the present climatic margins, where natural variability tends to be highest. Dryland agriculture in the subhumid tropics, for example, supports millions of people in Africa, Asia, and Latin America. This belt has seen unusually high rates of population growth in recent decades. Much of the real impact of climate will come, as it has in the past, from the occurrence of quite ordinary droughts or floods that in the days of lower population would have had little impact.

Climate and the food system

The shocks administered to the food systems by the climatic anomalies of the 1970s have had some impact on institutions, but not as much as they should have.

The price structure of the food system depends to an extent on the export prices of food and coarse grains. Only about a tenth of grain production enters into world trade, yet small perturbations of that trade cause wide price fluctuations that extend to small village markets in remote Third World countries. The 1972-1973 crop failures were quite local, but they hit both major producing and major consuming areas. The result was a wild escalation of price—a trebling for both wheat and rice—that caused great dislocation and distress in the poor countries. Yet the overall world production of cereals fell by only 1 percent. Since then a small glut has reappeared (in relation to demand that is price-sensitive rather than need), thanks to good growing conditions. Prices have sunk accordingly.

Such fluctuations are likely to continue unless the world arrives at a miraculous stabilization of the food system. They will continue to present us with difficult and perhaps tragic consequences.

There are several points to be made on the future role of climate in the overall system. Cereal supply, both coarse and food-grain, is highly susceptible to rainfall variation and especially to recurrent drought. There is virtual certainty that such anomalies will continue and that they will hit major export areas from time to time. On the world scale, it is unlikely that such "hits" will be simultaneous in all these areas. One consequence of the reduction in their number, however, is to make this calamity more likely. The major wheat exporters are now only four in number: the United States, Canada, Australia, and Argentina. In 1972-1973 all four areas were adversely affected by bad weather. The same year a major drought and winterkill induced crop failure in the Soviet Union. The Soviets' resultant massive purchases of stored grain precipitated the price inflation of 1973-1974.

However, there is no present evidence that such climatic anomalies are likely to increase in frequency. The major hazards seem to be twofold:

• The risk that severe, prolonged drought may return to the Indian subcontinent, where it has been remarkably absent in recent decades. The visitation of a Sahalian-scale desiccation upon India and Pakistan cannot be ruled out. It would undo the work they have done to increase their agricultural productivity and would put an unimaginable strain on world peace and security.

• The long-term probability that carbon dioxide heating will shift the rainfall patterns in the continental interiors so that there will have to be changes in the location of cereal production, especially of the high-protein hard wheats that are typically grown near the arid limit of cultivation. There may also be a progressive desiccation of some, but not all, of the densely populated dryland farming areas of the tropical world.

A more general anxiety is that possible countermeasures may prove politically impossible. The phenomenon of desertification, for example, will take a long time to reverse. What is happening to the desert margins of Africa and Asia is a progressive loss of biological productivity that depends more on human failures than on changes of climate. Rising populations and improved veterinary medicine combine to make necessary and possible higher livestock densities that put heavy pressure on grass, soil, and woody vegetation (also under attack by the gatherers of firewood). When drought comes, as it will always do from time to time, such overstressed land use systems may virtually collapse. There may be irreversible losses of soil, perennial vegetation, and livestock—even famine. The recent Sahelian crisis rehearsed the effects for a largely uncomprehending world.

The United Nations Desertification Conference drew up a plan of action that is now being put into effect. But the major burden of carrying out such remedial action often falls on governments that are poorly organized and short of technical capacities. Most are in regions lacking the needed infrastructure.

The advanced nations generally assume also that action on a world scale to prevent climatic deterioration is out of the question. The recent U.S. National Climate Program Act (Public Law 95-367) has as its purpose to "assist the Nation and the world to understand and respond to natural and man-induced processes and their implications." There is no talk of controlling or reversing the changes, but only of understanding and response (9).

At first sight this must be true. Considering only fossil fuel consumption, the stabilization of carbon dioxide content at its present atmospheric level would call for measures to avoid 60 percent of present consumption, or the storage of about 3 billion metric tons of carbon annually. This is about 6 percent of the annual net production of new biomass by living terrestrial ecosystems. Presumably this is beyond our technical and political skill to accomplish.

Conservation of soil and its vegetative cover is an activity that bears heavily on the control of the carbon cycle. It is estimated that terrestrial biomass storage of carbon is a little under 900 billion metric tons, while in soil humus and bogs storage may lie in the range of 1,000 to 3,000 billion metric tons (1). It is also widely believed that there has been a rapid transfer of carbon to the atmosphere through forest clearance and reduced organic content in soils.

If there is to be any attempt to regulate the rise of atmospheric carbon content with its potential climatic consequences, it will likely come from attempts on a worldwide basis to reverse this attrition of carbon storage in the world's soils and vegetation. The objectives of soil conservationists thus take on a new dimension. They bear on the earth's climatic future.

All this must take place in the presence of considerable uncertainty. Little of what I have said can be substantiated strongly enough to defend it as hard fact. Scientists, however, are apt to prejudge the question of what is politically feasible. If in a decade or so it becomes obvious that for strategic reasons it will be necessary to achieve control over climatic variation, and I have acquaintances in the Soviet Union who say this now, the political means will be found. I only hope that when and if that unlikely moment comes, we will also be able to come up with the physical means!

REFERENCES

1. Bolin, B. 1977. *Changes of land biota and their importance for the carbon cycle.* Science 196: 613-615.
2. Hare, F. K. 1979. *Climatic variation and variability.* In Proceedings, World Climate Conference. World Meteorological Organization, Geneva, Switzerland.
3. Hare, F. K., R. W. Kates, and A. Warren. 1977. *The making of deserts: Climate, ecology and society.* Economic Geography 53: 332-346.
4. Hays, J. D., J. Imbrie, and N. J. Shackleton. 1976. *Variations in the earth's orbit: pacemaker of the Ice Ages.* Science 194: 1,121-1,132.
5. Kellogg, W. W. 1977. *Effects of human activities on global climate.* Technical Note 156. World Meteorological Organization, Geneva, Switzerland.
6. Manabe, S., and R. T. Wetherald. 1975. *The effects of doubling the CO_2 concentration on the climate of a general circulation model.* Journal of the Atmospheric Sciences 32: 3-15.
7. Mason, B. J. 1979. *Some results of climate experiments with numerical models.* In Proceedings, World Climate Conference. World Meteorological Organization, Geneva, Switzerland.
8. Munn, R. E., and L. Machta. 1979. *Human activities that affect climate.* In Proceedings, World Climate Conference. World Meteorological Organization, Geneva, Switzerland.
9. National Academy of Sciences. 1979. *Toward a U.S. climate program plan.* Climate Research Board, Washington, D.C.
10. National Academy of Sciences. 1975. *Understanding climatic change.* Washington, D.C.
11. Parthasararthy, B., and D. A. Mooley. 1978. *Some features of a long homogeneous series of Indian summer rainfall.* Monthly Weather Review 106: 771-781.
12. Revelle, R., and W. Munk. 1977. *The carbon dioxide cycle and the biosphere.* In *Energy and Climate.* National Academy of Sciences, Washington, D.C.
13. Woodwell, G. M. 1978. *The carbon dioxide question.* Scientific American 238: 34-43.
14. World Meteorological Organization. 1979. *World climate conference, declaration and supporting documents.* Geneva, Switzerland.

3

On the relevance of lungfish, koalas, lilacs, wolves, bullfrogs, and spirit levels in the consideration of resource-constrained economies

John A. Livingston

I am not a soil scientist, an economist, or what you might call a resource manager. I am interested primarily in biological conservation—nature preservation. This interest requires me to investigate the relationships (past and present) between man and his environments, between man and nonhuman nature. I am interested in the process nature of those relationships, particularly in the historical role of cultural attitudes toward nature. And because man is a part of nature, it follows that human attitudes and perceptions of nature turn out to be attitudes and perceptions of people.

Clearly, it is one of the historic causes of our present predicament that we members of a highly technical civilization have always assumed that there were neat engineering remedies for any and all problems environments might throw at us. Even the most single-minded among us are beginning to acknowledge that we were wrong in this. Indeed, it is beginning to look as though we have not been asking the right questions. We have not even begun to understand the problems themselves.

There are changes going on in the environment, and we face a dilemma or a set of dilemmas in facing those changes. For purposes of this, I define

John A. Livingston is a professor in environmental studies, York University, Downsview, Ontario.

"change" as the perceived difference between what was and what is. I emphasize "perceived" because rarely do we know what was and even more rarely do we know what is. However, the difference in the buying power of a 1949 dollar and a 1979 dollar represents a change. There is a difference too in world human population in those 30 years. Nature paid a terrible price for human accomplishment over that period—from a change in the number of blue whales to synthetic pesticides that have contaminated the entire biosphere.

There has also been a perceived change in the availability of those parts of nature that we have customarily taken free for the asking and we call "resources." Clearly, there has been a change in how much of what is available to whom merely for the asking and also in the volume of nonrenewable pieces of nature to support our appetites. On the other hand, there has been no change whatever in the fact that natural materials of all kinds are finite. Resources were just as finite in 1949 as they are today. The essential change is that today we are just beginning to admit it. True, we have read about it for years, but today we are beginning to feel it. And that represents a qualitative change. There has been a change in our perception of nature and the human relationship with nature.

The nature of evolution

Another kind of change is quite different from the simple arithmetical exercise that reveals the difference between then and now. This second one is similar in that it also is only visible by hindsight: you use the reference point of what was in order to do your sum. But it is different in that it is a process as opposed to a net result. It is this continuous process of adaptive movement in concert with changing environments—the picture of biological adaptation to change—that we call evolution.

While the arithmetical assessment of change is quantitative, the evolutionary model is qualitative. Things change into quite different things, qualitatively different things. A lizard turns into a bird; another lizard turns into a furry little insectivore that turns into a man. All change, whether you can measure it or not, is evolutionary in that it turns things into other things, and the change is irreversible. That is in the most fundamental nature of things.

One of the most interesting and perhaps the most important thing about evolutionary process is that it is conservative. The drive is always toward maintenance of the status quo. It has been expressed as Romer's Rule after Alfred Romer, the great Harvard vertebrate palaeontologist (1). It goes like this: "The initial survival value of a favorable innovation is conservative, in that it renders possible the maintenance of a traditional way of life in the face of changed circumstances."

Romer thus explains the invasion of the land by the early air-breathing fishes, the famous lobe-finned lungfishes of the Devonian period that eventually turned into the first amphibians. They could breathe air and they had stumpy, strong fins. Occasionally, in a period of drought, they would find themselves stranded in a rapidly shrinking pool. At that point, the ability to breathe air and the strong, thick fins enabled them to struggle to a better hole. Some of these eventually turned into amphibians, but what the air-breathing and the stumpy fins really allowed them to do was to go on being the fishes they had always been. Indeed it was easier to go on being fishes because it was easier to get back into the water. The drive was to continue to be fishes. The drive was conservative. That they changed into something else in the process was, in this sense, an incidental result. Change was only visible by hindsight.

What this means is that adaptive process, innovation, is always trying to maintain the status quo, to maintain a balance. But balance is, of course, never achieved because environments are always changing. This is the evolutionary dynamic. In the process of being ultraconservative, living things change in spite of themselves. In the process of struggling back toward the water, the stranded lungfishes became amphibians, which they never intended to do.

Evolution and oil

Now, without apology, we apply Romer's Rule to current affairs. There is no better example of the conservative nature of innovation and adaptation than the contemporary oil problem. The problem is not oil; the problem is our machines that depend on oil. And then again, the problem is not really our machines; it is humanity. We did it out of our unswerving commitment to the ethic of production and consumption, to something we invented and christened "progress." It follows that in our conservative drive to continue to use our machines we will go to any lengths whatever to (a) obtain oil for them or (b) fabricate a substitute for oil to use in the same or a similar combustion process. We want to go on being fishes.

We are quite capable of fighting over oil or over the raw materials for some synthetic fuel, rather than peacefully launching an all-out search for other ways of doing things. It may well be that in our frantic thrashing around for ways to continue to use the present internal-combustion engine we may well stumble over some favorable innovations that will allow us to go on being fishes, or we may not. The technocrats hate to be reminded of the fact that evolution is unpredictable and uncontrollable.

The difference between the man and the lungfish is said to be intelligence: the ability to profit from experience, being able to apply past knowledge gained in new situations. We have, for example, plenty of data concerning the energy subsidy that is part of present-day agriculture. More energy goes into machines and fertilizers and pesticides than is produced by the crop. Deficit budgeting cannot go on forever. There are those who claim that there simply is not enough oil in the arctic to equal the energy invested in exploration, drilling, extracting, shipping, and refining. We seem to be in the position of a stranded lungfish, waiting for something in our circumstances to change us into something else, something more appropriate to changed environmental conditions. Something will certainly happen, and I wonder what it will be.

Changing our assumptions

Some of the innovations that will be required of us in due course cut even more deeply and painfully than the internal-combustion engine. Let us take soil for an example. Soil is a living thing. But we do not know it from direct observation. Without a microscope we cannot see soil's activity; we can only infer it. To our unaided eyes, it does not appear to be alive; it's still there in the morning, much as it was last night. It doesn't go away, at least not perceptibly. It does evolve and change, but slowly. We tend to treat it as though it were inert.

Since soil appears to be inert, and for all intents and purposes just lies there, waiting for us to use it, we take it as given. It is ours to do with as we wish; that is our right. We may abuse it or we may not, but it is ours to use. It doesn't talk back, and nobody talks back on its behalf. I wonder if perhaps our assumed right to the soil, like our assumed right to the oilfields of the world, may not be a kind of dangerous self-delusion. Indeed, I see the civilized human assumption of the right to nature for any and all human purposes as an assumption that has gotten us into a heap of trouble.

To examine our assumed right of proprietorship over the various aspects of nature is much touchier than examining our dependence on the internal-combustion engine. It reveals some deep-rooted difficulties. For example, I have property in rural southern Ontario that I deeply love and that I would defend to the last gasp were anyone to try to take it from me. It's mine, all mine. Or is it?

In the spring and fall, many migratory birds pass through that property. For a few days, twice each year, they are all over the place But obviously they are not mine; they are migratory birds. But there are other birds that stay there for part of the year; they breed there and spend the summer there and then spend the winter someplace else. Does the fact that they nest there make them mine in the summer and somebody else's in the winter? Then there are the grouse, hawks, and the owls that stay there the year round. Does that make them mine? I think not.

But what about things that are not as mobile as birds? The frogs in the ponds pretty much stay put, except when my neighbor digs a new pond, enough of them find it to colonize it. Whose are those colonists—his or mine? Or when my lilac sends suckers under the fence and rises in my neighbor's hedge-row, who owns the new plant? Is it a new plant? My neighbor might say that it is his, because there it is on his property. But I could say that it is the same old rootstalk, and it is mine. And so on. My neighbor's basswoods seed my property, and my sugar maples seed his. Nothing is static; things change.

Back to the soil. It also changes. Just because the soil lives, moves, and evolves and changes too slowly for us to see it happen, does that mean that it is not just as much a living thing as a sugar maple or a bullfrog? Does the fact that it does not run away mean that it is mine? I know the air is not mine, but I breathe it as though it were. I know that the soil is not mine either, but I treat it as though it were. That is because society permits me to do so. What goes on on my property, short of absolute mayhem, is nobody's business except mine, so long as it does not bother somebody else. I can mine my soil, poison it, hook it into an addictive dependence, and beat it into blow-dirt and get away with it, so long as it doesn't bother somebody else. But if I concoct some new and even more damnable weapon of war on the long-suffering soil than we have already, something that can spread to my neighbor's soil and infect it, I'll hear about it fast enough. Society declares limits to my freedom of access to my own property. A stream on my property comes to me from a neighbor's property. He cannot plug it up, and neither can I; that would prevent another neighbor's cattle from drinking. There are social limits to my right of proprietorship after all.

The education of society

Rights turn out to be accompanied by restrictions, often regulations, that really are duties to our neighbors. A right is accompanied by a concomitant duty. Changes have occurred so gradually and so subtly that, like the process of aging, it is difficult to pinpoint just when they happened. Society has evolved.

It has been said that totally free individual enterprise is only possible in environments of instant and abundant resource availability. It seems no coincidence then that the "religion" of individual free enterprise reached its fullest development where it did. In the North America of our ancestry there was no conceivable limit to resource abundance. It was only natural that society responded as it did. But now that we are beginning to learn, the hard way, that nothing in this world is unlimited and infinite, it becomes appropriate to ask questions about certain of those old presuppositions about the freedom of human access to nature, and about the notion of individual and collective proprietorship over nature.

Although this is most certainly a political issue, I hasten to assure you that I am not raising politics in the usual sense. It is one of my beliefs, one that arises from the evolutionary model, that things are as they are at any given moment in time because the then prevailing environmental conditions permit it. Currently prevailing forestry techniques create an environment for the spruce budworm that, in turn, creates an environment for fire. Just as mercantilism and technology provided the environment for the Industrial Revolution, so the Industrial Revolution provided an environment for dramatic social change. The superabundance of natural material wealth in North America provided a social, economic, political, and cultural environment for the emergence of the ideology of our individual and collective proprietorship over nature. Evolving in concert with that ideology, indeed as a symbiotic partner, was the urban-industrial production-consumption imperative.

I think we have to get used to the fact that, as times change, so too do environments, and that out of the crucible of change arise new beings and new phenomena. I suppose that had anyone in the pre-lungfish Devonian period predicted the emergence of creatures that would breathe atmospheric oxygen and bounce around on dry land, he would have been burned at the stake for heresy.

Now, let us acknowledge at this point that being an amphibian is not necessarily better than being a fish; it is just different. It is only humans who talk about the progress from fish to amphibian to reptile to mammal. Only humans see improvement in all of this. When you back off a bit, you see that all it is, really, is change. And change, in the evolutionary sense, is neither good nor bad; it simply *is*.

If we are to make a start in the confrontation of our present dilemmas, we have to accept that the same principle applies in human social affairs. Change *is*; you can't stop it, and the harder you struggle against it, the tighter the bind. Remember that in the Devonian period not all of the lungfishes became amphibians and not all of them got back to the water; many perished, high and dry.

Profound changes are coming, and whether we like it or not, we had better be thinking about them. And when we do think about it, we see that a great deal has already happened. The enormous complex of boards, tariffs, subsidies, penalties, equalizations, lobbies, regulations, and agencies that surrounds the agricultural industry today, for example, would have been just as unthinkable a couple of generations ago as was the first amphibian in its time. But it happened; we adjusted to it; and more is in store. More is going to impinge upon what we perceive as personal freedom, use of our land, for example.

The irrelevance of political ideologies

Having in mind our quite natural conservatism, I expect that fences between our fields will grow higher and stronger before they begin to shrink. Private ownership will be defended more fiercely than ever, the more restrictive the world becomes. This is the way I will react. The first person who tries to tell me to convert the hayfields to market gardens or the woods to pasture or the frog ponds to fish ponds will bring down the wrath of Jehovah on his head. But he will do it anyway. Environmental circumstances will be such that I am not going to be able to stop him. My acquiescence will be legislated, and in my acquiescence I will have changed; I will have evolved. I won't be any better or worse; I'll just be different. But it will be more painful than it would have been had I been slightly more flexible. In other words, it will behoove me to loosen up a bit.

I am aware that there is a strong political implication in all of this. But remember that I am not talking about politics in the sense of political ideologies. I am talking about politics in the pure and basic sense: the organization of human societies in their environments. That organization is going to change, and the change is going to have little, if anything, to do with customary political ideologies.

In fact, I find that political ideology has very little to do with conservation. If the soil is destroyed, who cares what the political beliefs of the destroyer may have been? Once the world's great whales are gone for good, what could it possibly matter where the profits went, who owned the whaling fleet, what flag his ships flew, or what his beliefs were? What earthly difference does it make to the shrimp beds and to the shrimp fishermen of the Gulf of Mexico that it was Pemex, a state-owned oil company, whose well blew up, rather than Exxon, a private corporation? None whatever. In spite of the politicians and the ideologists, the distinction is quite irrelevant from the conservation point of view. Conservation is about life not about belief systems.

I emphasize the irrelevance of political ideologies in these questions because it is important to separate and not confuse them with the political realitics that the short supply of raw materials is bound to generate. We know about the political realities of "commodity power," such as that wielded by the Organization of Petroleum Exporting Countries. One of these days we may see "wheat power"; I think we probably will. One serious implication in all of this is that any kind of "commodity power" represents by necessity a centralization of political power with respect to that commodity. If we persist along our merry, extravagant way, one day soon the growing shortage of resources is going to mean centralized control of that resource supply that remains. On the face of it, there would not seem to be any real alternative. The centralization of resource industries of all kinds would seem to be inescapable.

Future options

There has been abundant literature on the future of resources, much of it long before the Club of Rome and *The Limits to Growth*. A recent book, *Ecology and the Politics of Scarcity*, by William Ophuls (2) seems to encapsulate most of the critical dimensons of the problem in an unusually careful and persuasive way. "The essential political message of this book is that we must learn ecological restraint before it is forced on us by a potentially monolithic and totalitarian regime or by the brute forces of nature. We are currently sliding by default in the direction of one (or both) of these two outcomes. Only the restoration of some measure of civic virtue (to use the traditional term) can forestall this fate, and the necessary lessons in virtue are, again, better learned from political philosophy than from personal suffering." Ophuls describes his book as a "prologue to a political theory of the steady state." The only political alternative to totalitarianism that the author can see in the face of our shrinking resource base is the creation of small-scale, simple, and frugal steady-state societies. I am not going to pursue this further at the moment, except to remind you that the slide toward graver problems is accelerating at this time and that we seem to be staring an iron-fisted centralization directly in the face unless we relax our traditionally rigid positions in a hurry. The degree of centralization that is envisioned would represent a dramatic and drastic change in our quality of life.

Quality of life is a desirable goal for human societies. Everyone will have an individual and particular image of life quality. For me, it means the care and maintenance of options. Every lopping-off of an option is a reduction of life quality. Every option foreclosed is an escape route to quality barricaded off for keeps.

We all hear a good deal of talk about life quality nowadays, everybody seems to have something to say about it, but rarely does anyone tell us what it actually means. Among conservationists, the notion is often expressed as environmental quality. We can narrow the focus a bit if we suspend the wider sociocultural nuances of environment to concentrate on the biophysical. But even here there is a problem with definitions. Virtually everybody seems to agree on environmental quality as a policy goal, but I have not yet seen a firm statement of what it means. This is an important hindrance to implementation.

Complexity favors heterogeneity

To me environmental quality means, among other things, heterogeneity. It means variety, diversity, and options. Homogeneity (uninterrupted wheat fields, tree farms, cities, expressways, feedlots, suburbs) is a kind of ecologic heresy. The concept of a healthy ecosystem is one with many parts, many roles, many interrelationships, many alternatives, many structures and functions, and many ways of doing things. It is dynamic; it flows and changes. It is resilient. It provides options for its parts and processes in the event of disturbance. The monoculture, on the other hand, the pure culture of longleaf pine, rice, or people, is an open invitation to disease, parasitism, and collapse. The reduction of parts and pathways, roles and processes, and means and alternative means can weaken an ecosystem and make it vulnerable. Quite obviously, the same is true of a society or a culture.

Life quality means life options, options for change in the face of changing environments. To the student of evolutionary biology, every variation in every individual organism is an option for change. It may not be used immediately, or ever, but it is there, against possibilities. Evolution is opportunistic. New variations, each of which is an individual experiment, continually probe and test the changing environment for new opportunities. When the option presents itself, a new variant may become a new ecotype, a new race, perhaps even a new species. There are variations in anatomy, in physiology, and in behavior. These variations evolve in concert with changing environments over time.

There are also variations in human cultures, beliefs, values, superstitions, traditions, assumptions, and even perceptions. Or there used to be. The culture of our Western technomechanistic (we sometimes called it "developed") world seems to be pathetically homogeneous. A colossal irony is that we apparently perceive this creeping homogeneity (one world, in our image) to be good. We are certainly attempting to inflict it on the rest of the world as fast as we can. We connive with every means at our disposal to brainwash underprivileged countries into sharing our suicidal belief that industrial production and consumption is the measure of high civilization.

This creeping process of world homogenization has, more than any other factor, helped to mire us in the deepening pit in which we now find ourselves. World dependence on industrialization, with its frightening dependence on increasing consumption of energy, on machines, on pesticides, on synthetic fertilizers, and all the rest, can have but one consequence from the ecologist's point of view. Since the option to homogeneity is heterogeneity, the message for the agricultural community should be obvious. Industrial farming (agribusiness) will go, along with its monstrous machines; there seems little doubt. Smaller scale, mixed, individual family farming is a great deal closer to the ecologic model, because mixed farming, by definition, means options. The harder we struggle against the recovery of our sanity, the more traumatic will be the changeover when it does come.

In other words, there seems little doubt that industrial agriculture, as we presently understand it, is as doomed as the dinosaurs. I will applaud its passing, for its death throes will force us, like it or not, to review some healthy options that have been out of sight and out of mind for too long.

This is not romanticism. I am not suggesting the resurrection of old virtues and all the backbreaking, pretechnical hewing and hawing. But I am saying there is an alternative to the ravenous insatiability that characterizes urban-industrial production and consumption. I am urging an intelligent, informed, sensitive approach toward a sustainable and humanitarian relationship with each other and the land. The changeover will hurt. It will take time. But the alternative will hurt more, and time will not be our ally.

There is no simple recipe for all of this. There are many; none is simple. No single approach will be sufficient. As it is in ecosystems, so it is in all things: ecological communities and associations are site-specific; no two are exactly the same. One spruce bog may look like another and one woodlot like another, but no two are exactly the same. Each community, whether human or nonhuman, is the current end product of its local history, its local circumstances, and its local environment. Generalization is impossible because of the complex individuality of each situation, except at a level that simply is not very useful. No one can really tell us what the post-industrial, scaled-down, sustainable human society will look like except in the broadest way. Essentially, it's up to each of us—not all of us, collectively.

The population factor

Now there is one basic, fundamental and radical issue that must be addressed concurrently with our search for liberation from our technological-industrial dependence. That is the matter of human populations. Remember that there are two quite distinct population problems: one is the absolute number of people; the other problem is their distribution and concentration.

Over two years ago, I was in Malaysia for a time, and while there I saw some of the Vietnamese boat people. There were a lot of them, and more were arriving weekly. They came to the east coast of Malaysia, across the South China Sea, into the river estuary at a place called Mersing, north of Singapore. They came in rickety, rotten old boats, crowded to the gunnels, certainly sub-seaworthy; they would wait for high tide, then run the boats aground, pull the plugs, and scuttle them. At that point, the Malaysians were not seriously trying to put them back to sea. There were long lines of these boats resting high and dry on the mudflats. People were living on them and on a fenced-off area adjacent to them. The local people were helping them with food and so on, but they were not allowed to leave this compound. An offshore island was also being used to house these refuge boat people.

The boat people are there because there are simply too many people in Indochina for a characteristically thin tropical resource base to support. There are especially too many people if the goal of Indochinese governments, as it seems to be, is industrialization in the Western image. You cannot industrialize in the Western image without resources in the ground. There are too many people everywhere in the Far East for the local resource base, and so in Vietnam, thousands of people are pressured out. And if you want to reduce your population by way of mass emigration, you select for that purpose a group—ethnic, religious, political, or whatever—that is least appropriate to the prevailing sociocultural environment. I would see this as a process of artificial selection brought about by underlying, natural environmental stresses. Vietnam chose to single out the ethnic Chinese as their artificial selection.

Malaysia also has a bursting population and is not a rich country. It is also a Muslim country. There are many Chinese there who have been there for many generations, mostly Buddhists, some Confucians and some Christians. Chinese people are second-class citizens in Malaysia, and the government does not want any more of them, even if they could support them, which they cannot. Most boat people have the misfortune to be of Chinese ancestry, in addition to whatever political reasons there may be, such as the economic place they may have occupied prior to the present Vietnamese regime.

Whenever the pressure is on, whether it is population pressure, economic pressure, or some other, those who are different in some way are usually the first to pay the price. This is, by the way, the reason that nonhuman beings, such as whales and polar bears, have to pay the price for resource-constrained human economies. The unpleasant fact seems to be that the process is all quite natural. I expect and fear that we are going to experience large-scale racism in increasing measure, in direct proportion to population pressure and the shrinking availability of resources. It is important to attempt to understand what this is all about.

Small is natural

I say it is natural because we are, after all, biological organisms and carry a genetic inheritance that is manifest in our anatomy, physiology, and behavior. We are animals. We human beings, which means we socially co-operative primates, are not designed for high-density concentration. High population density is foreign to our most fundamental nature, and we pay the price for it. High-density centralization of vast numbers of people is foreign to our biology, and many people pay the very painful price for it.

It seems to be in our biologic background that we function best in groups in which every individual is recognizable and known to every other. This kind of group is loosely known as the extended family. But more than that, we are socially cooperative animals; there are many animal societies that are not cooperative. It is natural and inherent in us to cooperate in relatively small aggregations, like those of hunting dogs, lions, wolves, and, to some extent, chimpanzees. Social cooperation arose in our hunting past and gave rise to such phenomena as sharing, teamwork, babysitting, role functions, and so on that we share with wolves and others. There is a place for every-body, everybody has a place, and everybody knows everybody else's place. So it is even today with the hunting band of Australian aborigines, the tiny outport fishing village, the kibbutz, and the family farm. Small is natural.

The small aggregation works because it is in our nature. In natural group-ings such as this, strife is rare and tension minimal. On the other hand, as numbers increase beyond a certain point (the point at which individuals rec-ognize and know each other) it becomes necessary to use political, as op-posed to natural, behavioral devices to keep order. There is no longer a nat-ural bond to hold the aggregation together; an artificial one is substituted.

What our optimum group number might be, no one knows. It might be 40, 200, or even 1,000. This would vary according to environmental circum-stances, including the quality and quantity of the resources. But whatever it is, it is of this magnitude. It will not be 10,000, a million, or a billion. At those levels, the flow of order is concentrated and flows downward. Once you concentrate population beyond the natural "magic number," you have to add ever more contrived regulatory means of control, which becomes in-creasingly difficult to enforce and increasingly restrictive to the individual. The village cop in a town of 500 really isn't busy most of the time, and he hasn't got any riot gear. The policeman in a large city puts his life on the line every time he reports for duty.

Roots of racism

What I am saying here is that there is a biologic base for the small, frugal, cooperative, and sustainable human concentration over and above all of the social, economic, political, and other arguments that have been put forward by so many people in the last few years. I am saying also that there is a biological base for much of the nonsocial turmoil that we observe in Vietnam, Malaysia, Rhodesia, the black ghettos, or the local shopping center.

I am simplifying unconscionably here, but I do not want you to think that I claim war and such obscenities are natural. They are not. But they are the responses to an unnatural way of life, an unnatural way of doing things. Racism is one of its manifestations.

It is important to remember from the biological point of view that your average bigot is running scared. He behaves as he does because he is frightened. That is why he is so dangerous. And as often as not, he has good reason to be afraid. The stranger represents, to the bigot, the possible breakdown of everything that he believes and is. The stranger, the person who is different, represents a real and present threat.

Xenophobia, fear of the stranger, is well developed in all social cooperative beings. Such groups are extremely cautious about accepting any stranger into their midst. Many times they will drive a strange intruder away immediately; at other times there may be eventual acceptance after a long period of tentative approaches and rejections. There is some internal sensing mechanism that resists the unfamiliar, rejects that which is foreign, fears change, and steadfastly adheres to the maintenance of the status quo. Don't forget that a stranger is a changing circumstance. Our innate conservatism is strong and ancient.

Now, having in mind what I call the unnaturalness of human population concentrations and the artificiality of our resulting sociopolitical systems, by contrast with the naturally self-regulating system of the socially cooperative group, it seems logical to conclude that the first symptoms of any major environmental dislocation will be observed in the social organization. We begin to see the artificiality of our system on the South China Sea and around the California gas pumps. Environmental stresses are felt first in the human social organization, because that organization is not appropriate to the realities, as we presently understand them, of living in a biophysical system.

Reorganizing societies

Clearly the goal is human social organization that is appropriate to the realities of our being living organisms. The most fundamental prerequisite would be flexibility. Nowdays, environmental circumstances change more rapidly than they did, as the simple consequence of the acceleration of our race toward resource exhaustion. But the urban-industrial society has become so unyielding and inflexible that it would seem to be in real danger of suddenly snapping, rather than pliantly giving, under present-day stresses. Whether we already have passed the point of no return as the result of the stresses we have placed on our environment, no one yet knows. In case we have not, I suggest that the operative word from now on be flexibility.

Flexibility implies the capacity to recognize and to intelligently select options. There are unused options in every aspect of our lives. Clearly they exist in all organizational and institutional arrangements. There are alternatives to centralization, to ponderousness, and to the tyranny of growth. There is even an alternative to planning. It is called designing. There is an opposite to homogeneity. There are even two sides to extinction: one is to vanish without issue; the other is to be flexible enough to change into something new.

When it comes to keeping afloat in the biologic sense, the name of the game is hanging loose. Foreclosure of any possible adaptive option, any alternative route, is simply not in the individual self-interest, to say nothing of the larger interest. In its continuing dog-paddle to remain afloat, every individual living being acts in its own self-interest. Self-interest is the core of being.

Now, in what I am calling natural cooperative societies, those of wolves, or of hunting dogs, for example, actions that help the individual survive and prosper also help that social unit to do the same. One of the things that appears to be essential to group success is the absence of violence within the group. They will and do occasionally drive away outsiders, as we have seen, but within the group there is a level of peace and tranquillity that we would have every right to envy. From time to time there may be much roaring and demonstrating and elaborate shows of weaponry, but there is almost never any actual violence. It is all ritual, show, convention, and routine, mere posturing. Nobody is hurt, and the positive bond throughout the group is maintained.

Some notable exceptions to this rule have happened in zoos, where an unnatural number of individuals (baboons in one case I can remember) confined together have exploded into fearsome blood-letting. This is the direct consequence of unnatural density. There appears to be an upper limit, according to the species and the environmental circumstances, in which organization can be maintained. This is the magic number I mentioned earlier.

The "ethics" of wolves

In studying the individual interactions between members of such groups, various ethologists have pointed to inhibitions against fighting. As you may know, at the approach of the biggest or dominant male wolf, another individual may roll over on his back like a puppy, or slowly move his head to one side, exposing his throat, thus making himself entirely vulnerable to the fangs of the large male. But nothing happens. Many observers say that the big animal is thus inhibited from attacking; the action of the subservient individual prevents the attack. Scientists say that he is inhibited because they apparently assume that the wolf is by nature a bloodthirsty, slavering killer and has to be prevented from indulging his true instincts.

I think this interpretation is the victim of human presuppositions about nature. I know of no evidence whatever to show that the wolf or any other animal is innately savage. I have been watching living beings and trying to understand them for a very long time, and the one element that seems to me to cross all species borders and to be common to all things, is that phenomenon that we call compliance. The big wolf doesn't need to be prevented from attacking; he has no intention of attacking. Both he and the subservient wolf are complying with the social imperative against internecine fighting. In fact, by going through this little minuet, they are solidifying and reinforcing their social relationship. Nothing could be more destructive to the group self-interest than to have one or more of its members wounded or incapacitated when the time comes for the hunt.

However, fighting can and will take place when the appropriate signals of compliance are not forthcoming. In such cases, the dominant animal appears to be triggered to action by some perception of disorder or disorganization, which he swiftly moves to correct in the group self-interest. He strives toward equilibrium.

My perception of this is that the integrity of the socially cooperative group is maintained by mutual compliance. In human society we call mutual compliance ethics or civic virtue. Ethics are simply principles of good or appropriate behavior in the interest of the extended group we call society. And of course, it is thus in the interest of the individual member of the group. But remember that the integrity and well-being of the group comes first, for without it, the individual cannot function. So it is, I feel, that each of us as a biologic being, and as a member of a socially cooperative species, is genetically programmed to comply for the greater interest. This biologic drive to comply is not unique to the wolf, or to man, or to any other socially cooperative species. It is as basic as hunger, thirst, sexuality, or caring protectiveness of the young.

In dense super-aggregations, however, that drive is thwarted and frustrated simply because a recognizable group is gone, and with it goes one's own sense of place, one's sense of belonging. Belonging is a biologic imperative, but all one has left to belong to, or to comply to, is oneself. So we get such phenomena as the "me generation" with all of its familiar manifestations. I think the vulgarity of conspicuous consumption is the natural outcome of the loss of our sense of social place. Instead of the naturally-knit, cooperatively ethical community, in which organization is maintained by a web of compliant personal relationships, we find ourselves governed by codified ethics, such as laws, that must be intensified in direct ratio to increasing density. They are enacted and enforced for our protection against the extraordinary and anomolous forms of behavior that unnatural densities cannot help but produce. All of this derives from the stifling of our inherent, innate, compulsion to comply, our natural drive to be ethical.

A last lesson from the lungfish

Speaking of natural drives, while all this is going on, back on the Devonian beach the good old lungfish is still humping along overland toward the next pond. As we have seen, he is able to continue his struggle because he can breathe air and he has strong, sturdy fins. He has been carrying this equipment around with him, even though he hasn't used it before. But now that his conservative instincts are fully aroused, he dips into his bag of tricks and presto, he had the solution all the time. Such existing tools or talents, now being pressed into service in a new environmental circumstance, are called pre-adaptations. A pre-adaptation is some anatomical, physiological, or behavioral feature that may or may not be used extensively at any given moment, but may come strongly into play after an environmental change. It suddenly becomes important; indeed it may make the difference between survival and death.

So I think it is legitimate to ask the question: what is the human pre-adaptation, if there is one, in this time of a dwindling resource base? Some people would no doubt say our reason and our rationality. To that, I could only reply that our reason and our rationality at the present time show no promise whatever of extricating us from a bind into which our reason and our rationality got us into in the first place. I do not think that pure reason is capable of bailing us out of a situation that instrumental rationality created.

I am beginning to see human rationality as an interesting, but double-edged hyperspecialization. A hyperspecialization is the polar opposite to a pre-adaptation. An example would be the total dependence of the koala bear on eucalyptus leaves or the total dependence of North America on fossil fuels. Snatch away the eucalyptus or the fossil fuels and you have an abrupt extinction. Our rationality is such a specialization, because it demands for its smooth functioning one-to-one connections, simple cause-effect lineal sequences, and instant answers to black-or-white, right-or-wrong binary questions. All in spite of the fact that we are biologic beings, part of nature. And nature does not work that way. Connections in nature are mutual and systemic, not one-to-one. There are no simple causes and effects in nature, only relationships. There is no good or bad in nature, no aggression, no achievement, and no reward or penalty. Our high technical civilization simply cannot cope with these realities. This is because of our hyperspecialization.

It goes against the cultural grain a bit to admit that we may already have a clue as to the direction out of our contemporary dilemma. It goes against the grain because it is no compliment to contemorary rationality that the clue may be inborn, as part of our genetic inheritance. Our civilization would much rather pretend that the way must be rationally deduced, planned, fabricated, engineered, and executed. To suggest that the clue might lie in something as embarrassing as our animal nature would be a bit too much. Nonetheless that is where I think it may be found.

I think that the human pre-adaptation for unexpected environmental change is going to turn out to be our genetic capacity for cooperative social behavior, at low population density and in groups no larger than those that can be maintained through individual relationships. I think that our pre-adaptation is the drive to comply: the ethical imperative. Such ethics are not fancied; they are real.

You have heard the expression "small is beautiful." Small is also natural. That is what makes it beautiful.

REFERENCES

1. Hockett, Charles F., and Robert Ascher. 1964. *The human revolution.* Current Anthropology 5(3): 135-168.
2. Ophuls, William. 1977. *Ecology and the politics of scarcity.* W. H. Freeman and Company, San Francisco, California.

II. LAND RESOURCE CONSTRAINTS: RESPONSES IN JAPAN AND WESTERN EUROPEAN COUNTRIES

4
Land-constrained economies: Some answers from the western European countries and Japan

Yves Cathelinaud

For most people living in the Western European countries and Japan, there is no doubt that land is a finite resource. And this is the feeling not only among urban citizens, but also in the farming community. In those countries, the neighbor is rarely far away, and finding a plot of land, for whatever use it may be, is never a simple matter. Indeed, competition for land reached such levels that over the years it has become a subject of public concern and a policy issue. Moreover, it is being realized more and more that the use of land is not reflected merely in the number of acres devoted to each activity; what is also important is how that use of a given area may affect the area next to it. So it is a widely accepted idea that public policy is needed to assure wise land use.

However, individual countries are in different situations; pressures on land are obviously more acute in the Netherlands than in Spain. On the other hand, in the policy field, land use measures are never designed from scratch. They have been preceded by a long series of dispositions dealing with property rights that go back into history. These legal traditions necessarily have a profound bearing on subsequent land use measures, which

Yves Cathelinaud is principal administrator in the Directorate for Food, Agriculture and Fisheries, Organization for Economic Cooperation and Development, Paris, France. The views expressed in this paper are his own and do not necessarily correspond to those of the organization to which he belongs.

helps explain the variety of policies among countries. Some aspects of other countries' policies can suit North American realities and be of help when preparing the transition to a land-constrained economy or tackling problems that are indeed already present in North America at regional or local levels.

The extent of the land constraint in Western Europe and Japan

You can get an idea of the land constraints in Western Europe when you recognize that 19 countries gather 384 million inhabitants on a total area of not quite 4.4 million square kilometers (1.72 million square miles), while the 240 million North Americans have available 19.4 million square kilometers (7.57 million square miles), 4.4 times as much (Figure 1). While the average population density per square kilometer is 23 in the United States and 2 in Canada, it reaches 45 in Ireland, 97 in France, about 240 in the United Kingdom and Germany, 306 in Japan, and 340 in the Netherlands. Of course, when assessing the pressure exerted by population on land, it is preferable to eliminate all acreages that are of little or no use to man: deserts, mountains, internal waters, and certain types of forests. Density in remaining habitable (4) areas would then rise to about 9 per square kilometer in Canada and to 44 in the United States. But corresponding figures would be 141 in France, 398 in Germany, 479 in the Netherlands, and 1,390 in Japan—32 times more than in the United States. Under these conditions,

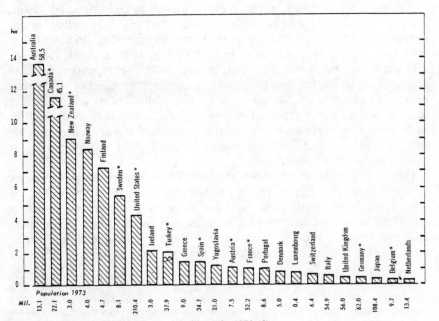

Figure 1. Total space available per inhabitant in 1973 (3).

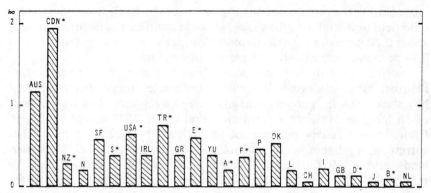

Figure 2. Cultivated land area per inhabitant in 1973 (3). The order of countries is the same as in figure 1.

land appears to the public at large as a finite resource; and even if there may be no agreement on solutions, there is a general awareness of the problem.

But what about agriculture in this context? The area of cultivated land per inhabitant may be an indicator of the scarcity of land. Figure 2 illustrates the difference between Canada (almost 2 hectares or 4.94 acres per inhabitant) and Switzerland or the Netherlands (0.06 hectare or 0.15 acre) or Japan (0.05 hectare or 0.12 acre). Here again, comparisons must be interpreted with prudence, because agricultural potential is also a function of climate, of intensive practices such as irrigation or glass-houses, etc. It remains that the availability of agricultural land is very limited and is an object of acute competition between farmers. On a square kilometer of agricultural land (cropland and grassland) there is 1 farmer in Canada, but there are 12 in Germany, 19 in Italy and the Netherlands, and 180 in Japan. A look in the past will show another difference between these countries and North America. In North America, the evolution since the 1950s has shown important movements in the use of land (for instance, reduction of agricultural land in eastern Canada and corresponding expansion in the West), while in Europe or in Japan these movements have been extremely limited, whatever the situation in agricultural markets. This indicates that there is no reserve of land and also that farmers are still numerous and that the average acreage of their holdings so limited that competition for land does not allow for any temporary idling of land (although marginal land may be abandoned in some remote areas).

Moreover, the trend has been, and still is, toward slow, but continuous reduction of the agricultural land base. One finds the same factors at work as in North America—urban expansion, industries, communication infrastructure, recreation, and also abandonment of marginal land and afforestation. The demand for nonagricultural forestry uses is the most preoccupying since it is, as a rule, almost irreversible; and contrary to what happens in North America, it cannot be compensated for through reclamation of new land. During the rapid economic expansion of the 1960s, the consumption of agricultural land for urban uses reduced the utilized agricultural area by about 0.20 percent each year in most European countries, but at a rate of 0.73 percent in Japan and 1.23 percent in Belgium.

I realize I have already made some abuse of figures, but let me mention the price aspect because in our market economies the price best expresses how the market feels about the availability of a resource. The average price of all land sold in France for agricultural use in 1977 was about $1,700 (United States dollars) per acre and in England about $2,500 per acre. The corresponding figure would be $4,400 in Germany, $9,500 in the Netherlands, and $61,500 in Japan. Of course, as soon as you would look for prime land or land not too far from a town, even though it would be for agricultural use, you would find prices two or three times as high ($128,000 per acre in Japan). You may not be surprised under these conditions that observers term agricultural land a scarce good.

Problems arising from a limited and shrinking land supply

It is useful to make a distinction between problems that interest the whole of a country or only certain regions.

The national issue: Food supply. There are, of course, differences in agricultural policy among these 20 countries. They may be more or less ready to rely on food imports, depending on their balance of payments, the capacity of their agricultural sector to supply food to consumers, and the need to maintain a decent income for farmers. But for security reasons their governments have to insure that this rate of self-sufficiency does not fall below a certain level. For example, in the United Kingdom, it is around 70 percent, expressed in calories. The net agricultural imports of Japan or Germany are equivalent to the net agricultural exports of the United States.

In the past, however, the increase in yields has more than offset the loss of agricultural land. For example, Belgium is one of the most densely populated among the countries in question, and it has the highest percentage of agricultural land taken over by other uses; in the 10-year period between 1960 and 1970, agricultural production showed a gain in volume of 35 percent, while some 11 percent of agricultural land was lost to other uses. Between 1965 and 1975, the value in constant terms of agricultural production went up 23 percent in Western Europe and 29 percent in Japan.

These figures should not lead to excessive optimism. On the one hand, the rate of increase in agricultural production is slowing down. The annual rate of increase for Western Europe diminished from 2.3 percent in the period 1961 to 1970 to 1.6 percent in the period 1970 to 1976. On the other hand, a part of this production is due to imports of intermediate agricultural products, essentially feedstuffs. The Netherlands provides us with a striking example of how part of the input is coming from land in other countries. On the basis of the yields in the United States, the Dutch import of feedstuffs around 1973, if grown in the United States, would have used 2.2 million hectares (5.43 million acres). It could be said that one-half of the final Dutch production was coming from its national territory and the other half from an equal area in a country like the United States or Canada (3).

Another reason why the European unused potential is far smaller than in North America is that the use of fertilizers, particularly nitrogenous fertilizers, is already more intensive. Western Europe uses 70 percent more nitrogenous fertilizer per acre of cropland than North America. Compared to the United States, the use of these fertilizers is about 2.4 times more intensive in Japan, Switzerland, or Norway, 4.3 times more intensive in Belgium, and 10.9 times higher in the Netherlands. Indeed, with the rise in energy prices, the use of these fertilizers will pose difficult economic problems. Resource constraints are really encircling European and Japanese agricultural sectors.

Moreover, like in Canada and often in the United States, it is the best agricultural land that is generally lost to urban expansion in Europe. According to various estimates, the agricultural productive capacity of land taken over in Great Britain in recent years was some 50 percent greater than the average for the cultivated land throughout the country. A similar situation exists with irrigated land taken over in Mediterranean countries for tourist development.

Finally, looking at the world situation does not lead to convincing certainties. The Food and Agricultural Organization estimates that only 11 percent of the world soil resources allow cultivation without serious limitations (1). The rest are hampered by drought, mineral stress, shallow depth, etc. More hectares could probably be put to cultivation, but this would necessitate appropriate technology and expertise, not to mention a good deal of money. In the majority of cases the productivity of these additional hectares appears to be much lower than that of the cropland already in use. The increase of the Third World population increases the need for food, but at the same time reduces the available agricultural area, either for its housing needs or through overuse and deforestation, which lead to erosion and desertification. Thus, Western Europe and Japan appear as land-constrained economies in a land-constrained world.

The local issue: Peri-urban agriculture. The links of agricultural land with neighboring uses, the insertion of agriculture in the local social structure, and the location of incoming uses replacing agriculture are aspects that are important at the local level. A good deal of attention has been given to areas near urban centers because that is where new changes in the economic system are situated (2). The resulting demand for land is concentrated there, leading to acute conflicts. These conflicts involve not only the appropriation of land, but also derive from incompatibility between neighboring uses, especially when various nonagricultural activities have interspersed the agricultural territory. On one hand, there are land losses and the tremendous increase in land prices, and peri-urban farmers are confronted with a climate of uncertainty as to the advance of urbanization that restrains them from investing and modernizing. On the other hand, there is a typical eco-logical problem, involving the functioning of the peri-urban system with all these various activities reacting on one another. These ecological and envi-ronmental aspects have now taken on importance in our societies. For agri-culture, urban encroachment may mean breaking up of farm units, traffic difficulties, disappearance of agro-business, high taxes, competition for water, disamenities, and pollutions of various types. Agriculture is not al-ways a pleasant neighbor with its possible smells or pollutions. This local aspect of the land issue is at the origin of most land use measures taken in the European or Japanese context.

Adjustment to the land constraint

To fully appreciate the measures taken in Western Europe and Japan in response to the limitations in land, it is necessary to grasp the differences in the sociological context and to consider the political environment that led to the current situations in the various countries.

Two political currents have worked to bring public intervention in the land use field. For a long time, they acted separately. On the one hand, for centuries the states or the towns have tried to regulate urban development, mostly for security or police reasons, but more recently for aesthetic or en-vironmental reasons. At the beginning of the century, zoning was already an efficient guide to city development in Germany. Over the years, the ex-tension of urban planning and the complication of building license proced-ures have been common features of most European countries. Citizens are aware, even though it may be with mixed feelings, that the slope or the color of their roof is no longer entirely their own choice, but must follow certain rules.

On the other hand, the land-hungry farmers have always been asking for more land. This has led to now defunct policies of land reclamation, such as the polders gained from the sea in the Netherlands or the bonifica programs bringing irrigation and drainage to underused land in Italy.

Other measures have tended toward a more efficient use of agricultural land already available. Land consolidation, amalgamation of holdings, and various programs for farm enlargement have been implemented in Europe and Japan. These measures impaired valuable advantages for the farming community, but in several countries they also brought some limitations to the free disposal of land. Some form of authorization for sale became nec-essary (as in Norway, the Netherlands, Germany, and France) with a view of maintaining the viability of farm units.

These two forces, urban and rural, have acted separately. In most coun-tries it was like two worlds each having its regulations. But strong economic development and the resulting demand for land for housing, industry, and highways have broken the balance of forces because it happened mostly at the urban fringe where urban regulations were not applicable and where rural regulations proved too fragile to face the pressure of private interests for intensive use of land. One result of this development has been a rapid degradation of the environment around cities and a high increase in city maintenance costs due to dispersion of activities. Thus, the case for land conservation and for a wider planning and management of the land resource gained importance.

In most of these countries, physical planning was introduced some time after World War II to ensure a better use of the available resources and a better balance between the developments of the various regions inside a country. Frequently, however, the effects of decisions such as road building or industrial incentives on land consumption were not taken into consideration; agriculture was considered merely as a reservoir of reasonably cheap land.

Since the mid-sixties however, planning objectives and methods have changed. Under what is now termed areawide planning and management, agriculture is taken more into account. A number of countries (Britain, Denmark, Finland, Japan, Norway, Portugal, Sweden, and Turkey), particularly conscious of the physical limits to their farmland, have taken action to protect their prime lands.

Zoning is being gradually integrated in this new type of planning. Although wide variations still exist in organization due to historical reasons, it is now possible to distinguish three general levels of planning having a bearing on land use: a national level; a regional level, more precise for land use; and a local level, which is expressed by zoning.

There is now an increasing effort to establish a greater degree of consistency among these three levels. However, this is not always easy since zoning plans have sometimes been designed without waiting for completion of regional master plans.

In the Netherlands a considerable effort of cross-consultation has been made among these various levels that has allowed this country to arrive at a complete coverage of the national territory with zoning in conformity with the various objectives of development. This result has to be put in its context: the Netherlands is a country where centuries of struggle against the sea engendered traditions of discipline in water control that prepared the public to accept a strict land use control policy. But zoning of a whole country is also possible under different conditions. Recently, Denmark has also been completely zoned, and in Japan all densely populated regions are covered by zoning. Belgium, Germany, and Switzerland also aim at complete zoning. But it is, of course, a process that requires time.

Although it currently represents a sort of central measure of land use policy, zoning remains a rather controversial issue in Europe and Japan. One aspect that raises problems is the area submitted to zoning. In some countries, zoning is compulsory only for localities of a certain population. This is the case in France, where the communes (townships) are numerous and consequently have small populations; small communes may be left outside zoning that is compulsory above 10,000 inhabitants, even though they are near an important urban center. In such an event, urban pressure that is held in check in the zoned areas may well overflow into this unprotected area of farmland, a problem familiar to unincorporated areas in North America.

The degree of protection of agriculture varies with the possibility of other uses being permitted in agricultural zones. In Denmark, Germany, Japan, and Switzerland, all utilization that is not bonafide farming or forestry is forbidden in these zones. In Finland or Sweden, however, recreational activities may be situated there. In the Netherlands some zones are designated as purely agricultural, while others may include recreational activities.

How long a farmer is guaranteed that his land will remain agricultural depends in theory upon the legal duration of the plan. There are great variations in this regard. In Finland, the definition is permanent; in Great Britain or France, no definite time period is set. In other countries, a period of 10 years has been retained. I find that the disposition adopted in Sweden is very interesting. There, local land use plans are broken down into two or three time periods corresponding to the stages of urbanization foreseen so that the farmer can plan his investments with full knowledge of how much time he has, according to the zone where he is located.

The area designated for urbanization, that is, left unprotected, is of course a function of the duration of the plan. Too often, municipalities find it tempting to make urbanization zones too large. There is currently much discussion concerning the respective advantages and disadvantages of large-scale urban zones in the framework of a long duration and smaller zones in a frequently revised plan.

The efficiency of zoning also depends on the existence of earlier measures that continue to play an important role in land use. Some precedents counter scattered urbanization by restricting building to equipped areas (Norway and Switzerland) or to lots adjacent to land already built on (frequent in Germany). Others counter change of use by preventing the splitting up of land (Denmark and Norway) or by requiring the reimbursement of state-subsidized improvement (Japan). Land purchased by local authorities in view of future expansion also have some influence by relieving the pressure on peri-urban land to a certain extent (Sweden, Finland, The Netherlands, Great Britain, and France).

Toward economic neutrality in zoning

Whether or not zoning will achieve a secure protection of farmland depends, as in North America, on how firm the public authorities will stand when faced with requests for special exceptions or revisions. Such requests are not surprising because an owner can hope to get 10 or even 20 times more from the sale of his farmland if he can have it included in a development zone. Efforts are presently being made to reduce the pressure of private interests, particularly by limiting the possibility of windfall gains. The measures taken vary with the attitudes of countries toward property rights and indemnity for easements.

Taxation has been used to help reduce these pressures. The impact of differentiated annual taxes has not really proved to be determinant. Transfer taxes and capital gain taxes seem to be more efficient, especially when they reach such levels as in Great Britain (a new tax introduced in 1976 levies from 67 to 80 percent of capital gains for development land).

In France and in Italy, it has been preferred to reduce the scope of property rights. The volume of buildings per acre is limited or, as in Italy, the right to build is practically detached from the right of property. These measures decrease the value of land itself for the buyer and, correspondingly, for the seller.

Denmark chose a different approach since the law provides that owners be compensated for limitations on the use of property imposed in the public interest; a once and for all payment has been made to landowners who might have valid reasons to hope to build but had been deprived of this possibility as a result of zoning.

Although public authorities are moving prudently in this field, there exists a current of ideas that point to schemes for equalization of land values. One formula consists of attributing the same amount of building rights (expressed, for instance, in cubic feet of building per square yard of surface area) to an acre in the development zone and to an acre in the agricultural zone. Only owners in a development zone are, of course, allowed to build. But as the building rights are spread over the whole territory (buildable and not buildable), the amount of building rights corresponding to a buildable plot is not sufficient to allow for building and the owner must complement it by more building rights bought from owners in an agricultural zone. This operation, that may take place in a sort of stock exchange, leads to financial transfers between owners who can build and those who cannot and consequently tends to reduce the interest of an owner to see his land classified in a development zone and, hence, pressure on zoning authorities. This is being tried in France and Switzerland.

Conclusion

I would also like to stress the difficulty of land use choices. In spite of the wealth of data and the sophistication of programming techniques, land use choices will always have a high policy content, for they entail a delicate balancing of individual interests against those of society and of the interests of the present generations against those of future generations.

I also realize that many will find the situation of agriculture in these countries so far removed from that in North America that measures taken there may seem excessive for the situation here. In particular, urban sprawl is certainly more a primary cause for alarm than it is in North America. But I think that the preservation of agricultural land may be also in the interests of exporting agricultural countries. By avoiding the destruction of resources and by maintaining their long-term production potential, they will be able to retain their export capacity. Moreover, the rise in energy prices will have important impacts on land use, requiring in particular more land for a possibly less energy-intensive agriculture and for extractive activities. From this perspective, these foreign experiences require reflection.

Many people are concerned by land use measures, and the interests they feel are at stake are so strong that the success of these measures needs public acceptance. This cannot be gained without a lengthy maturation of minds. I think that international cooperation can help convince people by illustrating the type of policies and programs that have proved their usefulness and feasibility in other countries.

REFERENCES

1. Food and Agriculture Organization. 1977. *The state of food and agriculture.* Rome, Italy.
2. Organization for Economic Cooperation and Development. 1979. *Agriculture in the planning and management of peri-urban areas. Volume I: Synthesis report; Volume II: Case studies and reports on certain policy issues.* Paris, France.
3. Organization for Economic Cooperation and Development. 1976. *Land use policies and agriculture.* Paris, France.
4. Organization for Economic Cooperation and Development. 1979. *The state of the environment.* Paris, France.

III. INSTITUTIONAL RESPONSES TO RESOURCE-CONSTRAINED ECONOMIES

5
Institutional constraints in managing resources in North America

Robert J. Sugarman

Institutional limits and capabilities are a topic of conversation in government halls all over our lands. It is a current if not urgent topic, and one not solely of academic interest to planners of food and land resources. For with the intensified search for new energy sources, the always-present but little noticed potential competition and interrelationship between human energy sources and machine energy sources is now coming to the fore. There is and will increasingly be competition for land, competition for use of crops, competition for consumption of energy for food production, and perhaps most important, competition for the consumption of air and water for energy and food. This is what I take resource limitations to mean as applied in the context of this book.

Resource limitations is indeed a massive topic, both in complexity and significance. Resource experts devote themselves daily to predicting how it will play out in redistribution of assets, manpower benefits, and costs; to finding the technical answers to make natural resources stretch to supply us; and to learning how far these resources can be stretched to this end, and how much we will have to pull in our belts. Similarly, political leaders of both the United States and Canada focus their personal energies and those of their principal staffs on this topic. Their dedication, commitment, and sensitivity to the issue is apparent. Their call for improved communication

Robert J. Sugarman is chairman of the United States Section of the International Joint Commission, United States and Canada, Washington, D.C.

and societal rededication is poignant and compelling. It is a challenge to all of us, and our future depends on our response. Perhaps of most concrete significance is the recognition by leaders of both countries that there is inherent interdependence between the United States and Canada. It implies coordinated management of the environment along our joint border.

If institutional management of resources implies aspects of generalized as opposed to wholly individualized control, institutions to manage the resources will be critical to optimum management. Our institutions must be analyzed, criticized, and adapted to today's needs. Let's look at one such institution for what it might indicate, through its strengths and weaknesses, about the shape of needed institutions and the obstacles to their realization.

The International Joint Commission

The International Joint Commission (IJC) is the child of the narrowest of reasons for generalized control, that is, control of levels and flows of the Great Lakes, its channels, and other waters running along the boundary. It was physically impossible for either country to control the levels and flows unilaterally, so Canada and the United States really had to negotiate a treaty to do so together, as they did in 1909, when they also created the six-member Commission, three from each country, to regulate the levels and flows. Yet, less cooperative responses could certainly have been found. The Boundary Waters Treaty could have specified levels and flows, or provided for bilateral negotiations to do so. Indeed, Canada and the United States could have simply impacted on each other without a treaty, accepting the common law of riparian duties to each other and perhaps recognizing a duty to notify and consult, a duty that is just now coming into general acceptance among developed countries.

It was both a limited and an innovative notion that a permanent Commission be created to regulate the levels and flows on the Great Lakes. While the governments kept a tight rein by specifying criteria and by the power of appointment of commissioners and budget, they took a daring step in authorizing decision by a majority of six members, regardless of national division and without unilateral recourse, except renunciation of the treaty.

Now, as I said, the governments conferred the right of binding decision on the Commission with regard to actions that affect the levels and flows of the boundary waters. The rationale was the manifest inconvenience of ad hoc cooperation or unilateral action. Having decided to create the Commission, they then allocated to it two forms of action without initial substance, two bottles without content. History would determine the content. One empty bottle was the jurisdiction to accept mandates from either government to study any issues concerning the boundary areas, and make recommendations for their resolution (Article IX). The other was to accept joint requests for binding arbitration of disputes (Article X). Finally, the treaty, in a single sentence, binds each party not to pollute the water of the other, but, significantly, no power was conferred on the IJC with respect to that duty (Article IV). The history of these four features of the treaty is instructive. Only one has evolved about as expected.

Protecting water quality

The obligation not to pollute has become by far the most complicated and visible of the four features, occupying much time of the governments, the people, and the Commission today. Contrary to plan or expectation and despite Article IV, pollution became a major and complex threat to the boundary waters, especially the Great Lakes, and has engaged the talents and resources of both countries. From pollution in the connecting channels to the near shore areas of the lakes, to the open waters, and now to the edges of the basin, the effort to cope effectively has spread wide the amount of concern and programming.

As a culmination, the governments in 1972 entered into an elaborate agreement within the umbrella of the treaty to restore and protect the water quality of the Great Lakes Basin and its boundary waters, and they have given the Commission today a general mandate with a substantial, joint staff to monitor Great Lakes water quality, critique the governments' performance, and give advice and recommendations (Great Lakes Water Quality Agreement of 1972). Most significantly, in November 1978, both governments reaffirmed their confidence in the IJC by continuing its mandate as an independent voice on Great Lakes water quality (Great Lakes Water Quality Agreement of 1978).

Arbitration and reference

The history of the Commission's arbitration and reference jurisdictions generally are equally interesting. The arbitration provision is interesting because it has never been invoked. In this context, it is curious that the countries agreed in 1978 to arbitrate their ocean boundaries off the East Coast, but specified a special ad-hoc panel. Although this draft treaty has not been ratified by the U.S. Senate, the hesitation appears not to be based on this aspect. Thus, arbitration as such does not seem objectionable; yet the IJC has never been used for this purpose. If one can guess, one might say that the governments want to choose their judges for each new dispute before they will cede sovereign decision-making power. To guess why would be to speculate, but I think it instructive that the parties do not so blithely accept a judicial process.

The reference power is noteworthy because it has been used repeatedly—almost 100 times—but never by one government, always bilaterally. It has been almost always used to resolve water problems, four times on air quality, once on a political science issue, and once on the aesthetics of Niagara Falls. Many recommendations have been implemented; others have died aborning. But in almost all cases the problem has been alleviated, if not eliminated. The process of study, which involves both countries working together binationally on IJC study boards, provides a workshop in which advocates can square off for a fair fight or a joint try at the facts—today, more likely, a joint effort to program the computer or predict such impacts of proposed projects' vegetative succession or aquatic success. Many of these study references have led to long-term monitoring responsibilities of which that covering Great Lakes water quality is the most notable.

Binding jurisdiction

Finally, the Commission's initial mandate, binding jurisdiction over levels and flows, has led, as one might have expected, to a body of decisions approving dams and providing for regulatory structures and permanent regulation plans to operate the project and protect those affected. Though this process was predictable, even here interests whose existence or concern was not anticipated have emerged, such as wetland and fish protection, and the Commission has had to evolve new rules and plans to deal adequately with them. Conversely, in some cases the governments have preempted the Commission by making special agreements on individual projects as provided in the treaty.

Viewing these activities in perspective, the Commission is not a powerful body. It does not enjoy a large staff, nor does it function broadly as an environmental ombudsman or a super-government. It is not directly involved in most of the great U.S.-Canadian issues of trade, energy, or finance; bilateral treaties and negotiations in those areas are much more elaborate. Yet it is the closest we have to a general jurisdictional international arrangement affecting land or water and its use.

One has only to observe the other developed countries of the world hardly agreeing on the principles of nonpollution and not yet able to agree even to notify or consult to realize how far we have come by comparison.

Learning from limits

Yet, here we want to learn more from our limits than from our achievement. To start with, what is it that permits us to go this far, but limits us from going further? The answers are clearly not demonstrable, but some reflections may be offered. In commencing this task, I would like to suggest that the issue of institutional limits in this period of resource limitations is essentially a reflection of the issue of power to distribute resources. I will therefore begin by reflecting on this power. In so doing I observe deep fears awakened by the prospect of control. Even in the best of times, humankind is slow to cede power over its lives and property. Even in eras when resources have seemed limitless, North American people have sought to keep power at home or as close to home as possible. This is especially true with regard to those resources that are most at risk by controls, such as real property. Real estate is most at risk because it is, almost by definition, a major asset—in many cases it is the only significant asset that a family owns; because it cannot be hidden, moved, or converted easily into other forms and is therefore the most vulnerable and because it represents home and even, in Freudian terms, the womb. It represents the most self-controlled source of food, a powerful psycho-economical component. It represents, of course, shelter, which satisfies another primitive, fundamental urge. It is largely these reasons that explain why so much blood has been spilled and so much resistance encountered in revolutionary countries over land and why, for similar reasons, land redistribution is such a significant issue.

Nor should lack of knowledge be overlooked in evaluating these fears. For example, one factor that appears to contribute to a deep distrust and suspicion of pollution control requirements is lack of awareness that certain farming practices can and do cause pollution. A study of Ontario farmers done for the IJC revealed that many of the respondents had adopted practices that had the potential for causing water quality problems (*1*). For example, 37 percent of livestock farmers spread manure within 50 feet of streams, thereby creating a potential problem of nutrient runoff to streams and lakes. Forty-six percent of the farmers actively cultivated less than 20 feet from streams or drainage ditch banks, which increases the likelihood of eroded soil particles reaching the lakes. Yet 80 percent of the respondents believed that farming activities contributed only to a minor extent or not at all to water pollution. This belief may exist because only seven percent had ever personally suffered any adverse effects. Thus, distance from the effects engendered ignorance of the relationship; and this, in turn expectedly provokes reluctance to change and accept limits.

In summary, we see that holding land and control over its use as close to home as possible is a traditionally held psychological-economic imperative augmented by lack of awareness.

In a lesser but still significant extent, this is also true of power over even the incidents of land ownership, that is, conservation practices, crop controls, pesticide use, etc. Powers over the attributes of ownership are tolerated, but with deep distrust and suspicion.

Need for and acceptance of regulations

Despite these fundamental values and needs, as with other human wishes, we see also that people generally acknowledge the need for some societal restraints on the use of land. Indeed, the exotic use of land and activities on land in an industrial society have gradually brought about considerable limits. Some have been narrow and others complex and broad. They range from prohibitions of tanneries to aesthetic controls, from pesticide limitations to controls on historic buildings. Moreover, the mechanisms are increasingly intricate, ranging from cost-sharing grants to tax preferences and penalties, from local zoning codes to national land classifications. Although we are familiar with them, it is worthwhile to dwell for a moment on the huge and fine web of controls that users and owners of land today accept. While it is impossible to describe in a phrase, perhaps the most accurate generalization is that there are today more controls than freedom.

The reason for this is that our industrial society and population growth have spawned an incredible plethora of land use problems—real or potential threats to public health and the community welfare—by which an owner-user of land can adversely affect others. In other words, we now have an interdependence and the ability to harm each other externally—caused insecurity—in ways that simply did not exist 50 years ago.

Yet in the face of all the accepted limits, there remains a strong and deep-seated resistance to land use controls. In the study of Ontario farmers (*1*), less than half (46 percent) of the respondents preferred strict government enforcement. Indeed, as recent events like Love Canal suggest, there are still significant, unacceptable gaps remaining in the control systems. Resistance ranges from American resistance to zoning and pollution controls in the courts and legislatures to Soviet peasants, whole groups of whom chose extermination by Stalin rather than give up control of their farms. The continuing, strong ambivalence with which our society regards control, I believe, finds its origin in the reasons I have suggested.

These are reflected in the variety of responses to the increasingly critical environmental conditions we have noted. Responses range the gamut from centralized collective management in the Soviet Union to local collectives in Israel, to essentially unrestrained individual or corporate control in, let's say, Paraguay or Liberia or Thailand, to the regulated compromise now practiced in the so-called developed nations, such as our nations.

It is important to try to understand the reasons for the different approaches, even though it is impossible to ever define precisely the formula for explaining them. The present degree of knowledge is so primitive that perhaps a few generalizations will provide what instruction we can expect.

It seems, through our knowledge of the history of the major evolutionary patterns of controls, that the key variables in determining the degree of individualism versus that of collectivism or regulatory control are the shortage or abundance of natural resources; the comparative degree of domestic and foreign tranquility, both in defense terms and the economic-health sense; the complexity of society, and the socio-cultural scarcity of resources or a sense of externally caused insecurity will draw people toward more collectivism or regulatory control, depending in degree on their socio-cultural commitment to individualism. Note that economics is a unifying thread running through all these variables. The economic concept of "optimality," in this case optimality of the quality of life, both objective and perceived, is the general theme. I say both objective and perceived, but I hasten to add that in dealing with quality of life, they are fundamentally a single notion.

I would suggest that, at least in our Western cultural tradition, outside interference is accepted in proportion to peoples' feelings of a necessity for it.

This tells us two things. One is that people will accept control. The second is that they want as little as possible.

Creating institutional arrangements

Thus far, I have not explicitly discussed the institutional limitations upon centralized resource management. But I have through my discussion of psychological economics, focused on some of the conditions in which institutions exist, are limited, and obtain authority and acceptance. Let's now apply, in Lockean style, our individualistic analysis to the institutional arrangements that we might conceive and that now exist to direct and mold the optimal development and preservation of resources. In this process we will identify, qualify, and come to grips with some of the basic public desires and fears about such institutions. We will find out in light of the human reluctance to cede individual control over the home, that it is understandable that collective institutions created to control, regulate, own, or manage land resources are regarded with skepticism, hostality, suspicion, and fear.

Institutions that control land use in both the United States and Canada range from local to international. Traditionally, land use decisions involving private land have been made on the local level. Although the states and provinces have had broad jurisdiction to implement land use controls affecting municipalities, until recently they had passed primarily enabling legislation that gave to local authorities the power to regulate land use. This cession of power to local authorities has been a concession to the psychological and economic factors just discussed. Local inhabitants have resented intrusion of authorities from outside their immediate area. They have, however, accepted some restraint on land use imposed by local authorities. A landowner is more likely to relax his individualism for the purpose of collective regulation if he perceives that that regulation comes from those who he believes share this economic interest in and understand his psychological identification with the land.

Essentially, local zoning and land use control represent an effort by those in the immediate vicinity of real property to optimize the local aggregate value of land use. In other words, landowners prefer to give up control of their use of land to only those who share their perceived interests and are immediately accessible. Indeed, such traditional local land use control has been adequate to affect the density, type, economics, and use of land as well as to control its effects on its immediate neighbors. It is not surprising, given this analysis, that those who control local power, that is, the local landholders, wish to keep their power at the local level. The requirements of public hearings and notice in all stages of the institutions of land use control—zoning, municipal planning, and subdivision control—reflect the acknowledgement by legislators that local citizen support is essential to acceptance of control decisions. Thus, if there were no threat of insecurity from forces external to the locality, we would logically expect to find that local landowners have exclusive control over local land use.

There are, however, broader external threats. For over a generation now, it has been perceived that downstream, downwind, and down-distribution chain peoples can be adversely affected by upstream actions. Water overflows, toxic substances, odors, and highway crowding are just some of the obvious environmental impacts, and I do not enter upon economic effects of one community's actions upon another. In response to these impacts, it was common for communities to zone their noxious uses at the downwind or downstream edge of town or on the boundary. Even in a primitive, analytical sense, however, interdependence is an old fact. In recognition of the nature of this interdependence, states, provinces and counties have gradually adopted generalized rules and created areawide bureaucratic agencies. Only in this way could economic and quality of life competition be prevented from undermining downstream local controls, especially where, in their absence, the adverse effects could be shifted downstream, thus optimizing local benefits while externalizing costs.

Some institutional arrangements

Areawide controls were instituted not only to prevent competition between municipalities but also where municipalities could or would not create control to prevent pollution emanating from use of the surrounding countryside. In Vermont, for example, most townships in the 1960s had not developed any type of land use regulation capable of controlling rapid development of second residences for weekending New Yorkers of the commercial enterprises built to serve them. The second residences were often built on hillsides and used septic tanks, which were unsuitable because they discharged sewage into settled communities in the valleys below. Many hillside municipalities, possibly because of the increase in land values or tax revenues, did not pass bylaws to protect the valley residents. Because of their pressure, the state re-evaluated its nonintervention policy and in 1970 passed Act 250 (10 Vt. Stat. Ann. s. 6001 *et. seq.*), a statewide planning program. The act regulates such specified types of development as commercial enterprises exceeding threshold sizes or construction of 10 or more dwelling units by requiring state permits. Power to grant necessary permits rests with the State Environmental Board, composed of eight district commissioners appointed by the governor.

Another example of the problem of land use activity in the surrounding countryside affecting established municipalities was a 1971 drought in three highly populated Florida cities. The drought was caused by widespread drainage, dredging, and filling wetlands, which had normally recharged the groundwater. To combat the problem and to prevent recurrence, the Florida legislature in 1972 enacted several pieces of environmental and planning legislation. The most significant was the Environmental Land and Water Management Act of 1972 (14 Fla. Stat. Ann. s. 380.012 *et. seq.*). The act establishes the state's interest in development problems and provides that the state guide and coordinate relevant local decisions.

Significantly, there is a complex power split. The Division of State Planning, the agency primarily responsible for administration of the act, recommends (based on nominations by affected local and regional authorities) areas of "critical state concern," which the governor may subsequently designate for development control. Local authorities where the wetlands are located may then prepare development regulations for the designated area in accordance with state guidelines. It is worthy of note that where the local authorities fail to make regulations within six months, the Division of State Planning promulgates the regulations.

Maine in 1970 and Wyoming in 1975 devised a series of statewide programs to prevent possible environmental damage from proposed oil refinery developments.

Under Maine's Site Location Act (38 Me. Rev. Stat. Ann. s. 481 *et. seq.*), all commercial, residential, or industrial developments that occupy a land or water area in excess of 20 acres or contemplate drilling for or excavating natural resources must obtain approval from the Maine Board of Environmental Protection.

Under Wyoming's statewide planning law (Wy. Stat. s. 9-849 *et. seq.*), a State Land Use Commission must adopt state land use goals, policies, and guidelines. Once adopted, the local governments must develop or cooperate with the county in developing plans consistent with the state guidelines.

Limitations on authority

These examples and others demonstrate the ceding by local landholders of some land use control power to a more generalized level of control in order to prevent damage caused to one community by its neighbors.

We must observe, however that only minimum power was conceded to the state governments. Procedural requirements for their exercise were carefully scoped and codified, and no powers that could be kept at home were transferred. Generally, such state and provincial agencies as planning boards provide a legislative framework that local authorities adopt, elaborate upon, and enforce. At the same time, it is not uncommon for these agencies to retain approval power over the actions of local governments. Under the Ontario Planning Act, for example, municipalities devise land use plans that must conform with the provincial policies. To ensure conformity, the Ontario Minister of Housing must approve the local plan before it becomes effective.

In many states the approval power goes even further. If local governments fail to act on a problem within a reasonable time period under a given statute, state agencies have the right, as in the Florida Environmental Land and Water Management Act of 1972, to adopt regulations for the municipality.

Although this approval power appears powerful on the surface in usurping local authority, two contervailing factors may attenuate its force. First, there is flexibility in interpreting "failure to act." "Reasonable" time periods vary, and local circumstances must be considered in each case. Second, extensive public participation required by the various state statutes guarantees nonofficial citizen input. The new Act No. 64 enacted this year in Michigan to regulate and site hazardous waste disposal facilities guarantees public input to a significant degree by inclusion of "One third members of the general public" as part of the state hazardous waste management planning committee, and assures that almost half of the committee acting to approve a proposed site be representatives of the community where the site is located. Thus, localism continues to prevail, although larger bodies have increased influence.

The inference seems clear. Localized control, where the individual has direct access, still dominates institutional arrangements. Only in those areas where there is a strong sense of insecurity is a more general governmental control level permitted, and then only to the extent necessary.

Institutional arrangements at the federal level

Now, it is an easy task to carry this analysis to the federal level. It was not until this decade that the states' and provinces' inability to provide adequate protection was conceded. And the threat came from, once again, outside forces.

First, states or provinces were downstream or downwind from one another. Second, economic competition among states and provinces made it impossible to control adverse environmental impacts without federal uniformity.

So, once again, faced with insecurity, the United States reached to a more general level of control to optimize benefits. But just as the people had reserved power to themselves and had kept much of what they gave to local government at that level, so they withheld as much power as they thought feasible from the federal government.

Others are more intimately familiar than I with the inability to secure passage of national land use regulation at the federal level in the United States or even the Environmental Protection Agency's inability to implement what many thought was a mandate for federally supervised land use planning in Section 208 of the Federal Water Pollution Control Amendments of 1972. Many people are also probably aware of the trend in the United States toward regulatory decentralization, where increasingly, money collected and regulatory standards enunciated at the federal level are being retroconsigned to the state levels. Thus, while Public Law 92-500, the Federal Pollution Control Amendments of 1972, provided strong federal control is setting standards for priorities in treatment works grants, much of that control was returned to the states by an elaborate amendment in the 1977 Clean Water Act. In the Surface Mining and Reclamation Act of 1977, passed to obtain minimum requirements for state mining reclamation, Congress required that implementation be left to states that desired and agreed to do so;

and states and industry have contended that they need not conform to the federal regulatory minimums, but only to their interpretation of the general language of the statute. Once again, generalized regulation is ceded to a more distant government only reluctantly and then only to the extent perceived necessary. I can't speak authoritatively on the Canadian experience, but my outside perception is that it is modest to say it is similar. Indeed, I recently heard an authoritative source indicate that distribution of power to the provinces is a political limitation upon the federal government of Canada even in its existing international relations. It has been argued that the federal government lacks the capacity to pass legislation affecting property and civil rights matters under provincial jurisdiction, even for the purpose of meeting an international obligation, such as under the British North American Act of 1867.

International institutions: The IJC example

Now, if this is the way our peoples regard the transfer of power to their own central government, which they elect, to which they pledge allegiance, and whose flag they serve and bear arms, it does not require much imagination to estimate how ready they are to cede power to a supernational entity responsible to them only indirectly, not elected, little known, and at best somewhat remote. Conceive of the enormity of release of sovereignty involved in such an action, when the sovereign is the ultimate transferred focus of self-sufficiency. Imagine also the limitations and safeguards with which they would surround such a delegation of authority.

Is it necessary for me to stress the small powers and carefully confined limits upon it with which your IJC lives? Need I explain for you the sometimes excruciating confines within which such an agency operates? Indeed, the news is not that the IJC has limits, but rather that it enjoys any life at all. Is it surprising that the IJC can issue no order to cease and desist from pollution, nor refuse a license to discharge? I say, in light of the history and psychology, it is remarkable, if not astounding, that the governments have invited the Commission to criticize them and dischargers, and to do so in public, for their inadequacies in cleaning up the Great Lakes.

Now, in this context, we can understand the limitations upon the IJC, their origin, and the limits of their use.

Let me focus on one or two features of the Commission in light of this analysis.

First, one consequence of the caution accompanying the Commission's functioning is the comprehensiveness of its approach. Problems may seem overstudied to insure full recognition of all interests. As one example close to home, IJC studied nonpoint pollution, especially from agriculture, for six years at a cost of some $14 million, and the agency is not finished yet. In short, overcoming the gulf of separate nationalities requires a bridge of heavy, solid construction. Today, however, it is a fact that economics, time constraints, and the enormity of the questions make comprehensiveness an elusive pot of gold at the end of a limitless rainbow. Today, the Commission is confronted with a need to make judgments without all the conceivable facts. Fortunately, comprehensiveness is an inadvertently defective notion. There are always unintended consequences. A corollary of that fact is that we are usually best served by minimizing our interventions into nature and targeting them by fine tuning. The increasing general acceptance of this fact of life has made the Commission's approach viable.

Second, the Commission is an intrusion into national sovereignty, no matter how it tries to serve the true will of the sovereigns. Since Pericles and before, states have struggled with the tension between openness and security, and today it is no different. In the case of the Great Lakes, for example, the Commission must call the players out even when they are sure they are safe, and players who pay the umpire feel aggrieved. As a hired gadfly, the Commission is always at risk. Its exercise of what power it has is inevitably inhibited by its consciousness of the political as well as the legal ease with which the grant of power can be revoked because of what it says. This also leads to search for consensus, watering down, and sometimes delay.

Third, as the winds of adversity begin to blow, the first reaction to the feeling of insecurity is to clutch to one's own bosom, one's own possessions, and to shed or reduce responsibilities to others. Thus, it is sad but true that the harsh realities of the energy shortage, the environmental and economic constraints have inspired such a trend in both our countries. It is not a pretty thing, but it is an inevitable stage. Cooperation depends on trust, and trust is reduced in the initial states of situations of scarcity; it returns, relatively, only when cooler heads are allowed to go to work. And, as I suggested, trust in others to control our land use is a fragile notion to begin with. This leads to reluctance to confide problems to an impartial process based on fact-finding where this could limit national exploitation of resources.

Another important factor is that the IJC is extremely limited in its resources. This is not a plea for a higher budget, nor a suggestion that the work cannot get done. Rather its significance is that we depend for almost all our data, analysis, and expertise on civil servants, on the departmental personnel of each country. These are organized into bilateral "boards" in which complementary groups of such people serve as a task of their employment. It provides us with a strong infusion of expertise as well as the domestic perception of the issues and facts in both countries; it should not, however, be misperceived as always providing a truly non-national institutional construct. It is instead binational. This is, of course, not intended as an adverse reflection on anyone; it is only a recognition of reality; and many believe its benefits outweigh its costs. Some, including me, see the Commission, at the same time, as having essentially a non-national mission, that is, to resolve issues as if they arose within one nation, and to the extent this view obtains, the Commission can be constrained in its ability to act nonnationally by a gap between its non-national sense of mission and the binational concepts that pervade the civil service in the various governments, federal, state, and provincial. In some important situations, some have suggested, this ultimately reflects a hesitation on the part of the two countries to cede too much to too powerful a body. In fact, whether so intended or not, this practical limit on the strength of the non-national body is real indeed.

A final limitation on the Commission's strength is the fact that it has little tradition of law to draw upon, and it has, as well, little tradition of relying upon or developing such law. Some applaud this situation, urging that legal principles are not particularly useful in a situation where there is no shared body of such principles and no mandate for developing one. In this view, the Commission is perceived as a searcher for a "good," that is, sensible solution to each problem even though the principles seemingly underlying such a solution may seem inconsistent with those seeming to underly another seemingly similar problem. The qualifier "seeming" is vital, because it is likely that six Commissioners seeking to do good or satisfy a general public would not in fact apply inconsistent principles to similar problems; the point is that a perceived difference (nonsimilarity) may lie in political circumstance, not in environmental or natural facts upon which principled people could comfortably decide equitable questions. Put otherwise, our legal systems accept that socioeconomic optimality requires general rules that may not achieve such optimality in each case; the need for the general rule is thought to outweigh the loss in some specific cases. An example is the requirement that guilt be found beyond a reasonable doubt in criminal cases.

The reluctance to develop general principles in the Commission's work seems to reflect a preference for more freedom to seek optimality on a case-by-case basis, which, as applied to the "reasonable doubt" example, would permit the jury to apply whatever standard of proof it thought most useful in each case, taking into account such factors as the public opinion about the defendant.

While I respect the view just stated, I believe that the development of general principles by the Commission would usefully reduce the areas of uncertainty and dispute and enable disputants on both sides of the border to feel their concerns had been equally considered, regardless of their political or economic power, and thus enhance the effectiveness and credibility of the Commission. Though I am convinced of the wisdom of this approach, I recognize that my preference is both American and lawyerly and, therefore, cheerfully co-exist with those who are members of neither group, or only one.

Whatever one's views on these matters—ceding of power, resources, and development of independent nonnational principles—it seems to me clear that the common feature of the Commission's limitation is the fear or reluctance to allow power to move further away from home. This is a fundamental human fact.

But as the history of the Boundary Waters Treaty shows, not far behind fear in our history has been a spark of reaching out for common mutual security, as I indicated earlier, a willingness to cede individual power where necessary for individual preservation. Our North American common, successful perception of knowing we can work together, as shown by the IJC experience, fans that spark into flames, and will keep fear from hiding the necessity for us to do so. Thus, I believe there will occur an increasing degree of recognition that just as we share common watersheds, so we share airsheds, a humankind, and an energy base and economy to a considerable extent. Perhaps someday it may even be seen that all these "sheds" are part of one "farm."

Recognition of these realities will lead in time to a broadening of our joint efforts to optimize the use of all our resources. My sense of our peoples' fundamental fear of big government, detailed earlier, tells me that our movement toward joint control will be gradual and hemmed about with restrictions, restraints, and reserve, but I do not regret that. Ultimately the perception and the objective reality of the quality of life of a people are one, and I for one believe with the people that the individual dignity and independence of human beings is fundamental, if not identical, to the quality of human life. Our task is to meet the need for mutual security without imposing unworkable or stifling bureaucracy and rules. It is no mean task. It is tempting to use secrecy, to sell vast schemes, to impose solutions, to cover over problems because the complexity of the facts seems unmanageable. But we have made some strides; and if we now proceed with sensitivity and an awareness that our roots are one with those of our people and trust in ourselves, we can make institutions that serve our ends. Our people know we are of them and do not expect perfection from us; we should not purport to have it. But we must do our level best. If we do this, we North American peoples will be able to enhance our quality of life with constrained resources, for the resource of humankind will never be constrained.

REFERENCE

1. Bangay, G. E. 1979. *Agriculture and water pollution—an assessment of the practices and attitudes of Ontario farmers.* International Reference Group on Great Lakes Pollution from Land Use Activities, International Joint Commission, Windsor, Ontario.

6
RCA: A new approach to conservation policies and programs

David G. Unger

Congress asked the U.S. Department of Agriculture (USDA) in the Soil and Water Resources Conservation Act of 1977 (RCA) to assess USDA soil and water conservation programs in a far more systematic way than ever before. Congress also directed USDA to reach out to a wider variety of organizations and citizens than ever before to obtain their concerns, ideas, and preferences. Why? At the heart of the RCA process are the problems of constraints on natural resources, constraints on expenditures to meet resource problems, and constraints on, or caused by, the institutional arrangements that are in place or may be needed for effective resource conservation.

Congress asked USDA through RCA to report by 1980 on the status and condition of America's natural resource base, the present and likely future demands on these resources, the kinds of programs needed to protect and enhance those resources for sustained use, and any new approaches that may be needed.

Passage of RCA followed an earlier request from the Senate Committee on Agriculture, Nutrition, and Forestry that USDA provide information about its soil and water conservation programs for use in Congressional oversight activities. The RCA process has meshed well with this ongoing work. RCA also has meshed well with a companion act, the Forest and Rangeland

David G. Unger, former deputy assistant secretary of agriculture for natural resources and environment, is the associate administrator of the Soil Conservation Service, U.S. Department of Agriculture, Washington, D.C.

Renewable Resources Planning Act (RPA), administered by the U.S. Forest Service (USFS).

Overall, RCA is bringing about the most fundamental look ever taken at soil and water resource problems, policies, programs, and institutions. The documents that will be forwarded by the president to the House and Senate early next year, and the documents that will follow them at one- to five-year intervals, will substantially influence future appropriations, policy mandates, and institutional relationships. That influence will be felt far beyond the Soil Conservation Service (SCS) or any other single agency. It will be felt beyond USDA or any other department. It will be felt in every state and locality in the land.

The process is evolving in a different way from what was thought at the beginning: USDA is taking a more fundamental look, digging deeper, involving more people and agencies, looking at broader issues, and investigating in more detail the nation's basic approaches to soil and water conservation.

Public participation in RCA

I have been greatly encouraged by several developments as the RCA process has unfolded over the past year. First, I have been encouraged by the widespread public response to the RCA meetings of last spring and summer and the suggestions and comments that have come along since then. Whether the attendance at any one of the 8,700 meetings was large or small, the expression of ideas and concerns about natural resource problems and opportunities in the United States has been extremely helpful in shaping the RCA process.

This year, we are extending our public participation process in additional directions. Several meetings have been held with representatives of interested groups—agricultural, conservation, state and local government, civic, and environmental. We have assembled five panels of distinguished academic consultants who have given us their detailed reactions to central elements of our effort to date, and we will call in at least two other groups or panels to aid in the "mid-course corrections" before the RCA appraisal and proposed program are completed.

Reaction from the public to our proposals will be important as we develop final recommendations. To help obtain this input, two national RCA public meetings will be held in August 1979. When the draft appraisal and program are completed, we will hold 18 regional public meetings. There will be other opportunities for public involvement in the states.

To supplement these sessions, we plan to conduct a national public opinion survey with the aid of Louis Harris and Associates, Inc. This will collect the views of a representative sample of the American people regarding their perceptions of soil and water conservation and their preferences among alternatives for action. We have set up a response analysis center in Athens, Georgia, to handle upwards of 200,000 comments. This entire public participation process, which is called for in the Act, is vital to shaping the final proposed program and ensuring its acceptance.

RCA a department-wide effort

Second, I have been encouraged by the elevation of RCA from a single agency concern to a truly comprehensive departmental effort to evaluate the past, present, and future of some 34 conservation programs of USDA. The USDA national interagency coordinating committee has been meeting almost continuously to give overall guidance to the RCA effort.

The committee, which I chair, has representatives of eight USDA agencies concerned with soil and water conservation: SCS; USFS; Science and Education Administration (SEA); Agricultural Stabilization and Conservation Service (ASCS); Farmers Home Administration (FmHA); Rural Electrification Administration (REA); Office of Environmental Quality; Office of Budget, Planning and Evaluation; and Economics, Statistics and Cooperatives Service (ESCS). The Council on Environmental Quality (CEQ) and the Office of Management and Budget (OMB) also are represented.

We are realizing together that we must struggle with and settle on some innovative options in soil and water policy. We cannot afford to approach conservation policy from the "least-common-denominator" method, where the only changes that result are those that meet no objection from an agency or its interest groups. Past performance suggests some changes are needed, and Secretary Bob Bergland has said that the precept "nothing is sacred" should guide us. But in the final equation, we need to focus our efforts on policies that can realistically be expected to be implemented successfully.

Initiatives by nonfederal groups

Third, I am encouraged by the initiative taken by conservation districts, ASCS county committees, state soil and water conservation and natural resource agencies, and other groups in many states to do something right away with the facts being generated through RCA, rather than wait for our national recommendations. Developing and strengthening local and state soil conservation programs will be a most important result of RCA.

More than $6 million in RCA funds have been granted over the past two fiscal years to state soil and water agencies and individual districts for that purpose. They are being aided by sample outlines for long-range programs prepared by a special task force of the National Association of Conservation Districts (NACD). The increased and innovative action in the states toward better natural resource decisions is good news.

The future and flexibility

Fourth, I am encouraged by the interest generated during and after a futures conference held in Washington in January 1979 with participation by USDA, Congress, interest groups, and some professional futurists. The purpose was to expand our understanding of the possibilities for the United States within a world context in the near-term and long-term future. We learned that USDA must function in far more flexible ways if it is to deal with the uncertainties and extraordinary challenges of the next half-century in a society and economy characterized by uncertainty, rapid change, telecommunications, shifting social values, and conflict. The conference really served to open up our imagination in connection with RCA and other efforts.

This meeting has the same potential for broadening our collective perspective and understanding of the need for creative decisions amid a future of resource constraints.

Data generated by RCA

Probably the best knowledge we have ever had of the resource constraints is represented by the 500-page RCA *Appraisal Part One*, which sets forth a wealth of natural resource data, much of which was available before but never systematically combined. In part two of the appraisal, we will piece together or evaluate what all that information means—to describe not only the physical setting that exists but also the institutional setting and the capability of soil and related resources and institutions to meet projected future demands for various goods and services.

To aid in this evaluation and comparison, RCA is using a linear programming model, updated from one that USDA used in the agricultural portion of the Second National Water Assessment two years ago. The model computes gross erosion and sediment deliveries, uses alternative sets of crop yield projections to reflect different assumptions about improvements in production technology, and compares alternative conservation policies.

As one example, let's say that a national policy were established to limit annual soil loss to 5 tons per acre. The model would remove from consideration all crop production activities and practices that yield over 5 tons gross erosion. The required output then must be met through less erosive activities at minimum cost of production. The model would show how any particular policy would raise or lower commodity prices and describe any regional land use or crop production shifts associated with such a policy.

The printouts would not be the decision, but rather aid the making of decisions on objectives and policies, along with the appraisal data, public comments and suggestions, and the counsel of program managers.

Designing public programs

Carving a program out of all of these facts, figures, and experience is an exceedingly complex and difficult task. I cannot overemphasize the complexity and the potential difficulty. The present program didn't just happen.

But I am excited about the RCA process as a new approach to designing public programs. Rather than considering how USDA might incrementally make some changes in an individual program to improve its effectiveness or start with some broad goals, we began by establishing seven areas of concern that all USDA conservation programs need to address: (1) The quantity and quality of soil resources necessary to provide an adequate supply of food and fiber through the year 2030. (2) State and national water quality objectives. (3) Water supply and conservation. (4) Fish and wildlife habitat improvement. (5) Reduction of upstream flood damages. (6) Energy conservation. (7) Attention to other related resources.

Next, our job is to establish proposed levels of accomplishment for each of the seven areas of concern based on a comparison between the situation now and our best determination of what ought to be. We want to express these objectives of a national soil and water conservation program, for that is what they will be, in quantified terms to the maximum possible extent.

The next step is to explore alternative strategies for reaching these objectives. Some basic and difficult questions have guided our discussions:

• How can incentives to practice soil and water conservation be built into USDA programs?

• How can disincentives in existing programs be removed?

• Can a totally voluntary program succeed in meeting conservation needs?

• Should some sort of cross-compliance among programs be initiated?

• How can a coordinated cost-sharing program be established that is effective and acceptable to all major interests?

• How can we design a program to reinforce the nation's environmental goals of water quality improvement, fish and wildlife habitat protection, and wetlands preservation?

• What should be the role of research and education in the soil conservation program?

• Should federal assistance be tied to matching funds?

• Can a program be designed that will target personnel and financial resources toward the most critical conservation needs?

• How can we make sure that the people who need help the most, including small farmers and minority groups, receive assistance?

• What elements of programs need to be combined or better coordinated?

• How can we most effectively maximize the historical relationship between USDA and local and state entities in an effective program?

The next step is to turn these questions, data, and concerns into three to five alternative program strategies that will be incorporated in the draft program that goes out for public review. Each alternative will be a relatively complete "package" of possible actions and activities by USDA. Each alternative will have been evaluated in terms of the following criteria: Capability of meeting the natural resources objectives within specified time-frames, ability to target on the resource problems, cost-effectiveness, rea-

sonableness and practicability, compatibility with other authorities, degree
of nonfederal involvement, social distribution of cost and benefits, benefit
cost ratio, land use implications, avoidance of internal USDA duplication,
response to market changes, environmental impacts, regulatory impacts,
maintenance of soil and water conservation, and political viability.

Some themes for the strategies

Let me recite briefly some of the main themes for strategies being sifted
right now, in no particular order.

Present approach would be things about as they are now with some adjustments. USDA's programs of research, education, and financial and
technical help have evolved over many years. They offer local people a
variety of means to become aware of soil and water conservation, to identify their own problems, to design solutions and to get organized for group
action. They basically respond to landowners' initiative to seek assistance.

This approach has produced good results. It has evolved to meet questions and changing priorities and needs, but many people question whether
the evolution has been fast enough and whether cost-effectiveness and concentration on critical problems have received sufficient attention.

Green ticket is another strategy being considered. Most of us heard about
it last year when Neil Sampson, executive vice-president of NACD, proposed an idea for incentives for landowners and users who are doing a good
job of soil and water conservation, according to some objective set of standards. It would be a voluntary program—no penalty for not participating
and no regulation requiring participation.

Cross-compliance is another approach, which Secretary Bergland referred to in February at the NACD convention. Under this strategy, effective soil and water conservation performance would be a requirement for receiving assistance under certain USDA programs, perhaps along with some
tax adjustments.

The CARE strategy (stands for *Critical Areas, Resources, and Environment*) would keep the present incentives in a large share of the United
States, but would take special steps in selected counties, regions, or
hydrologic areas where it does not pay the individual land user to do what is
"socially productive." USDA and others would take an extremely close
look at some areas, restructure costs or long-term contracts, and put together a fundable package for the total area. It would likely involve a multidisciplinary planning effort and interagency approach. It would blend national and local priorities. A variation on this theme would be to formulate
national models to set program priorities.

Expanded state role as an alternative program strategy would encourage
state agencies to become more involved and to exert a different level of control. This might be through transfer of funds to develop increased staff of
their own, or it might be through asking them to contribute funds to share
national program costs.

Many states already have implemented measures to increase their role. The redirection could be for voluntary programs, regulatory action, or a combination of the two. It likely would result in a greatly reduced federal role over time.

These are among the major choices under consideration at present. They are not necessarily mutually exclusive: The strategy or strategies ultimately selected by Secretary Bergland and President Carter may well combine elements of several of them. And between 1980 and 1985, the RCA process and congressional action will provide a way of continuously adjusting USDA strategies.

All of this work is still in draft form and is being continuously refined and revised. USDA needs and welcomes people's views. There will be continuing efforts to weigh alternatives, make choices, fine-tune old programs, and weigh new options.

Melding economics, environmentalism, and stewardship

No proposal can be worth very much unless one other thing happens:

A few people always have seen that confidence in the future comes from careful, prudent, and wise use of the resources that we have now. For some this kind of thinking has been an extension of faith; for others, it is an understanding that freedom to use property brings with it responsibility. For others, it has taken the form of a commitment to a longer view than immediate economic or social gain; for the rest, perhaps, it is simply an interest in the public good as well as private welfare.

In the face of the resource and institutional constraints, it is time for widespread adoption of a view of land and water that incorporates economics, environmentalism, and stewardship.

It is time for the landowners, environmentalists, and economists to do more than accept each other, more than just understand one another's position. It is time for them to adopt part of each other's objectives as their own.

The Soil and Water Resources Conservation Act, first conceived as an aid to the Congress in weighing programs, can become an invaluable tool in designing programs acceptable in the state and local network of institutions. The information generated from RCA, with the aid of thousands of local people, may likewise provide part of the foundation for a new way of thinking about America's natural resources, a new conservation ethic.

A new way of thinking may alter the way we act, in time to assure our future.

As John Schaar wrote, "The future is not some place we are going, but one that we are creating. The paths to it are not found but made, and the activity of making them changes both the maker and the destination."

IV. WATER ISSUES IN RESOURCE-CONSTRAINED ECONOMIES

7
An assessment of water resources in the United States, 1975-2000

Lewis D. Walker

Rhetorical persuasiveness is no longer needed to convince the public that an adequate supply of water is essential for the physical, economic, social, and environmental well-being of the United States. The increasing, and often competing demands for water are forcing attitudes away from the view that water is an inexhaustible luxury to the realization that water is a finite, though renewable, resource. Because it is finite, water is a limiting resource in the development of economic activity. This finite resource perception differs from the perception of water either as a component of various functional uses or as an issue to be addressed and regulated via institutions. Although the Second National Water Assessment examines the functional uses of water, it does so from a finite resource perspective. The examination of water as a supply and demand issue brings to light the problems that public and institutional entities must address. With this objective, the U.S. Water Resources Council prepared the Second National Water Assessment.

The Water Resources Council was established under the Water Resources Planning Act of 1965 (Public Law 89-80). Its members are the secretaries of agriculture, army, commerce, energy, housing and urban development, interior, transportation, and the administrator of the Environmental Protec-

Lewis D. Walker is assistant director for policy with the U.S. Water Resources Council, Washington, D.C.

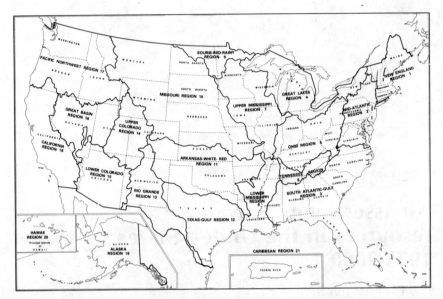

Figure 1. Water resources regions.

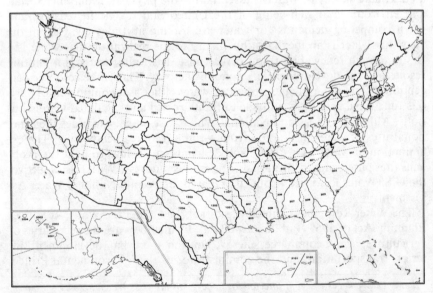

Figure 2. Water resources subregions used in the Second National Water Assessment.

tion Agency. A primary function of the Council is an ongoing program to assess the adequacy of water supplies to meet water requirements of each water resource region in the United States. Two national assessments have been completed, the first in November 1968, the second in December 1978.

The two national water assessments

The scope of the second assessment goes beyond the groundwork done in the first assessment. While the original goals of identifying, quantifying, and showing the extent and seriousness of water and related land problems remain, the second assessment refines the data-gathering process and enlarges the problem areas introduced in the first assessment.

To get a more refined perspective on regional problems, the second assessment revised the 20 hydrologic water resources regions into 21 regions, then further divided those 21 regions into 106 smaller hydrologic units called subregions (Figures 1 and 2). Data from the 106 subregions were then aggregated to present more precise information on the regions.

In addition to the more precise hydrologic and geographic focus, the second assessment also narrowed the time range for projections. Because pro-

Table 1. *Streamflow frequency—"1975."* (Italic numbers not included in total because these are inflows to another region.).

| Water Resources Region and No. | Streamflow (billion gallons per day) | | | | |
| | | Percent Exceedance | | | |
	Mean	5	50	80	95
New England (1)	78.2	107.7	77.4	62.7	48.3
Mid-Atlantic (2)	79.2	115.1	77.8	61.2	48.4
South Atlantic-Gulf (3)	228.0	356.6	219.3	164.1	121.8
Great Lakes (4)	72.7	103.9	71.7	57.3	44.9
Ohio (5)	*178.0*	*254.0*	*178.0*	*141.0*	*105.0*
Tennessee (6)	*40.8*	*57.9*	*40.8*	*35.9*	*31.4*
Upper Mississippi (7)	*121.0*	*189.0*	*121.0*	*91.8*	*65.3*
Lower Mississippi (8)	433.0	757.0	433.0	282.0	202.0
Souris-Red-Rainy (9)	6.0	11.4	5.6	3.4	1.8
Missouri (10)	*44.1*	*74.3*	*43.2*	*29.9*	*17.6*
Arkansas-White-Red (11)	*62.6*	*120.7*	*59.1*	*37.4*	*21.6*
Texas-Gulf (12)	28.3	62.4	22.9	12.3	6.3
Rio Grande (13)	1.2	4.4	.6	.3	.2
Upper Colorado (14)	*10.0*	*15.6*	*10.0*	*7.0*	*3.9*
Lower Colorado (15)	1.6	1.7	1.6	1.4	1.2
Great Basin (16)	2.6	4.7	2.4	1.6	1.2
Pacific Northwest (17)	255.3	344.7	254.3	213.3	179.7
California (18)	47.4	87.4	44.3	29.8	19.5
Total, regions 1-18	1,233.4	1,956.9	1,210.9	889.4	675.3
Alaska (19)	905.0	1,030.0	898.0	795.0	705.0
Hawaii (20)	6.7	10.3	6.3	4.9	3.8
Caribbean (21)	4.9	7.1	4.5	3.3	1.6
Total, regions 1-21	2,150.0	3,004.3	2,119.7	1,692.6	1,385.7

jections for a 50-year period are uncertain, the second assessment confined its horizons to a 25-year period, from 1975 to 2000, whereas the first assessment used a 55-year forecast period extending from 1965 to 2020. The base year "1975" represents an assumed average rather than an historical year and is shown with quotation marks.

With the tighter data-gathering unit and the narrower time scope, the second assessment enlarged the treatment of water issues. It covers population; income; water for domestic and commercial uses, manufacturing, food and fiber, energy and minerals production, recreation, fish and wildlife, natural and historical areas, navigation; erosion, sedimentation, and flood management; and water treaties and compacts. Other considerations include a more detailed evaluation of groundwater use, a quantification of instream use, and an analysis of pollution sources. The report also shows specific problems by regions and compares the federal and state regional projections for 1985 and 2000.

Resolving the many complex water and related land problems is no simple matter. The demands made on our water resources by the nation's growing population, expanding economy, and ever-increasing complexity of tech-

Table 2. Ground-water withdrawals and percentage of overdraft—"1975."

Water Resources Region and No.	Total Withdrawal (mgd)*	Overdraft		Subregions		
		Total (mgd)*	Percent	Number in Region	Number with Overdraft	Range in Overdraft (Percent)
New England (1)	635	0	0	6	0	-
Mid-Atlantic (2)	2,661	32	1.2	6	3	1-9
South Atlantic-Gulf (3)	5,449	339	6.2	9	8	2-13
Great Lakes (4)	1,215	27	2.2	8	1	30
Ohio (5)	1,843	0	0	7	0	-
Tennessee (6)	271	0	0	2	0	-
Upper Mississippi (7)	2,366	0	0	5	0	-
Lower Mississippi (8)	4,838	412	8.5	3	3	7-13
Souris-Red-Rainy (9)	86	0	0	1	0	-
Missouri (10)	10,407	2,557	24.6	11	10	4-36
Arkansas-White-Red (11)	8,846	5,457	61.7	7	7	2-76
Texas-Gulf (12)	7,222	5,578	77.2	5	5	24-95
Rio Grande (13)	2,335	657	28.1	5	4	22-43
Upper Colorado (14)	126	0	0	3	0	-
Lower Colorado (15)	5,008	2,415	48.2	3	3	7-53
Great Basin (16)	1,424	591	41.5	4	4	7-75
Pacific Northwest (17)	7,348	627	8.5	7	6	4-45
California (18)	19,160	2,197	11.5	7	5	7-31
Regions 1-18	81,240	20,889	25.7	99	59	1-95
Alaska (19)	44	0	0	1	0	-
Hawaii (20)	790	0	0	4	0	-
Caribbean (21)	254	13	5.1	2	1	5
Regions 1-21	82,328	20,902	25.4	106	60	1-95

*Million gallons per day.

nology make a national policy and coordinated management even more imperative. Moreover, environmental protection measures have added still another dimension to the challenge.

The ultimate goal of the assessment program is to help bring about improved and coordinated management of the many federal water-related programs. While specific management recommendations are not given, the second assessment identifies specific problem areas and outlines key policy implications.

Organization of the second assessment

The second assessment discusses three general aspects of water: water supply, water use, and critical water problem areas.

Water supply. Nationally, the United States has an ample overall supply of water from both surface and underground sources. Table 1 shows the amount of water available in streams on a regional basis in "1975." To reflect the random nature of streamflow from year to year, table 1 gives mean flows as well as percent exceedance flows. A 5 percent exceedance flow means that the given value is an average high flow exceeded in only 5 out of 100 years. Table 2 shows the "1975" groundwater withdrawals and degree of overdraft (net depletion of supply) for the 21 regions.

In spite of the adequate national supply, uneven distribution of precipitation causes regional or local water shortages. These shortages can occur in any season and in any part of the United States. They are generally associated with the arid West. Many humid eastern localities also have periodic water supply problems. At times, the poor water quality or economic, social, and environmental constraints can also constrain water supplies. For example, water rights laws may enable an upstream user to deplete a streamflow or deteriorate its quality so that a downstream user cannot depend on the flow.

Water use. The assessment deals with two types of water use: instream use and offstream use that involves groundwater use.

For offstream uses, the water is withdrawn from the surface water or groundwater sources and conveyed to the place of use, such as in irrigation or steam electric generation. For instream use, the water is used in the river channel itself, such as for navigation or fishing. "Water consumed," "consumptive use," or "consumption," refer to that part of the withdrawn water that is evaporated, transpired, incorporated into products and crops, consumed by humans or livestock, or otherwise removed from the immediate water supply. Total withdrawals and consumption, by functional use, for the 21 water resources regions are shown in table 3. These figures are given for the three case years considered in the assessment—"1975," 1985, and 2000. The same information is displayed graphically in figure 3 (withdrawals) and figure 4 (consumption). Total freshwater withdrawals and consumption by region are shown in table 4 for the three case years.

In "1975," the United States withdrew 338 billion gallons per day of fresh water (surface and ground) for offstream uses, such as agriculture, manufacturing, minerals production, domestic and commercial use, and steam electric generation. By the year 2000, this amount is projected to decrease to 306 billion gallons per day, a 9 percent reduction from "1975." This decrease will be due to more efficient use of water as a result of conservation efforts, better technology in recycling, and similar procedures.

Of the 338 billion gallons per day withdrawn in "1975," 107 billion

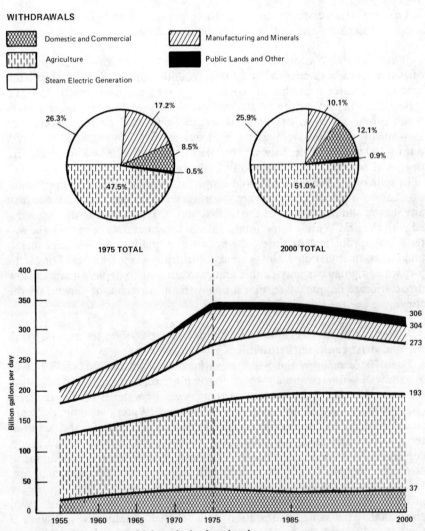

Figure 3. Total freshwater withdrawals, by functional use.

Table 3. Total withdrawals and consumption, by functional use, for the 21 water resources regions—"1975," 1985, 2000.

Functional Use	Total Withdrawals (million gallons per day)			Total Consumption (million gallons per day)		
	"1975"	1985	2000	"1975"	1985	2000
Fresh water:						
Domestic:						
Central (municipal)	21,164	23,983	27,918	4,976	5,665	6,638
Noncentral (rural)	2,092	2,320	2,400	1,292	1,408	1,436
Commercial	5,530	6,048	6,732	1,109	1,216	1,369
Manufacturing	51,222	23,687	19,669	6,059	8,903	14,699
Agriculture:						
Irrigation	158,743	166,252	153,846	86,391	92,820	92,506
Livestock	1,912	2,233	2,551	1,912	2,233	2,551
Steam electric generation	88,916	94,858	79,492	1,419	4,062	10,541
Minerals industry	7,055	8,832	11,328	2,196	2,777	3,609
Public lands and others*	1,866	2,162	2,461	1,236	1,461	1,731
Total fresh water	338,500	330,375	306,397	106,590	120,545	135,080
Saline water† total	59,737	91,236	118,815			
Total withdrawals	398,237	421,611	425,212			

*Includes water for fish hatcheries and miscellaneous uses.
†Saline water is used mainly in manufacturing and steam electric generation.

gallons were consumed. By the year 2000, consumption is expected to be about 135 billion gallons per day, an increase of almost 27 percent. The projected increase will result from growth in manufacturing and mineral industries, steam electric generation, and agriculture. Another significant cause will be the increased evaporation that will result from higher water temperatures needed to increase recycling. Agriculture is, and will continue to be, the major consumptive user of water. Except for consumptive losses caused by recycling, consumption is more critical than total withdrawals because water consumed is not available for other downstream uses.

Fish and wildlife maintenance, hydroelectric generation, navigation, and recreational activities are instream flow uses. Of these, maintenance of fish and wildlife habitat requires the greatest amount of streamflow. For the conterminous United States, the estimated ideal flow for fish and wildlife is 1,035 billion gallons per day, somewhat below the estimated average daily streamflow of 1,233 billion gallons. Although the average daily flow for the nation is more than enough to meet the need for fish and wildlife, the adequacy of streamflow to meet instream flow needs is similar to that of water supply; it varies from region to region.

Critical problem areas

To identify the critical water problems of the United States, a water supply adequacy analysis model was developed. It is based on the concept of a balance between water use and water supply for both groundwater and fresh surface water. This model, shown graphically in figure 5, allowed analysis of each of the 106 water resources subregions. Subregions have water inflow or supply from upstream subregions, interbasin imports, precipitation, runoff, and groundwater. Water losses include interbasin exports, consumption, and evaporation; these are deducted from the potential supply. Groundwater recharge is accounted for in the model but is not considered a loss because the recharged groundwater aquifer also supplies water to the stream.

The results of the adequacy analysis suggest that the intensive use and

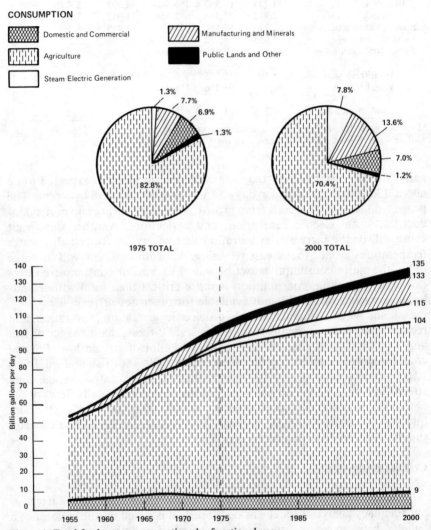

Figure 4. Total freshwater consumption, by functional use.

Table 4. Total freshwater withdrawals and consumption—"1975," 1985, 2000.

Water Resources Region and No.	Withdrawals (million gallons per day)			Consumption (million gallons per day)		
	"1975"	1985	2000	"1975"	1985	2000
New England (1)	5,098	3,939	3,230	481	647	1,063
Mid-Atlantic (2)	18,300	15,857	13,873	1,843	2,472	3,548
South Atlantic-Gulf (3)	24,510	25,457	28,340	4,867	6,772	10,053
Great Lakes (4)	42,813	32,666	25,624	2,598	3,300	4,693
Ohio (5)	34,934	27,838	16,925	1,798	2,527	4,332
Tennessee (6)	7,412	7,131	6,013	313	647	1,105
Upper Mississippi (7)	12,401	10,386	7,910	1,145	1,604	2,688
Lower Mississippi (8)	14,567	17,453	24,841	4,027	4,554	5,511
Souris-Red-Rainy (9)	336	329	587	112	204	446
Missouri (10)	38,016	48,037	44,359	15,469	19,206	19,913
Arkansas-White-Red (11)	12,868	13,799	13,337	8,064	8,769	8,887
Texas-Gulf (12)	16,925	15,932	14,991	11,259	10,227	10,529
Rio Grande (13)	6,321	6,204	5,633	4,240	4,320	4,016
Upper Colorado (14)	6,869	7,841	7,519	2,440	3,018	3,232
Lower Colorado (15)	8,917	8,528	7,857	4,595	4,754	4,708
Great Basin (16)	7,991	7,316	7,258	3,779	3,765	4,036
Pacific Northwest (17)	37,495	38,098	33,852	11,913	14,610	15,196
California (18)	39,636	40,549	41,265	26,641	27,932	29,699
Total, regions 1-18	335,409	327,360	303,413	105,584	119,328	133,655
Alaska	305	433	745	58	207	459
Hawaii (20)	1,879	1,619	1,349	605	636	666
Caribbean (21)	907	963	890	343	374	300
Total, regions 1-21	338,500	330,375	306,397	106,590	120,545	135,080

competition for water to satisfy a wide variety of purposes have created a number of problems. The ten problem areas identified are as follows:

• *Inadequate surface water supply.* Localized problems of inadequate surface water supply have been identified in all 21 water resources regions. However, 17 subregions have or will have a serious problem of inadequate surface water supply by the year 2000.

• *Overdraft of groundwater.* The most dramatic cases of groundwater overdraft are in the High Plains area from Texas to Nebraska. Central Arizona and parts of California also depend heavily on groundwater. In some of those areas groundwater levels are declining 7 to 10 feet per year.

• *Pollution of surface water.* Occurrences of surface water pollution were reported in most of the 21 water resources regions. Dispersed agricultural sources, municipal and industrial wastes, acid mine drainage, and associated urban runoff are the significant sources.

• *Pollution of groundwater.* Groundwater pollution, whether existing or potential, natural or manmade, poses a significant health threat since 40 percent of the population derives drinking water from groundwater sources. Groundwater pollution has been recognized in nearly all 21 regions.

• *Quality of drinking water.* Pollution of surface and underground sources of public water supplies has serious potential public health conse-

82 LEWIS D. WALKER

quences. Thus, maintenance of both surface water and groundwater quality for drinking is of concern nationwide. At the community level, most surface water receives extensive monitoring and treatment, and groundwater receives at least chlorination. In rural areas, however, where many people obtain drinking water from individual domestic wells, the water receives little or no treatment, yet the potential health hazard is significant.

• *Flooding.* In 1975, 107 people were killed by floods and property damage was estimated at $3.4 billion. By the year 2000, potential flood damage is expected to increase to $4.3 billion annually unless floodplain management and the regulation of floodplains are expanded.

• *Erosion and sedimentation.* The "1975" average cropland soil loss from erosion was nearly 9 tons per acre; in some areas the soil loss exceeded 25 tons per acre. In addition, forest and pasture lands sustain soil losses of about 1 ton per acre per year. The consequent sedimentation from runoff frequently degrades the waters nearby.

• *Dredging and disposal of dredged material (dredge and fill).* The large volume of sediment deposited each year in navigable stream channels, reservoirs, and harbors requires regular removal and disposal. To maintain the

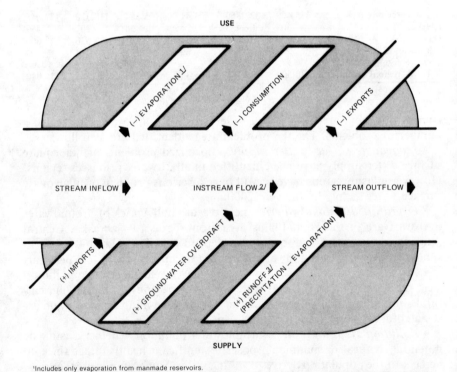

¹Includes only evaporation from manmade reservoirs.
²Includes flow requirements for navigation, hydroelectric, conveyance to meet downstream treaty and compact commitments, fish and wildlife habitat maintenance, waste assimilation, recreation, sediment transport, and fresh-water flow to estuaries.
³Includes precipitation minus natural evaporation from land surfaces and plant transpiration and drainage to ground water.

Figure 5. Water supply adequacy analysis model.

national navigation network, continued dredging is necessary. However, disturbance of the water bottoms by dredging frequently disperses pollutants settled into the sediment, thereby introducing high concentrations of pollutants in the surrounding water.

• *Wet soils drainage and wetlands.* Wet soils comprise an estimated 400 million acres, of which about 104 million acres are used for cropland. An estimated 43 million acres need improved drainage. An additional 70 million acres of wet soils in forest, pasture, or other types of wetland could be converted to cropland. However, it is estimated that by the year 2000 only 11 million additional acres will have been converted to cropland. This conversion will be offset to some degree by croplands that revert to wetlands and by the creation of new wetlands. Competition between agricultural and wildlife interests is particularly acute in some wetland areas.

• *Degradation of bay, estuary, and coastal water.* Much of the coastal area water is being degraded by domestic and industrial waste, particularly in the densely populated New England, Mid-Atlantic, and Great Lakes Regions. These coastal waters provide major recreational opportunities for more than 80 percent of the population. In the Texas-Gulf Region, reduced streamflows to the bays have upset the fresh saline mix of water, affecting the marine life in those areas.

Figures 6 to 14 give geographical summaries of some of these problems.

Methodology and growth assumptions

The assessment process was divided into three phases: (1) nationwide analysis, (2) specific problem analysis, and (3) national problem analysis. In these analyses, data were developed on the nation as a whole, in the 21 water resource regions, and in the 106 subregions. In the third phase, to establish a basis for defining the management problem, the focus was on the water resource itself rather than on its end uses alone or on the institutions that regulate its use. If there were no constraints on the water, then a problem was not identified.

Nationwide analysis. This phase was to provide nationwide information on water requirements and water supplies and display the results against a nationally consistent set of projections. This was done to identify existing and potential water problems. These projections include population, agriculture, and forestry needs; water quality problems; electric power demands; flood damages; navigation needs; fish, wildlife, and recreation requirements; and land and water preservation. In the assessment, this set of projections is referred to as the national future.

The nationwide analysis produced a nationally consistent data base to gather information on water fluxes so that from a hydrological standpoint all water within and among the regions would be accounted for. However, getting data from the regions to agree with the national data, where agreement was necessary, proved to be a formidable task because regional

criteria for data gathering differed—some times significantly—from the
criteria established in the nationwide analysis.

Specific problem analysis. The specific problem analysis was to set forth
the state-regional viewpoints in a common format and in sufficient detail
for use in the national problem analysis. The state-regional study teams
identified and described (1) water-related problems, (2) geographic areas
having significant problems of a complexity that warrants preparation of
comprehensive plans or data collection activities, and (3) effects of not
resolving specific problems. Based on the above identification and descrip-
tion of problems, the 21 state-regional sponsors reported their conclusions
and recommendations. These reports on state-regional futures reflect local
viewpoints that are little influenced, if any, by the federal perspective. The

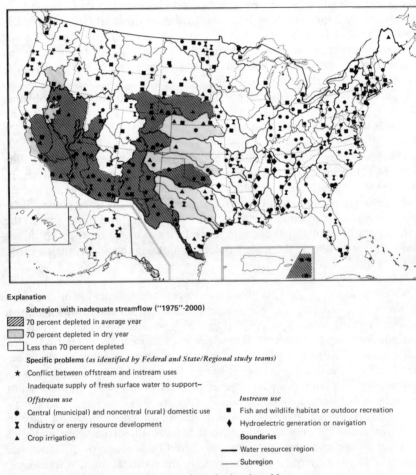

Explanation

    Subregion with inadequate streamflow ("1975"-2000)

  70 percent depleted in average year

  70 percent depleted in dry year

  Less than 70 percent depleted

    Specific problems *(as identified by Federal and State/Regional study teams)*

★ Conflict between offstream and instream uses

  Inadequate supply of fresh surface water to support—

Offstream use

● Central (municipal) and noncentral (rural) domestic use

Ⅹ Industry or energy resource development

▲ Crop irrigation

Instream use

■ Fish and wildlife habitat or outdoor recreation

♦ Hydroelectric generation or navigation

Boundaries

── Water resources region

── Subregion

Figure 6. Inadequate surface water supply and related problems.

state-regional futures are the regional counterparts of the national futures in the nationwide analysis.

National problem analysis. The final phase of the assessment was the national problem analysis. This analysis compared federal and state-regional viewpoints and identified, from a national perspective, the most serious water and related land problems in the United States. First, procedures and guidelines for the analysis were developed. The Council's National Programs and Assessment Committee then identified and described the water and related land problems, designated the geographic areas where these problems are or will be severe, and prepared a report on their conclusions and recommendations about the federal role in resolving these problems. Data from the nationwide analysis (first phase) and specific problem

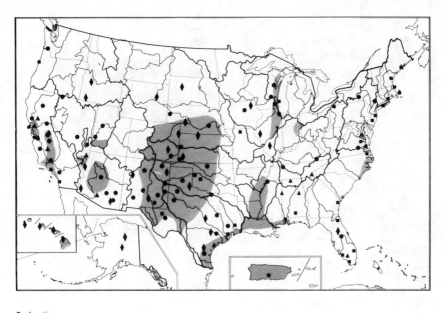

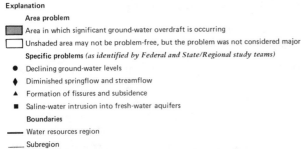

Explanation

Area problem

▨ Area in which significant ground-water overdraft is occurring

☐ Unshaded area may not be problem-free, but the problem was not considered major

Specific problems *(as identified by Federal and State/Regional study teams)*

● Declining ground-water levels

♦ Diminished springflow and streamflow

▲ Formation of fissures and subsidence

■ Saline-water intrusion into fresh-water aquifers

Boundaries

—— Water resources region

___ Subregion

Figure 7. Groundwater overdraft and related problems.

analysis (second phase) provided the basis for the national problem analysis (final phase), which has as its primary objective the identification, quantification, and articulation of problems of national significance.

Growth assumptions. In resource analysis, key variables, such as population or Gross National Product (GNP), are often taken to be independent or forcing variables whose values are simply extrapolations of past and current data into the future. Resource problems or requirements are then defined on the basis of those extrapolated values. However, these key variables are known to be dependent to some degree on the resources available. For example, excessive demand (as indicated by population or GNP) can lead to water shortages; however, the level of demand in turn can be influenced as technological development, governmental policies, and

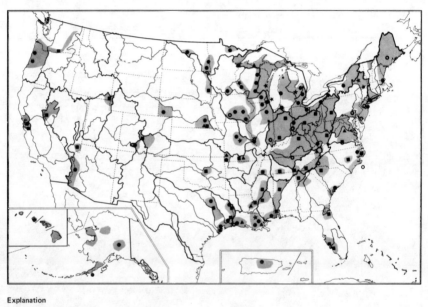

Explanation

Area problem

Area in which significant surface-water pollution from point sources is occurring

Unshaded area may not be problem-free, but the problem was not considered major

Specific types of point-source pollutants

● Coliform bacteria from municipal waste or feedlot drainage

★ PCB (polychlorinated biphenyls), PBB (polybromated biphenyls), PVC (polyvinyl chloride), and related industrial chemicals

▲ Heavy metals (e.g., mercury, zinc, copper, cadmium, lead)

■ Nutrients from municipal and industrial discharges

○ Heat from manufacturing and power generation

Boundaries

—— Water resources region

___ Subregion

Figure 8. Surface water pollution problems from point sources—municipal and industrial waste (as identified by federal and state/regional study teams).

consumer lifestyles respond to the supply of water available. To represent this feedback relationship would require a complex model beyond the scope of the assessment. Instead, the socioeconomic assumptions basic to the 1985 and 2000 water projections are independent of the influence that water supply may play on future growth.

The assumptions on which the two scenarios are based include:

• Population will grow about 0.9 percent a year, reach 268 million people in the year 2000, and reach zero growth early in the next century.

• GNP will increase about 4 percent a year, doubling by the year 2000.

• Water quality goals will be largely achieved by 1985.

• Attainment of water quality goals and higher monetary values for water will influence water use effectiveness.

• Agricultural production and marketing, after appropriate modifica-

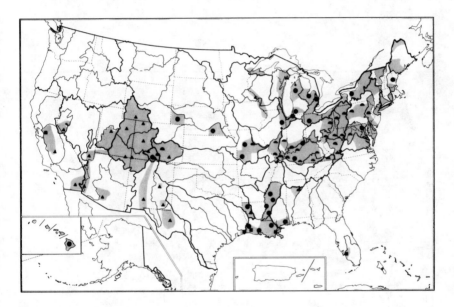

Explanation

Area problem

▨ Area in which significant surface-water pollution from nonpoint sources is occurring

☐ Unshaded area may not be problem-free, but the problem was not considered major

Specific types of nonpoint-source pollutants

● Herbicides, pesticides, and other agricultural chemicals

▲ Irrigation return flows with high concentration of dissolved solids

■ Sea-water intrusion

◆ Mine drainage

Boundaries

━━ Water resources region

──── Subregion

Figure 9. Surface water pollution problems from nonpoint sources—dispersed (as identified by federal and state/regional study teams).

tion, will reflect recent trends in per capita consumption and export levels.

• Current trends to increase emphasis on fish and wildlife and recreation needs will continue indefinitely.

• Levels of floodplain regulation will increase in the future.

• Current trends in waterway shipments as a proportion of total shipments will continue.

Actual and projected values for two critical use-related variables, population and GNP, are shown for the period 1950 to 2000 in figure 15.

Water problem profile analysis

For each problem area, the fundamental management questions of the assessment were these: What are the uses of the resource, and is there an ade-

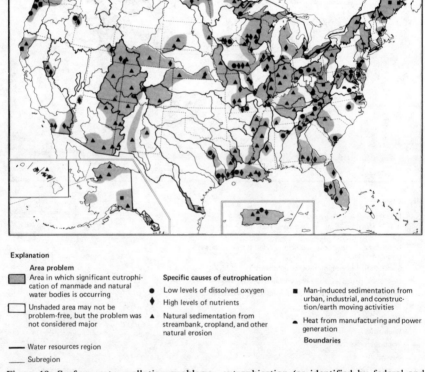

Explanation

Area problem

⬛ Area in which significant eutrophication of manmade and natural water bodies is occurring

◻ Unshaded area may not be problem-free, but the problem was not considered major

▬▬ Water resources region

___ Subregion

Specific causes of eutrophication

● Low levels of dissolved oxygen

◆ High levels of nutrients

▲ Natural sedimentation from streambank, cropland, and other natural erosion

■ Man-induced sedimentation from urban, industrial, and construction/earth moving activities

▲ Heat from manufacturing and power generation

Boundaries

Figure 10. Surface water pollution problems—eutrophication (as identified by federal and state/regional study teams).

quate water supply to provide for those uses? Central to the expected use analysis is the amount available. Even though water quality is implicitly included in the amount available, water quality is not addressed in the following discussion of surface water and groundwater supplies. Of the 10 water problems analyzed in the assessment, two critical water problems are highlighted below, inadequate surface water supply and overdraft of groundwater.

Inadequate surface water supply. Given a finite water supply, the time must come when the quantity available is no longer adequate to meet necessary competing demands. In the case of surface water, the problem is principally a conflict between instream and offstream demand. Offstream uses of water for energy, agricultural, domestic, and industrial needs must be

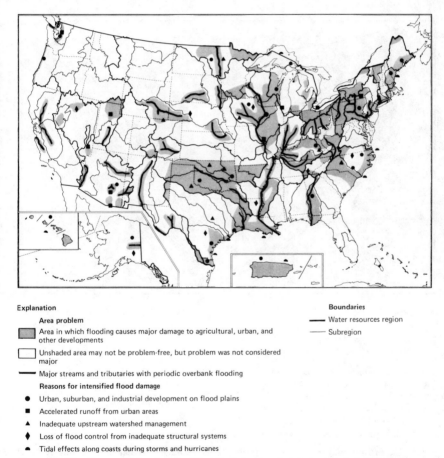

Explanation

Area problem

▨ Area in which flooding causes major damage to agricultural, urban, and other developments

▢ Unshaded area may not be problem-free, but problem was not considered major

━━ Major streams and tributaries with periodic overbank flooding

Reasons for intensified flood damage

● Urban, suburban, and industrial development on flood plains

■ Accelerated runoff from urban areas

▲ Inadequate upstream watershed management

◆ Loss of flood control from inadequate structural systems

◄ Tidal effects along coasts during storms and hurricanes

Boundaries

━━ Water resources region

── Subregion

Figure 11. Flooding problems (as identified by federal and state/regional study teams).

weighed against such instream uses as recreation, navigation, hydropower, and maintenance of fish and wildlife habitat. Where an inadequate supply exists or will exist, these uses must be carefully evaluated. By the year 2000, the problem of inadequate surface water supply will be severe in 17 subregions located mainly in the Midwest and Southwest (Figure 6). During low flow months, more subregions, including some in the East, will also be faced with this problem.

In response to the growing concern for environmental quality, the assessment focuses on the maintenance of instream flows for fish and wildlife. The geographical problem areas shown in figure 6 were identified through a stream depletion analysis that translated a certain level of streamflow into a corresponding degree of habitat quality. The results of the analysis indicate that the average current streamflows on the national level are adequate for

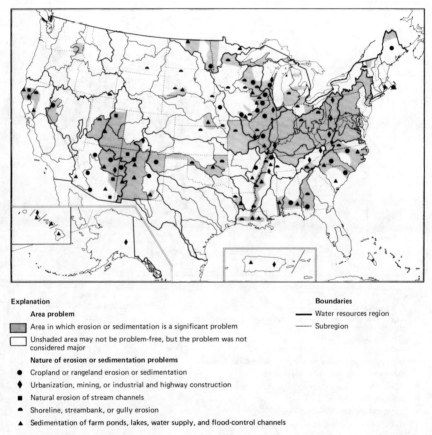

Explanation

Area problem

▓ Area in which erosion or sedimentation is a significant problem

☐ Unshaded area may not be problem-free, but the problem was not considered major

Nature of erosion or sedimentation problems

● Cropland or rangeland erosion or sedimentation

◆ Urbanization, mining, or industrial and highway construction

■ Natural erosion of stream channels

◆ Shoreline, streambank, or gully erosion

▲ Sedimentation of farm ponds, lakes, water supply, and flood-control channels

Boundaries

━━ Water resources region

── Subregion

Figure 12. Erosion and sedimentation problems (as identified by federal and state/regional study teams).

fish and wildlife. However, extreme regional variations can cause major shortages in certain areas. For example, the Lower Colorado region has an average flow of 1,550 million gallons per day, well below the 6,964 million gallons per day considered ideal for fish habitat.

Overdraft of groundwater. Generally, the volume of groundwater in the United States is estimated to be far greater than the total capacity of all the nation's lakes and reservoirs, including the Great Lakes. However, the supply is not infinite and current uses of groundwater are already creating major problems of overdraft in such areas as the High Plains from Nebraska to Texas, in south-central Arizona, and in parts of California.

The groundwater above the deeper, impermeable layers of rock is naturally renewed, primarily by percolation of rain or snowmelt. Pumping from

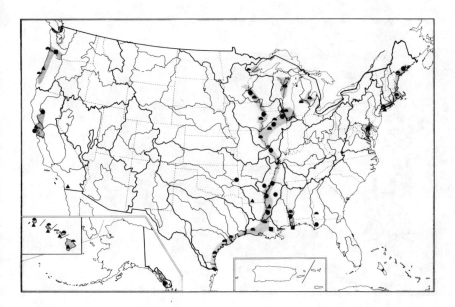

Explanation

　Area problem

　▨ Area in which there is a waterway with significant dredge and fill problem

　▢ Unshaded area may not be problem-free, but the problem was not considered major

　Specific dredge and fill problems

　● Channel maintenance for normal traffic

　■ Channel deepening and maintenance for deep-draft vessels

　▲ Land and waterfront development

　◤ Damage to fish and wildlife habitat

　Boundaries

　— Water resources region

　— Subregion

Figure 13. Coastal and inland waterways with dredge and fill problems (as identified by federal and state/regional study teams).

this source is termed "groundwater withdrawal." As mentioned in the water adequacy discussion, this renewable type of groundwater to some extent is also supplied by, and in turn supplies, streamflow. Since about 30 percent of groundwater naturally seeps into streams, groundwater availability is important to the continuity of streamflow. Excessive groundwater withdrawals can therefore affect the streamflow needed to support other uses.

The other nonrenewable groundwater that lies deeper, below a barrier of impermeable rock, may take years, centuries, even millennia to be replaced. When water is withdrawn from these deep aquifers, the term "groundwater overdraft" is applied.

Groundwater overdraft is substantial in some areas of the nation. For example, in the Texas-Oklahoma High Plains area, the amount of annual overdraft is estimated at more than 12,500 million gallons per day, an

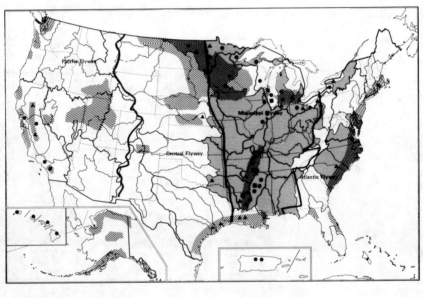

Explanation

▨ Subregion in which 50,000 acres or more of wet-soils are amenable to agriculture if land is drained.

Specific problems *(as identified by Federal and State/Regional study teams)*

▨ Wetland waterfowl breeding habitat needing protection

▨ Wetland waterfowl wintering habitat needing protection

▲ Farmland needing drainage

■ Urban areas with inadequate drainage

● Conflict between wetlands and wet-soils use

Boundaries

— Water resources region

— Subregion

— Flyway of migratory birds

Figure 14. Wet soils drainage and wetlands problems.

amount about equal to the natural flow of the Colorado River. Some observed indications of overdraft include diminished artesian pressure, declining streamflow, land subsidence, and saltwater intrusion. Figure 7 shows the areas of significant overdraft as well as locations of specific symptoms of the overdraft problem. The assessment estimated that 8 of the 106 subregions currently have critical overdraft problems, while 70 have moderate overdraft, and 22 have only minor overdraft.

Continued overdraft ultimately will lead to the drying up of aquifers as

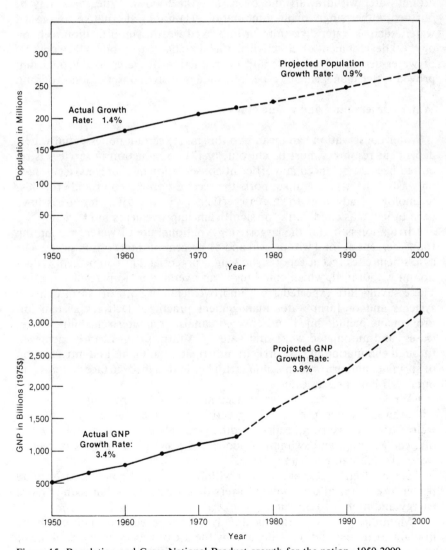

Figure 15. Population and Gross National Product growth for the nation, 1950-2000.

an economic supply of water. It will simply become too expensive to pump the remaining water. In a time of rapidly increasing energy costs, this point may not be too far off. As a result, irrigated cropping may have to be abandoned if no other source of water is available at a reasonable cost. This economic setback is considered more likely for irrigation than for other uses because the groundwater demand for irrigation is so great. In "1975," irrigation used about 68 percent of the groundwater withdrawn for all uses.

To avert these depletions, their negative hydrological consequences, and the impending economic setback to agriculture that result from excessive groundwater withdrawals and overdraft, the following measures may be pursued, either singly or in combination: (1) use of alternative sources of water, such as water diversions or improved weather modification technology; (2) development of effective artificial recharge methods; (3) relocation of water-depleting activities; and (4) reduction of water use through improved water management, especially an aggressive conservation program.

Water conservation and augmentation

Water conservation can mean two things: (1) certain nonessential water-dependent resources must be cut out, or (2) no reduction in services is required because balanced and efficient conservation measures have cut back on waste. The assessment supports the second option. To provide for this, technological advances to increase efficiency in the following areas have been targeted as candidates for significant improvements in efficiency.

• Irrigation is by far the largest single national use of water, accounting for 47 percent of total withdrawal and 81 percent of total consumption. The assessment cites recent reports showing a potential 20 to 30 percent reduction in withdrawal, which could mean an overall 9 to 14 percent lowering. These savings are expected from improvements in both off-farm delivery systems and on-farm water management practices. Delivery system improvements include lined and covered canals, computer scheduling of releases, and automated weirs and gates. On-farm savings can be achieved through elimination of over-irrigation, irrigation at night, and introduction of sprinkler and drip systems along with better designed surface systems and improved land preparation.

• While domestic use of water accounts for only 6 percent of the total withdrawals, water use can be greatly reduced at relatively low cost. Retrofitting showers and toilets; reduced outside use, such as lawn watering, car washing, and swimming pools; and prevention of leaks in central water systems can result in savings.

• Steam electric generation water withdrawals could be reduced 25 to 30 percent by means of dry cooling towers that use no water but require more energy and money to operate.

• Manufacturing withdrawals already are being reduced significantly by in-plant treatment and recycling and by the use of processes and equipment that require less water.

In addition to areas for conservation, the assessment also addresses the problem of increasing water supplies. Some potential sources of additional fresh water are highlighted below.

• *Improved surface-water management.* This includes both improved operation of existing facilities and development of additional storage reservoirs. Where temporary surpluses of surface water occur, artificial recharging of groundwater aquifers offers another way to augment supplies.

• *Weather modification.* Cloud seeding in the West has increased precipitation in some areas as much as 25 percent, resulting in increased snowmelt and runoff. Summer cloud seeding is a more complex process but remains a potential source of additional supply.

• *Desalination.* Since 1955, the number of desalination plants has increased from about a dozen, producing 2 million gallons per day, to more than 330, producing almost 100 million gallons per day. While it is a feasible additional water source, the development of desalination is constrained by the significant amounts of energy it requires.

• *Water reuse.* Limited supply, increased delivery costs, and water pollution control laws for higher quality wastewater discharges have increased the national interest in water reuse and wastewater reclamation. Some ways of reusing water are treated wastewater used for manufacturing, steam-powered electric generation, and irrigation; stormwater routed to recharge basins for later aquifer recharge; treated wastewater used to augment water supply either by aquifer recharge or blending in surface water reservoirs; and treated wastewater used to create a pressure barrier to protect freshwater aquifers from saltwater intrusion.

Both conservation and augmentation of supplies will be crucial to any comprehensive and farsighted water policy.

Summary

Water resources planners and policy-makers will continue to face hard decisions in weighing the trade-offs that are necessitated by limited water availability and quality. The economic implications of such trade-offs are also painfully evident. Unconstrained economic development is past. By the year 2000, higher demands will force more drastic action in the allocation of water. If the use of water is to be compatible with a healthy environment, which it must, agricultural production, industrial growth, and consumption of conventional forms of energy must be carefully scrutinized in the light of a water resource constraint. The Second National Water Assessment stresses the need for improved water resources management to solve current as well as future problems. The improved data base, the expansion of the set of problem areas addressed, and the clarification of key issues represent significant steps toward the realization of this goal. More detailed analysis planned for future assessments should provide an even more useful source of planning information for all levels of water resources management.

8
Economic and environmental effects of regional water limitations

D. A. Davis

Canada has abundant freshwater supplies, estimated at 6 percent of the world total. However most of the country's 22 million people live in a narrow ribbon of land north of the 49th parallel. For example, 75 percent of Canadians live within 100 miles of the Canadian-United States border, 95 percent within 200 miles. Canada is even more urbanized than the United States—76.0 percent versus 73.5 percent in 1970. For most of these people the abundance of water farther north has no practical significance in terms of usable local water supply, although hydroelectric power generation and recreational uses are important and will grow in significance. Very real is the fact that Canada already shares a significant part of its water resource with Americans all along the 8,800 kilometers of common border.

Water supply and demand

Because the populations in our two countries are in the convenient ratio of 1:10, it is fairly easy to make rough comparisons using United States and Canadian statistics (*1, 2, 20*). For example, the per capita withdrawal of water is almost twice as high in the United States as it is in Canada (1,302 versus 741 imperial gallons/capita/day), whereas consumption is even more disparate (410 versus 74 imperial gallons/capita/day). Irrigation accounts

D. A. Davis is regional director of the Inlands Water Directorate, Western and Northern Region, Environment Canada, Regina, Saskatchewan.

for 47 percent of water diversions and 83 percent of water consumption in the United States; 11 percent of all farmland is irrigated. The 5 percent of Canada's farms using irrigation (on only 1.7 percent of the farmland) divert only 10 percent of the total water used by Canadians, but these farms account for 46 percent of the total water consumed. In both countries, irrigation is concentrated in the West, those very sections of both countries that have the smallest natural endowment of water.

Groundwater is exploited to a much greater extent in the United States than in Canada. The rapid and intensive development of irrigation in the Texas-Oklahoma High Plains area in the last decade is a stark example of the rate at which resource development can occur today. The estimated overdraft of 10,400 million imperial gallons per day (20) has already made its impact felt, resulting in a $6 million study by the U.S. Department of Commerce to find alternative water supplies.

This development attests to the short-term viability of subsidized irrigation in the face of the lack of a long-term assured supply. The rapid development of center-pivot irrigation would seem to be related directly to high corn prices in the United States, which (19) made it economically feasible to grow crops on marginal, formerly nonirrigable lands using a surface or groundwater supply that was not available on a continuing, firm draft basis. Either the costs of production will increase rapidly with the increased costs of ever deeper pumping (exacerbated by fast-rising fuel prices), or the marginal surface water supply will make irrigation nonviable at lower crop values.

Need for long-term planning

The rapid rate of installation of center-pivot sprinkler systems can bring regional water supplies to a critical balance in a matter of a few years. Other developments that proceed without due regard to regional water limitations can produce similar results. Water policy must stress economic stability and long-term productivity, rather than maximum economic production.

This implies long-term water planning and management, the type of planning envisioned under the Canada Water Act, an act that makes provision for the federal and provincial governments to plan jointly and cooperatively for water resource management and, where appropriate, to implement these plans jointly. It obviously will have to be different from the kind of planning of the past, which was directed to maximum regional economic development based on an essentially unused resource.

The last major water project on the Canadian prairies, the Gardiner Dam and Lake Diefenbaker reservoir, was completed in 1967 at a cost of $130 million (18). It provides an interesting and recent case history of what can happen. Its main initial justification was the potential irrigation of 500,000 acres of land. Its actual use now is almost exclusively for power production and urban-municipal water supply. Only 31,000 acres are presently being irrigated from this reservoir, with interest growing slowly. We are extremely lucky to have the reserve capacity of the Lake Diefenbaker reservoir extended longer into the future, but it certainly was not according to plan. Massive developments of this sort are rare nowadays, with only incremental portions of the water resource uncommitted for the future.

New water supply projects for the southwestern corner of Saskatchewan have been proposed and studied for years. This area has a chronic water shortage. Again and again they prove uneconomical. In fact, there may be a basic problem with the original indiscriminate settlement and the suitability of the soil and the land for agriculture. A more crucial issue is the way such projects not only shore up the firm supply for existing uses, but invite new uses and thereby help to develop new dependencies, which then require yet another round of investment.

A recent study of the Oldman River sub-basin in Alberta illustrates a new approach to water resource development (10). It is interesting to note how the Oldman River Study dealt with irrigation, which now consumes 93 percent of the water in that sub-basin and has great potential for expansion. Instead of relying on the development of new storage facilities alone, considerable attention was paid to increasing the efficiency of use of presently available supplies. A $200 million canal and headworks improvement program by the government of Alberta and similar efforts by the federal government on its facilities go in that direction. All major conclusions point to the need for careful reconsideration and evaluation in the context of the South Saskatchewan River Basin as a whole. That larger study is now underway. Smaller and more manageable projects are preferred to big projects, with evaluation of each stage being part of the process.

Establishing a reliable data base

As we approach the limit on available resources, the margin for error decreases. It is astounding how little we know about water demand and use, despite the importance attached to water—and this not only in the arid West. We simply have to know who is using how much water of what quality, when, and for how long. We also have to know what the trends have been, and what influenced them. We must know what we are starting from before we can hope to figure out where we should be headed.

We are making a concerted effort particularly in western Canada to do just that. In the three Prairie Provinces of Alberta, Saskatchewan, and Manitoba the bulk of the runoff in the eastward flowing rivers originates on the eastern slopes of the Rocky Mountains in Alberta. Many years ago the provinces recognized the difficulty of trying to plan for the rational development of water resources when the rivers flowed across the provincial boundaries and developments or demands in one province could affect the water uses planned by its neighbor. Eventually a four-party agreement between Canada, Alberta, Saskatchewan, and Manitoba was signed that established the Prairie Provinces Water Board and also determined the share of the eastward flowing streams that each province could count on.

The Prairie Provinces Water Board started the first phase of a water demand study last year (*11*) for the three provinces. The study will cost $880,000 and take three years to complete. The intent is to establish a common data base for the historic water demand. There is not only a dearth of reliable, detailed statistics, but the statistics that are available often are not compatible because they were collected for other purposes.

The 10-state Missouri River Basin Commission, on which Canada has an observer, is proposing a similar cooperative water data analysis system adequate for assessing the current and future water uses within that basin (*7*). This can only be a start, for the matter of forecasting, let alone planning for and managing toward a specific water demand, is public policy-making of a high order. That has to be so, for several compelling reasons:

1. Water as a free good is a thing of the past. Rates for "new" water will be three to 30 times the present rates. New schemes will cost billions rather than millions of dollars, if they are at all feasible environmentally and politically (*15*).

2. High energy costs will drive costs up even further. For example, the Los Angeles Metropolitan Water District estimates it will be forced to raise its wholesale water rates by 700 to 1,000 percent in 1983 simply because current contracts for electricity must be renegotiated (*15, 16*).

3. The water resource is now over-committed in some areas, with reliance on water in groundwater storage, which is rapidly being depleted, or reliance on surface water, which is not available in a series of dry years.

4. The competition for water is not only with other human uses but with the instream and wilderness uses as well.

5. Native claims to significant tracts of lands and their water resources is further shrinking previous notions about the availability of water.

5. Many shortages are the inevitable results of past policies. This is a complex, difficult topic, which I will use to develop thoughts on the need to do some hard forward thinking now about the future allocation of water before future options are foreclosed.

Twisted water economics

There is little to be gained by being Simon-pure about the discovery that a water resource is overcommitted or developed to a degree that forecloses future options. However, we are in a better position today to analyze effects that are associated with large water resource investments, and as long as a sustained economic multisector approach to evaluation is taken, we can work toward a better balance of social interests. In the water field, irrigation is an obvious choice for evaluation because it consumes by far the largest percentage of water (83 percent in United States, 46 percent in Canada) and because the direct benefits per unit of water are lower in agriculture than in most municipal, industrial, and even energy uses.

"Tremendous conflicts among major federal (U.S.) programs and the very high cost of these conflicts have been noted" (*6*). It is not only that many projects are not defensible on economic grounds, they can even interfere directly with others already producing benefits.

Low water prices √

As the most accessible and easily developed resources were used up, prices had to rise. This natural process was masked by the way cheaper and cheaper energy in the 1940 to 1970 period allowed us to overcome the higher basic cost of development and transport. Meanwhile, all of this became anchored in an affluent style of life, wastage, and a set of expectations that is unequalled in history.

To name but one example: Canadians have benefited from the low prices and the convenience of fresh produce in the off-season that past water developments and pricing policies made possible. We are every bit as dependent as Americans are on the Imperial Valley salad bowl. Even in-season, Canadian-grown produce has difficulty competing because of the subsidies involved in these massive water developments to the south and the present low costs of transportation. Let us be candid. Neither nation has so far been willing to make the necessary attitudinal and practical adjustments that would make best use of available resources for society as a whole. Governments are interested, but the public does not give the concept much support.

Even now we in Canada and the United States are continuing to support and subsidize consumption (and waste) rather than conservation by: subsidized fuel prices, when we already use at least twice as much per capita as the next largest user in the world; lower water and power rates for large users, the very users that need the powerful incentive of increasing rates to make the big adjustments required in technology and processing; and depletion allowances, write-offs, and many other special formulas that promote high consumption and waste generation, rather than conservation and reuse.

Growth versus no-growth

Questioning the currently prevailing trends is not akin to being against development. Sachs (14) makes an eloquent case "for ecodevelopment," which he sees as "an instrument of prospective thinking and exploring development options." Benjamin Franklin is one of three thinkers who symbolize for him the new concept of practical knowledge and resourcefulness, and he quotes this delightful story:

"Having by chance awakened at six in the morning on a lovely summer day, Franklin noticed that his room was already bathed in sunlight. He immediately set to calculating the waste of candles due to the lack of synchronization between human activities and daylight. According to his calculations, Parisians could save 64 million pounds of candles each year. Taking his reflections to their logical extreme, he thought of proposing three measures to the government: a tax on shuttered windows, the rationing of candles, and a morning cannon shot 'to wake the sluggards effectively and to open their eyes to their true interest.' Happily, Parisians narrowly escaped this first version of daylight saving time.''

This amusing, but instructive anecdote gives hope that adjustments will be forthcoming to resolve some of the ultimate conflicts in allocation, but hopefully not through draconian measures involving massive government intervention. Nevertheless, wrenching decisions are now having to be made as limits on the water resource are approached. We have to know what the competing alternative uses are, their linkages and socioeconomic importance, substitutability of their products and technology, and the size and length of the required resource commitment. We must not preclude future options in our choices for the resource today.

In Canada, the 1976-1977 drought was a painful reminder of the "Dirty Thirties" and provided a practice run of conditions under a general water shortage. When it was all over and the excitement died down, some worthwhile long-term measures had been taken (3). There is now continuing federal-provincial consultation on drought through a federal drought task force. A three- to five-year study program on the economic effects of drought is commencing under federal-provincial agreements. These agreements also include demonstration activities, development of new technologies and crops, and productivity improvements measures (3, 4).

This is a step in the right direction, but we must eventually go beyond that. More needs to be known about the patterns of immobility of populations and resources in a region under major economic change (6): We should know who can and who cannot move quickly to other areas or jobs and what costs are incurred in making these moves. We should know what characteristics of the area and population determine these responses. What happens to capital equipment of different types and what proportion can be expected to be employed in alternative activities should also be known. We should know more about the social factors, costs and losses, involved in the process of job change or migration.

Far more inclusive evaluations in water resource planning and management are needed. Close technical and policy-level coordination within and between governments is essential. Financing and repayment policies must be revised to reflect the purposes established through more comprehensive planning.

Water conservation

The western provinces and states depend primarily on Rocky Mountain runoff for their water. Conservation traditionally has meant storing this water for use later in the year; a valid approach. Major projects were developed to provide a firm water supply base for all essential uses. Through subsidization or low initial development cost of an unused resource, water was available at cheap rates. Also, cheap energy rates for handling or pumping water resulted in profligate use. It is the disregard of the true value and significance of the conserved water that is causing concern today. The growth of irrigation is one example; the growth of major cities in dry regions is another.

Economics, environmental concerns, and sheer exhaustion of feasible sites have reduced the number of practicable major storage developments. The conservation that now needs to be practiced is not different from that implied in the original development; it is a parallel, delayed phase of it. Instead of using all the water we can just because it's there, we must defer its use where possible to keep open future options. The quandary is that the excess water goes to waste if not used; and yet, once a dependence on it has developed, it remains committed forever. Unused water must be looked upon as a cushion for the drought years and a heritage for future generation.

More and more, future or additional demands should be met through careful husbanding or reuse of what we have now. The energy that is least expensive and ecologically most beneficial is that which is saved. Energy saved and products recycled also mean less water used in energy production and processing of raw materials. We can therefore ill afford to ignore conservation, since water is an ingredient in practically every product or process. Likewise, the water that is least expensive and without additional environmental impacts is that which is saved. It is this compounding of benefits that we have yet to grasp and put to full use.

Water quality √

In addition to being an exploitable and renewable, if finite, resource, water is also an important environmental resource. The assimilative capacity of water has considerable economic value, but it too has been over-exploited. As use intensifies, water quality normally degrades unless water quality objectives are set and pollution control programs are established and enforced to protect future uses. However, if objectives are based on average conditions and existing levels of consumptive use, how will we meet the objectives in critical dry years? The point again is that some margin for extreme fluctuations in supply or future demand should be maintained.

Perhaps as a conservation measure we should give serious consideration to dual distribution systems—freshwater for drinking and reclaimed water for all the convenience and transportation uses to which we have so heavily committed our good water. Flushing toilets, washing streets and cars, watering lawns, and thousands of other uses can do with water of safe but lesser quality. We need not and should not experiment with people in the use of recycled water (9).

Recycling conserves freshwater and reduces the cost considerably, to as low as one-third the cost of new potable water. But an even more powerful reason for reserving the highest quality freshwater for drinking purposes is the mounting concern over environmental risks and how they might be managed. "Some of the potentially most serious problems are the hazards associated with nuclear power, carcinogens in drinking water, ozone depletion, buildup of carbon dioxide, pesticides and toxic chemicals generally. These have a number of common characteristics that make them particularly difficult to analyze and to manage. Among these characteristics are latency; irreversibility; potential of very high, but unknown, environmental and human damages; and presumed low probability of these damages. 'Potential' and 'presumed' are used here because lack of understanding of the underlying mechanisms is another characteristic common to many of these problems'' (12).

While we do not yet have to answer the ultimate question—What happens when there are no new natural resources, including environmental resources, to exploit?—we must act as if we did. The case has to be made strongly for greatly reducing the physical resources locked into material objectives and for carefully maintaining and extensively reusing all materials, both to reduce the use of resource inputs and to control the wastage of resources already in use (1).

Conclusion

There is no easy answer, but there definitely is a need to change our attitudes toward resource management and planning. Are we meeting our responsibility to future generations and leaving options for development open? Water, air, and land use policy must stress economic stability and long-term productivity, rather than the maximum economic production. The decisions we make must, where possible, be reversible and consider priorities of use for society as a whole rather than a specific agricultural, industrial, or energy production section.

The quandary we face is that the more information we have, and the more understanding we have of the environment, the greater the number of alternatives that can be explored and examined without perhaps making the future more certain or predictable. The range of options are multiplied and to some degree the opportunity for the unwise as well as the wise options are increased. But to admit that knowledge is a flawed good is not to recommend ignorance in its stead. We can and must learn a great deal from the developing energy crisis, which has caught two of the best-educated populations in the world in a shocking state of ignorance and confusion. It confirms the view that the kind of wise resource planning and public participation and education we have stressed in studies under the Canada Water Act must be continued, strengthened, and improved.

REFERENCES

1. Ayres, Robert U., and Allen V. Kneese. 1971. *Economic and ecological and effects of a stationary economy.* Resources for the Future, Washington, D.C.
2. Canada Department of the Environment, Inland Waters Directorate. 1975. 1976. 1977-78. *Canada water yearbook.* Ministry of Supply and Services, Ottawa, Ontario.

3. Canada-Saskatchewan. 1979. *Interim subsidiary agreement on water development for regional economic expansion and drought proofing.* Ottawa, Ontario; Regina, Saskatchewan.
4. Canada-Saskatchewan. 1979. *Subsidiary agreement on productivity enhancement and technology transfer in agriculture.* Ottawa, Ontario; Regina, Saskatchewan.
5. Canada-United States International Joint Commission. 1977. *Annual report.* Ottawa, Ontario; Washington, D.C.
6. Howe, Charles W., and K. William Easter. 1971. *Interbasin transfers of water. Economic issues and impacts.* Johns Hopkins Press, Baltimore, Maryland.
7. Missouri River Basin Commission. 1979. *Priorities report.* Omaha, Nebraska.
8. Novick, David. 1976. *A world of scarcities: critical issues in public policy.* Halsted Press, New York, New York.
9. Okun, Dr. Daniel. 1979. *Water should be segregated by use.* Water and Sewage Works (March): 52-53.
10. Oldman River Study Management Committee. 1978. *Oldman River report.* Department of the Environment, Edmonton, Alberta.
11. Prairie Provinces Water Board. 1978. *Annual report.* Regina, Saskatchewan.
12. Resources for the Future. 1976. *Annual report.* Washington, D.C. 107 pp.
13. Resources for the Future. 1977. *Annual report.* Washington, D.C. 94 pp.
14. Sachs, Ignacy. 1977. *Environment and development—a new rationale for domestic policy formulation and international cooperation strategies.* Environment Canada and Canadian International Development Agency, Ottawa, Ontario.
15. Salisbury, David I. 1979. *Coming to the bottom of the water barrel.* Christian Science Monitor (February 28): 12-13.
16. Salisbury, David I. 1979. *Water fights: The West goes to court.* Christian Science Monitor (March 1): 12-13.
17. Salisbury, David I. 1979. *Will people drink recycled water?* Christian Science Monitor (March 2): 12-13.
18. Saskatchewan-Nelson Basin Board. 1972. *Water supply for the Saskatchewan-Nelson Basin.* Project catalogue (appendix 3). Regina, Saskatchewan.
19. Sutton, Richard K. 1977. *Circles on the Plains.* Landscape 22(1): 3-10.
20. U.S. Water Resources Council. 1978. *The nation's water resources 1975-2000. Vol. 1: Summary.* Washington, D.C.

9
Water conservation potential in irrigated agriculture

Jan van Schilfgaarde

Agriculture, the largest consumer of water, competes with other users that often can afford a higher price. This makes agriculture particularly vulnerable when supplies do not meet demand. Especially for irrigated agriculture, the limitations imposed by water supply are apparent in the United States, as elsewhere. A recent review of global water resources concluded that in the year 2000 water limitations will be a decisive factor in economic development on most continents (7). In the western United States we need not wait untill 2000 to be in that predicament.

Water supply questions deal not only with quantity, but as often with quality. Surface runoff may carry a heavy load of sediment. Irrigation return flows tend to have increased concentrations of dissolved salts. Municipal wastewater may be high in nitrates or a variety of heavy metals.

No discussion of water conservation can avoid consideration of the institutional setting in which conservation measures must be implemented. From the outset a caution is warranted. Whereas both the on-farm water use efficiency—water used by the crop compared to that delivered to the farm—and the distribution system efficiency frequently are extremely low in comparison to the obtainable level. Such low efficiencies do not *a priori* demonstrate the potential for conservation. Whether water lost through low efficiency is truly wasted depends on circumstances. Frequently, it is

Jan van Schilfgaarde is director of the U.S. Salinity Laboratory, U.S. Department of Agriculture, Riverside, California.

effectively reused. We face an unfortunate dichotomy of opinion: some zealots demand unrealistic water savings in irrigation, while others take an adamant stance that irrigation farming is as efficient as it can be.

The need to irrigate

The purpose of irrigation is to supplement soil water to meet the plant's need. This need consists primarily of the evapotranspiration required to grow the crop, plus enough leaching water to prevent excess accumulation of salts in the soil solution. For a crop with a closed canopy, total dry matter production is related linearly to water consumed in evapotranspiration. Thus, a reduction in evapotranspiration tends to reduce plant growth; and generally speaking, limiting the water supply to less than the evaporative demand will reduce total dry matter production.

Two observations are in order. First, it is often not total dry matter production that is wanted; the marketable product may be the seed or fruit. Properly planned deficit irrigation may then produce the same yield with less water, or a reduced yield for a greater reduction in water consumed. Second, a certain amount of water is needed to establish the crop. Thus, if all available water (T) is taken into account (irrigation plus rainfall plus stored soil water), maximum total dry matter production per unit of water consumed (Y/T) is expected when T approaches the potential evapotranspiration; but when we distinguish between rainfall (P) and irrigation water (I), the maximum water use efficiency (Y/I) will occur when $I = 0$. This relationship, illustrated with arbitrary units in figure 1, shows the difficulty of discussing irrigation efficiency. At times, it is reasonable to distribute a limited quantity of irrigation water over an extended area to maximize total production (9). Just the same, in most cases conservation of water by under-

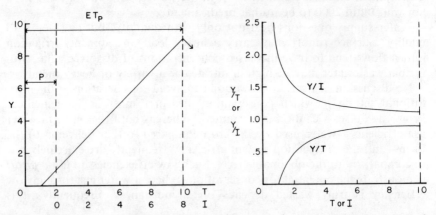

Figure 1. Schematic representation of water use efficiency by crops considering either the total water use, T, or the irrigation water used, I. Note that $T = I + P$; Y represents total dry matter yield.

irrigation is counterproductive. As a corollary, reduction of the evaporation component of evapotranspiration early in the growing season of a crop can be an effective conservation measure.

The second purpose of irrigation, to help leach excess salts, is equally important if there is to be sustained production. The leaching requirement can be calculated from crop tolerance data (8) and the irrigation water quality. It generally is a relatively small percentage of the amount of irrigation, but ignoring it can be disastrous (14, 18, 19).

Leaching water is not used consumptively, but contains more salt than the original irrigation water. As it is remixed with the irrigation water source, the water quality downstream is reduced. Remixing drainage water is a common and viable practice; it increases the overall efficiency of water use even where sloppy irrigation is practiced, and it provides for modulation of downstream flow through temporary underground storage. However, remixing never increases the total amount of water available for plant growth. Whether plants concentrate the salt in the soil solution to the maximum level possible in one pass or several, the amount of water they can extract is fixed. Only by using the water for more salt-tolerant crops can a greater fraction be used.

Effective irrigation

The key to effective irrigation is to provide the proper amount of water at the proper time. The optimum irrigation scheme provides water continuously to keep the soil water content in the root zone within a narrow range, although carefully programmed periodic stresses may be desirable to obtain maximum economic yield by inducing flowering in preference to vegetative growth or simply by avoiding excessive vegetative growth (11).

Historically, high labor costs made it advantageous to irrigate as infrequently as possible. The advent of new technology, including automation, has drastically reduced this dependence on labor. Whatever the frequency of irrigation, careful control of timing and amount applied is a prerequisite for high efficiency. This calls for water delivery on demand, which, in turn, requires close coordination between the management of the water delivery stystem and on-farm irrigation management. It also calls for devices to measure flow rates or volumes delivered or, as an alternative, for feedback devices that determine the water supply in the root zone. Furthermore, accurate delivery to a field is not enough; the areal distribution of water intake (not just water applied) also must be uniform.

Few reliable data are available on the efficiency of water application. The U.S. Department of the Interior (17) recently released a report containing a preliminary evaluation of the opportunities for water conservation on 61 irrigation projects. The project efficiencies quoted ranged from 7 to 80 percent, with an average of 44 percent. California's Department of Water Resources (2) reported hydrologic basin efficiencies ranging from 64 to 96 percent. On-farm efficiencies may be higher or lower, but no doubt also range from about 30 to over 90 percent. Thus, opportunities for improvement clearly exist. What the consequences might be is a separate question.

On-farm efficiency can be enhanced by a combination of physical facilities and management techniques. Neither alone is likely to achieve the best results. The most obvious way to improve efficiency is to transfer control of water distribution from the soil to an engineering apparatus. In any gravity irrigation system, basin or furrow, the irrigator attempts to provide equal water intake opportunity time across the field. When soils are not homogeneous, a uniform intake opportunity time does not guarantee uniform intake. In a closed conduit system, such as by sprinkler, bubbler, or trickle, the uniformity of application is subject to equipment control and, if the application rate does not exceed the lowest intake rate encountered, the actual intake is as uniform as the application. Thus, closed conduit systems have an inherent advantage. Another advantage is that they lend themselves more readily to automation.

Closed conduit systems also have disadvantages. They generally require some pressure for operation, thus increasing energy requirements. Sprinkler systems are subject to distribution pattern distortion by wind and to evaporative losses. Capital costs can be substantial, especially when a gravity system is adapted to a closed conduit system, so that a dual investment is required. Furthermore, poorly designed or operated sprinkler or trickle systems are likely to operate at far lower efficiencies than well-operated gravity systems. Especially, the extravagant claims for trickle systems must be carefully evaluated against actual field performance.

Some trends in irrigation

Nevertheless, new developments make some closed conduit systems attractive candidates for effective water conservation. The newer pivot sprinklers have lower energy requirements than earlier models. They and newly introduced low-pressure, linear-move systems, some dragging hoses to reduce application rates, can distribute water uniformly at reasonable cost. Efficiencies of 80 percent are reasonable to project. For tree crops, a low-pressure bubbler system (10) enables extremely uniform distribution of water, with a variation of water applied to individual trees less than two percent, while requiring only a nominal pressure head as low as one meter. Such systems can be operated to obtain the prescribed leaching fraction very closely.

Equally great opportunities exist with gravity irrigation. The choice depends on the water supply, the crop, the soil properties, and farmer preference. The typical graded furrow system generates a substantial amount of tailwater runoff. With furrow lengths compatible with mechanized farming operations, uniform intake opportunity time requires that water be permitted to flow out of the end of the furrow. This often leads to significant erosion. It clearly reduces the on-field efficiency. If the tailwater is reused on a lower field, or pumped back for reuse, the water use efficiency is increased.

Another approach was investigated by Worstell (*20*). By reducing the furrow length, typically from 150 to 50 meters, uniformity is increased and runoff is reduced or eliminated. To make the system compatible with cultural practices, Worstell's multiset system uses shallow, buried laterals across the furrows at appropriate spacings. The water bubbles up into the furrows from orifices in these buried laterals that are sized to give uniform discharge rates. Combined with automatically operated valves, this system holds substantial promise for conserving water and soil as well as labor.

It was demonstrated years ago in Arizona that high efficiencies could be obtained by use of dead level (no grade in either direction) basins. The commercial development of laser beam grading equipment provided the impetus for farmer adoption of this method. Dead level basins from 2 to 15 hectares in size can be irrigated effectively if the stream size (head) available to the farmer is adequate, if the land can be leveled without undue cost, and if the water outlet structure(s) is properly designed to minimize erosive cutting. The method has been used with single turnouts as high as 30 cubic feet a second (0.90 m^3 sec^{-1}) and with multiple outlets using smaller streams by modifying existing ports in laterals (*4, 5*). In either case, the development of reliable devices to automate gate or port opening and closing, so that the water is sequenced from field to field, was crucial in gaining farmer acceptance.

As a package, dead level irrigation, laser plane grading, and automation offers the opportunity, in the right circumstances, to substantially increase water use efficiency and reduce energy and labor costs (*3*). The labor savings are obvious. The energy savings come about because a smaller amount of water needs to be handled both for irrigation and for drainage while fertilizer requirements are reduced as well. Dead level irrigation is popular in parts of Arizona and is being evaluated in California and Colorado. It is no panacea, but its use is likely to spread rapidly in areas for which it is suited.

Each of the system innovations described has the potential to deliver high on-farm efficiency. None will do so unless properly managed. A first step toward good management is the use of measuring devices, such as flumes for open channels (*13*) or meters for conduits; another is proper scheduling. A number of groups have advocated irrigation management services. The concept uses climatologic data, together with information on the soil and the consumptive use of the crop, to project the right time for the next irrigation and the proper amount (*6*). Such service is currently provided by a number of commercial companies, by the Bureau of Reclamation, and by some irrigation districts. Originally, the concept was based on computer modeling of water use, combined with feedback information from the fields scheduled to fine-tune the predictions. Recently, some groups shifted to greater dependence on field measurements of soil water content and less on computers. Whether the recommendations are based on calculated daily evapotranspiration values or measured trends of soil water depletion is immaterial; the principle is the same: irrigations are scheduled, and presumably consummated, on the basis of actual need rather than on casual observation and experience. In some instances, the results have been less than spectacular. In others, they have been very positive in terms of farmer acceptance. Actual water savings are hard to quantify.

One important component of irrigation scheduling is that effective on-farm irrigation depends on an effective delivery system. As more irrigators shift to careful management, the demands on the distribution system will increase. In principle, irrigation scheduling programs should be useful in upgrading distribution network operations. One must recognize that there is an inherent conflict in the objectives of operating a reservoir and distribution system and the objectives of meeting crop water requirements by timely irrigation. The former is enhanced by regularly scheduled, sequential water delivery. The latter is enhanced by having water available on demand as the crop on a particular field needs it. This dilemma has been illustrated clearly with reference to Northern India (12), but the problem is ubiquitous. In any case, as water demands increase, the substantial losses in distribution systems from seepage from unlined canals, from spills, and from unneeded deliveries become prime candidates for ameliorative action. It is likely that the potential for water conservation in distribution systems is at least as high as it is on the farm (17).

Besides the obvious possibilities for water conservation through improved on-farm irrigation practices and more effective water delivery systems, there are two other important areas that deserve consideraton: drainage water reuse and crop selection and management.

Drainage water reuse

Most drainage waters from irrigated areas in the United States, although increased in salinity, still have substantial value for irrigation (15). Through remixing, many of these waters are routinely reused. However, in a number of instances they are considered waste and a price is paid for their disposal. Water resources can be stretched and drainage disposal costs reduced if this potential is recognized and utilized. Furthermore, the most effective use is obtained if the drainage water is used directly to irrigate salt-tolerant crops rather than mix it with less saline water for general use on a mix of crops. Even relatively saline water can be used in this manner. Table 1 lists the relative crop yields expected for selected tolerant species if the sole source of water available has the salt concentration indicated. These calculations are based on a leaching fraction of 0.35, a conversion between electrical conductivity of the irrigation water (σ_i) in decisiemens per meter and its concentration in milligrams per liter of 650, and a ratio (CF) of the average root-zone saturated extract conductivity to that of the irrigation water of 0.9, together with the tolerance data of Maas and Hoffman (8). Comparison of this table with the drainage waters considered by Rhoades (15) show that none exceeds the range of salinities in table 1. Most fall well below that range.

When drainage water is too saline for irrigation of commercial crops, it still may have value for the production of biomass. Halophytes can readily be identified that would produce a respectable yield while consuming saline water. Such production could serve a variety of purposes. The biomass produced could be used for the generation of methane or the extraction of pharmaceuticals; the vegetation could serve as wildlife habitat and a recreational resource; and the productive use of such waters could reduce the volume of water needing disposal through extensive drainage systems. Such use, however, would not conserve water for agriculture in the sense of making more water available for crop production. In a broader sense, it would make productive use of a now useless resource. For the concept to be economically viable, additional research is needed to select appropriate species, to develop practical means of processing the biomass as an energy source, and to identify marketable products that can be extracted. Additional prob-

Table 1. Expected relative crop yield as function of salinity of irrigation water.

	Irrigation Water Salinity (milligrams per liter)		
Crop	4,500	6,000	7,500
Cotton	1.00	0.97	0.86
Wheat	0.98	0.84	0.69
Bermudagrass	1.00	0.91	0.78
Barley	1.00	0.98	0.88
Sugarbeet	1.00	0.92	0.80
Sorghum	0.84	0.69	0.55

lems needing consideration, applicable to both drain water reuse for crops and to biomass production, may be grouped under the heading "systems analysis," or development of equitable systems for collecting and using the waters within the framework of existing physical systems and institutions.

Crop selection and management

Next, we turn to crop selection and management. Two ways seem to offer promise for water conservation while maintaining agricultural production. First, through breeding or selection of cultivars within species, varieties can be obtained that are more salt tolerant or that produce more marketable product per unit of water used. Breeding for salt tolerance is a neglected area. There seems to be no doubt, however, that substantial progress is possible (16) and intraspecific differences in salt tolerance have been observed for a number of species (1). Such increases in salt tolerance would be especially attractive in relation to the reuse of saline drain waters. Similarly, breeding can lead to selections that make better use of seasonal rainfall, that mature more rapidly without loss of yield, or have a more favorable ratio between marketable product and total dry matter production.

An entirely different approach is the substitution of crop species that use less water or that grow during periods of lower evaporative demand than currently grown species. An example might be growing two grain crops in sequence in place of alfalfa. Cultural practices also offer the opportunity to reduce water use per unit of production. Donald Grimes (personal communication), for example, found that increased planting density of cotton resulted in an earlier development of a closed canopy and thus in a reduction in evaporative loss and earlier maturity. As a result, essentially the same yield was obtained with less water.

There are other ways water can be saved by reducing the evaporation component of evapotranspiration, such as the removal of the cover crop in deciduous orchards, breeding plants that provide full cover earlier in their growth cycle, and changing irrigation practices. Germinating lettuce with sprinkler instead of furrow irrigation and using trickle irrigation to localize the soil area wetted fall in this last category.

Limitations to water conservation

So far we have looked at a wide range of options to reduce water use. To the extent these options reduce evapotranspiration and maintain crop yield, they are true conservation measures. To the extent they reduce water application but do not reduce evapotranspiraton, they may not result in any water savings and may even be detrimental. Two examples illustrate this important point.

The Sacramento and San Joaquin Valleys together constitute the Central Valley of California. Both valleys drain into San Francisco Bay. The Sacramento Valley to the north has a surplus of water (2). Some of this surplus is transported to the San Joaquin Valley to the south; some is used to provide water to the San Francisco Delta for a variety of uses, including the avoidance of saltwater intrusion.

There is no question that substantial improvements in on-farm irrigation efficiency are feasible in the Sacramento Valley. However, reduction in diversions to agriculture there could require a comparable increase in reservoir releases to satisfy needs in the Delta and in southern California. It would also tend to change the timing of water delivery to the south by eliminating the desirable delay in water deliveries through temporary groundwater storage. It would also probably reduce the water used by phreatophytes, increasing water available for commercial uses but reducing wildlife and recreational values. In short, the benefits from increasing irrigation efficiencies, in this instance, at best are in question.

In the San Joaquin Basin a similar situation exists in that return flow from the San Joaquin (of lower quality than that from the Sacramento Valley) is used to supply part of the Delta requirements. However, in the Tulare Sub basin at the most southerly end of the Central Valley, a different situation prevails. There, inadequate water supplies are supplemented with excessive groundwater pumping and with expensive water imported from the north via the State Water Project. Also, since the Tulare Sub basin does not have a natural outlet, drainage and salinity problems are increasing at an alarming rate. Provision for drainage not only would be expensive, but plans therefore have also run into opposition from Delta interests because of the high salinities the drain water would have when discharged into the Delta from a proposed central drain. In this case, reduced diversion requirements resulting from increased efficiencies would have inherent advantages. Furthermore, reuse of drainage water for irrigating salt-tolerant crops would not only reduce net water requirements but also the volume of drainage water needing disposal. A rough estimate is that 300 million cubic meters per year might be available for such reuse.

Imperial Valley obtains all of its irrigation water from the Colorado River. The drainage flow is discharged into the Salton Sea, where it ultimately evaporates. Here again a decrease in water applied would result in reduced diversions. Such savings could, considering California's legal entitlement to Colorado River water, be transferred to other uses. Reuse of drainage water would further augment savings.

In contrast, consider the upper reaches of the Colorado River Basin. In many irrigation districts in Utah and Colorado the irrigation efficiency is low. Generally, the surface and subsurface return flows are recovered later for downstream use. Except for their effect on phreatophyte use and permanent loss to groundwater, changes in irrigation practices would have no impact on total water supply, while reductions in irrigation diversions resulting from increased efficiency could result in accelerated streamflow with possibly adverse effects on the timing of water availability downstream.

This scenario has led to assertions that there are no large opportunities for water conservation in agriculture. One flaw in this argument is illustrated by Colorado's Grand Valley. Irrigation return flows from this valley contribute about 650,000 tons of salt per year to the main stem of the Colorado. Water that percolates into the soil displaces groundwater that has equilibrated with the underlying salt-laden shale formulations. Any reduction in groundwater flow results in a proportional reduction in salt return.

Similar shale formations are extensive through Utah and Colorado. In fact, under the authority of Public Law 93-320, the federal government developed plans for a program estimated to cost $160 million to reduce the salinity in the river by reducing canal, lateral, and on-farm seepage in the Grand Valley. This program will include measures to substantially increase on-farm irrigation efficiency and should result, in the process, in increased agricultural production and farm income. It will also reduce water lost to phreatophytes, but this water savings will be partly offset by measures to mitigate alleged losses in wildlife habitat.

Conclusions

The foregoing discussion has skipped over many important details. However, it illustrates several points. There is tremendous opportunity to increase on-farm irrigation efficiency and to reduce water losses from the distribution system. The prevalent pattern of reuse of irrigation return flows suggests that such changes may, in many cases, have limited impact on the actual amount of water made available for new uses and may even have adverse effects in terms of timing. On the other hand, even in those cases, the beneficial effects on water quality of increased efficiency can be substantial. In contrast, the use of saline drainage water for crop production and changes in the crop selection and management can be expected to conserve water without adverse impact on agricultural production. The problems and opportunities are highly site specific and only through careful evaluation of specific circumstances can valid projections be made.

Some technical options are cost-effective to the individual farmer. An example is precision leveling for dead-level basin irrigation in areas where this system is suitable. Others are not, especially if the beneficiary is not easily identified. This observation leads to a new set of concerns. The technical aspects of agricultural water conservation, complicated as they are, are simple compared to the institutional problems.

Historically, irrigation agriculture in the western United States developed under a set of laws and policies devised with the objective of encouraging development. The Reclamation Act of 1902 is a good example. These policies and institutions worked well toward this goal. Now that we have entered a period in which conservation of resources is more to the point than further development, these institutions are found to be wanting. There is great urgency in finding and implementing constructive ways to modify the existing institutional framework to better meet the needs of the present.

In particular, I would like to call attention to water pricing. The farmer generally pays so little for water that his incentive for water conservation is minimal. Where new water supplies need to be developed, the costs can be a hundredfold more than typical prices charged today. If an equitable system could be developed whereby the charges for water were based on marginal costs, the incentive for conservation would be greatly enhanced. Such a system would have little value unless it were combined with the possibility of transferring water rights, either on a lease basis or permanently. Clearly, such a basic change in policy could not be implemented without safeguards of established rights and would require careful study. Even then, any changes might take decades to implement. That no serious study of these questions appears to have been made, except for some limited academic work, illustrates a serious deficiency in our effort to use the same ingenuity to solve social and institutional questions as has been applied to technological questions of water use.

We face a serious problem of adjustment to an era of limited resources. We have on hand a number of technological options to help us make the needed adjustments, and through research new tools can and will be developed. It is far less clear that we shall take timely action to develop the corresponding tools in the social sciences that are at least as important as the technological ones if we are to meet the challenge.

REFERENCES

1. Abel, G. H. 1969. *Inheritance of the capacity for chloride inclusion and chloride exclusion by soybeans.* Crop Science 6: 697-698.
2. California Department of Water Resources. 1976. *Water conservation in California.* Bulletin 198. Sacramento, California.
3. Dedrick, A. R., and L. J. Erie. 1978. *Automation of on-farm irrigation turnouts utilizing jack tracks.* Transactions, American Society of Agricultural Engineers 21(1): 92-96.
4. Dedrick, A. R., J. A. Replogle, and L. J. Erie. 1978. *On-farm level-basin irrigation—save water and energy.* Civil Engineering 48(1): 60-65.
5. Erie, L. J., and A. R. Dedrick. 1979. *Level-basin irrigation: A method for conserving water and labor.* Farmers' Bulletin 2261. U.S. Department of Agriculture, Washington, D.C.
6. Jensen, Marvin E., David C. N. Robb, and C. Eugene Franzoy. 1970. *Scheduling irrigation using climate-crop-soil data.* Journal of the Irrigation and Drainage, American Society of Civil Engineering 96: 25-37.
7. Lindh, Gunner. 1979. *Water and food production.* In M. R. and A. K. Biswas [eds.] *Food, Climate, and Man.* John Wiley, New York, New York.
8. Maas, E. V., and G. J. Hoffman. 1977. *Crop salt tolerance—current assessment.* Journal of the Irrigation and Drainage, American Society of Civil Engineering 103(IR2): 115-134.
9. Musick, J., L. L. New, and D. A. Dusek. 1976. *Soil water depletion—yield relationship of irrigated sorghum, wheat, and soybeans.* Transactions, American Society of Agricultural Engineers 19(3): 489-493.
10. Rawlins, Stephen L. 1977. *Uniform irrigation with a low-head bubbler system.* Agricultural Water Management 1(2): 167-178.
11. Rawlins, S. L., and P.A.C. Raats. 1975. *Prospects for high frequency irrigation.* Science 188: 604-610.
12. Reidinger, R. B. 1974. *Institutional rationing of canal water in northern India: Conflict between traditional patterns and modern needs.* Economic Development and Cultural Change 23(1): 79-104.
13. Replogle, John A., and Albert J. Clemmens. 1978. *Measuring flumes of simplified construction.* Paper 78-2506. American Society of Agricultural Engineers, St. Joseph, Michigan.
14. Rhoades, J. D. 1974. *Drainage for salinity control.* In Jan van Schilfgaarde [ed.] *Drainage for Agriculture.* American Society of Agronomy, Madison, Wisconsin.
15. Rhoades, J. D. 1977. *Potential for using saline agricultural drainage waters for irrigation.* In Proceedings, American Society of Civil Engineering Irrigation and Drainage Division Special Conference on Water Management for Irrigation and Drainage. New York, New York.
16. Shannon, M. C., and M. Akbar. 1979. *Breeding plants for salt tolerance.* In Proceedings, Workshop on Membrane Biophysics. International Union of Pure and Applied Biophysics, Faisalabad, Pakistan.
17. U.S. Department of Interior. 1978. *Report on the water conservation opportunities study.* Washington, D.C.
18. van Schilfgaarde, Jan. 1979. *Salinity management for soybean production.* In Proceedings, Conference on Irrigated Soybeans, INTSOY. University of Illinois, Urbana.
19. van Schilfgaarde, Jan, Leon Bernstein, James D. Rhoades, and Stephen L. Rawlins. 1974. *Irrigaton management for salt control.* Journal of Irrigation and Drainage Division, American Society of Civil Engineering 100: 321-338.
20. Worstell, Robert V. 1979. *Selecting a buried gravity irrigation system.* Transactions, American Society of Agricultural Engineering 22(1): 110-114.

V. FOOD AND FIBER ISSUES IN RESOURCE-CONSTRAINED ECONOMIES

10
Resource constraints affecting future production of food and fiber

Raleigh Barlowe

Until recent times, proponents of economic growth in the United States and Canada have been little constrained by prospects of land or natural resource shortages. Inadequate supplies of labor, capital, and technical know-how have sometimes played decisive roles in preventing desired developments, but needed inputs of land and other natural resources have usually been plentiful.

It has been typical practice for captains of industry and their followers to treat natural resources as though their supplies were endless and inexhaustible. This view of natural resources as a bountiful and inexpensive input has gained wide acceptance. During the early 1950s, a prominent industrialist wrote of "our inexhaustible resources" (3), while a highly respected economist concluded that "agricultural land has been declining markedly in its economic importance" and will probably continue to do so (5, 6). A group of the nation's leading economists argued a few years later that natural resource availability had only a secondary impact on prospects for national economic development (7).

Anyone who has kept up with new developments during the last decade knows that this situation has changed. Land and other resource prices are rising at above-average rates; people are asking if we have enough land and water to handle our production needs; and whole nations are squirming

Raleigh Barlowe is a professor of land economics in the Department of Resource Development, Michigan State University, East Lansing.

because of shortages of energy and mineral supplies. The natural resources that played an essential but always-available and commonplace role in past production decisions have suddenly become critical inputs. With rising consumer and industrial demands and a limited resource base, we have discovered that we live on a finite earth and that the time may come when natural resources will be the strategic factors that determine what we can and cannot do in production.

Land and natural resources are indeed acquiring greater significance as production inputs. They also have a powerful potential for posing resource constraints for the future production of food and fiber. But viewing the situation realistically, we must note that they do not stand alone. Other factors can exert equally strong constraints on future production. In appraising the joint potential of these factors, it is important that we start by bringing the issues into focus. First, we must identify what we mean by resources and resource constraints. With this background, we can consider changing attitudes about resources, the implications of resource constraints for food and fiber production, and the important question of what we can do about it.

Resources and resource constraints

Discussions of resource constraints are obviously concerned with the presence or absence of particular factors or items that keep desired things from happening. A constraint is a barrier to action, and the concept of resource constraints suggests that desired developments are delayed or prevented by shortages of needed resource inputs.

By what specifically do we mean when we speak of resources? Resources represent sources of support. Economists go further to assert that ideas and physical objects become resources when we learn how to use them, when we assign values to them and begin to compete for their ownership and use (10). Thus described, resources involve a variety of production inputs. They can represent capital, credit, labor, and management as well as natural resources, such as land or water. They can involve ideas, human ingenuity, community infrastructures, and institutional resources, such as education, law, and governmental programs.

When we talk of resource constraints to food and fiber production, there is a natural tendency for people to emphasize physical and biological factors. But these natural resource factors represent only part of the total picture. Viable production programs call for operations within a threefold framework. Adequate physical and biological resources must be available to make production operations possible. Operations must be feasible from an economic and technological view, and they must pass the test of institutional acceptability. Resource constraints can arise from any or all of these basic frameworks.

Physical and biological framework. The requirement of physical and biological capability calls for the presence of needed physical resources,

such as land, water, minerals, sunlight, and climate, and for biological resources, such as plants, animals, and man. The absence of any of these
natural resources can make production impossible. Shortages can impose
severe production constraints. How we treat these resources depends on
their differing characteristics. In this respect, it is meaningful to classify
them into three major groups: flow resources, fund resources, and a composite group including the subclasses of biological, soil, and man-made
resources that have both fund and flow characteristics (2).

Flow resources represent those sources of support that become available
for use in a steady or predictable flow over time. Sunlight, changing
climate, wind, tides, rain, and the flow of streams are common examples.
Some of these resources (water and solar energy) can be stored for later use.
But most of them must be used at the time of their flow if their resource
value is not to be lost.

Flow resources are essential to and can pose production constraints for
agriculture. For example, farming operations can be seriously hampered by
lack of sunlight, too much or too little heat, and too much or too little
moisture. Until we learn how to better control these natural constraints, we
must accept most of their effects as givens.

Fund resources involve those natural sources of support that occur in
fixed quantities on or near the earth's surface. Minerals are a classic example, but the concept of fund resources also includes the earth's fixed supplies of air, water, and surface resources.[1] As their name suggests, fund resources are both fixed in supply and relatively irreplaceable. Some, such as
the mineral fuels, can be exhausted through use; while others, such as
metallic minerals, can be reused indefinitely as long as their basic supplies
are not dissipated through poor management.

The chief constraint problems associated with fund resources spring from
the fixity and exhaustibility of their supplies. With the destruction of their
resource values through use, steps should be taken to save mineral fuels for
their more productive and essential uses until alternative sources of energy
are developed to take their place. Conservation practices also are needed
with metallic resources to ensure that once used they are kept available for
possible recycling and reuse.

The composite class of natural resources involves physical and biological
resources that have characteristics of both fund and flow resources. At any
given time, these resources could be treated as a fund that is fixed in supply
and that could be totally liquidated through exploitative use. But if care is
taken to protect necessary seedstock and if good husbandry practices are accepted, the resources have a potential for restocking themselves over time
and for providing a predictable future flow of resources. Biological resources, such as plants and animals, provide prominent examples of this

---

[1]Although the total supply of water can be viewed as a fund resource, the operations of the
hydrologic cycle in causing rain and flowing streams makes it a flow resource. Solar effects and
gravity cause wind movements, changing climates, and tides. Biological processes and the action of flow resources make soil a distinctive composite type of resources.

composite class. Soils, which have characteristics of fund, flow, and biological resources, represent a second important subclass. Man-made (or man-organized) resources, such as water reservoirs and drainage works, constitute a third subclass.

Resource shortages can occur with each class of composite resources. But practical considerations dictate that they always be used in ways that permit the regeneration of their flows of resource values. Wise management of biological resources requires the protection of fragile and endangered resources and careful observance of the ecological laws of nature. Periodic or continuing disinvestments are possible and logical with each of the three subclasses, but these disinvestments must be balanced with timely reinvestments if the resources are to continue in productive use.

Economic and technological framework. Many operations that are possible from physical and biological standpoints are not feasible for economic or technological reasons. Experiments may demonstrate possibilities of production, but no businessman will undertake commercial production operations without first asking: Will it pay? In the production process, operators combine inputs of capital, labor, and management with physical and biological inputs, and they will not and cannot be expected to proceed unless they envisage prospects for gross returns that will more than cover their production costs. Harsh circumstances can force operators to cut back on the costs they associate with their labor and management. But in no case can they operate without the promise of profit that indicates a surplus of returns above production costs.

Any of several economic factors can pose resource restraints for food and fiber production. The problem may be low product prices, above-average production costs, inadequate labor productivity, insufficient capital, lack of credit, location disadvantages, high transportation or marketing costs, or unimaginative management. Economic restraints may also stem from arrangements affecting the allocation and distribution of incomes. Examples of this occur with leasing, working, and other arrangements that allocate the costs borne by participants on a different basis than the benefits received.

What happens in production also depends to a large extent on the state of technology. As man has succeeded in opening the gates of knowledge, he has discovered thousands of new ways for increasing productivity. Moving from the sail and the waterwheel to modern engines and power plants, he has found new ways to harness the forces of nature. Automobiles and planes have increased his mobility; radios give him almost instantaneous communication; chemistry and biology have shown new ways to use the resources of nature; and the development of improved input-output combinations has greatly expanded the potential for production.

Technological developments have done much to remove resource constraints in the past and have great potential for continuing to do so in the future. We have no guarantees though that the flow of new knowledge will continue endlessly into the future. Miracle answers to today's problems or even additions commensurate with those generated during the last century can do much to soften and solve problems caused by resource constraints. A slowing down or cessation of the flow of technical know-how, however, could create new restraints for farmers and others in both Canada and the United States.

Institutional framework. In addition to being physically and biologically possible and economically and technically feasible, production programs must be institutionally acceptable if they are to operate successfully in today's world. This test requires that a program be legal, administratively workable, and in tune with prevailing political and social goals.

Food and fiber production have enjoyed high institutional acceptability in the past. People must eat, and agriculture accordingly has enjoyed a traditionally high priority as a national activity. It would be nice if we could expect continued acceptance of this priority. But changing conditions almost always bring new attitudes and responses. Agriculture in a sense may be a victim of its past successes. Increases in productivity in the past have permitted a shifting of most of the population to urban environments. As these people have become affluent and further removed from agriculture, they have often tended to assume the availability of food supplies and have gone on to emphasize other priorities. Important among these new priorities are demands for additional housing, for open space and recreational opportunities, and for environmental enhancement.

Among the new priorities that are now competing with the needs of agriculture are the claims of land developers that diversion of prime farmland to urban uses will not be missed because there is plenty of good farmland in the next county, the environmentalist's claim that farm uses of chemicals must be banned because of their uncertain spillover effects on the environment, the suburbanite's charge that nearby farming operations must be curtailed because of unpleasant odors, and the trucker's demand that farm fuel allocations be reduced to accommodate nonfarm users. As these examples suggest, acceptance of conflicting priorities can pose problems for future food and fiber production.

Changing attitudes about resources

Students of resource attitudes and policies can argue that the new emphasis given to natural resources during the 1970s is only a stage in a long-evolving process. The preindustrial world of three centuries ago was a resource-constrained society. Recurring famines, severe epidemics, and frequent wars had kept total population numbers more or less in balance for several centuries. Levels of living were low for most people, and the seeming inability of the available land resources to provide more food, fiber, and other products was a major constraint to economic growth and to improvements in public welfare.

Discovery of the New World; the Industrial Revolution; increased commerce with other nations; and most important, the opening of the gates of knowledge with the development of new technologies, the discovery of new facts about life and disease, and the devising of improved strategies in production brought revolutionary changes in this earlier situation. Nowhere were these new conditions more important than in Canada and the United States. Settlers in both nations benefitted from the capital and ideas they brought from the Old World and also from opportunities to exploit a vast natural resource heritage on the new frontier. With thousands of acres of forests and prairies before them, it was easy for settlers to treat nature's bounty as the flow from a bottomless pitcher. Resource disinvestments were accepted as normal. Little thought was given to possible future needs to reinvest in biological and soil resources.

This frontier attitude about resource availability and use has continued with varying modifications to the present day. Yet, stirrings of change started slightly over a century ago when George Perkins Marsh pointed in his prophetic volume on *Man and Nature* to man's emerging power to modify and destroy his physical environment (*4*). Others raised the call for forest, soil, and grassland conservation in the decades that followed. These calls fell on deaf ears at first but gradually were heard and finally triggered the conservation movement of the early 1900s.

With this movement, people became more aware of the need for conserving vital natural resources; and governments, along with thousands of their citizens, adopted conservation practices and policies. These policies, for the most part, have dealt more with the husbanding and improved management of biological and soil resources than with the problem of resource constraints. Conservationists have recognized that a day of reckoning is in the offing; but while they have worked to save some resources, they have often joined their neighbors in demanding more and more resources for the workings of industry and the fulfillment of consumer goals.

Examples of these demands are easy to find. Approximately 388 million acres were homesteaded in the western United States in the 45 years following the Census Bureau's official ending of the frontier in 1890 (*8*). Total food production more than doubled in the United States in the 50 years following the 1920s, at a time when acreage of farmland was decreasing. Annual timber consumption increased and in all but a few years exceeded the levels of the 1890s, when numerous early calls were made for timber conservation. Consumption of minerals and mineral fuels increased at an exponential rate. Calculated on a weight basis, world demand for our 25 most important minerals rose from an annual rate of 15.8 trillion tons in 1965 to 22.2 trillion tons in 1974—40.5 percent (*9*).

Are these trends good or bad? Obviously, we have been successful in stepping up production. But have we been feasting on resources that should be saved for the future? As one might expect, opinions vary widely on this point. For almost a century, prophets of gloom and doom have confronted us with dire predictions of famine, resource shortages, and overall diminishing returns. Outpourings of neomalthusian predictions concerning the dreadful ultimate consequences of our actions have come in four great waves: first during the conservation movement years at the beginning of the century, again in the years following World Wars I and II, and most recently with the blossoming of the environmental movement in the late 1960s and 1970s.

The latest outpouring of concern has had the greatest impact on public thinking and policies. Among the reasons for this, one can point to the fact that the maturing of the industrial age has foreshadowed what many thinkers envisage as a transition to a postindustrial era in which relatively more emphasis will be given to services than production.[2] Degradation of certain environmental resources, in combination with the relative affluence enjoyed by large sectors of the population, has favored programs for environmental enhancement. And with the oil crunch of the early 1970s, the United States experienced its first real brush with resource shortages.

It is too early to tell how much the experiences of recent years will affect future attitudes and policies concerning the conservation and protection of vital natural resources. At this point, however, it appears that we are on the path for adopting policies that will translate several social concerns about resource and environmental constraints into programs of action. Among other things, such programs may well call for more intensive land and resource planning, the protection and conservation of farmland and other resources, and encouragements for the development and increased use of biological and flow resources.

Current constraints and their implications

What are the major resource constraints to food and fiber production? These constraints can be grouped into six classes: (1) those factors we must accept as they are, (2) land and water supplies, (3) other natural resource inputs used in production, (4) economic factors, (5) technology, and (6) institutional factors.

Man now enjoys far more control over his working environment than at any time in past history. Yet there are several basic flow resources he must accept as givens. Important among them are access to sunlight, climate, duration of growing seasons, exposure to winds, and amounts of normal precipitation. Future operators may grow their crops in green houses or benefit from man-regulated climate. For now, though, we must treat these factors as givens around which farmers must accommodate their operations.

Land and water supplies. Operators have more choices available when they make decisions concerning the use of land and water resources. The

---

[2]This transition has prompted arguments for zero population growth and for shifts to a steady-state or no-growth economy.

available quantities of these resources are fixed from the standpoint of society but highly variable to individual operators. Of the two factors, the supplies of water that become available through normal precipitation often operate as the more important constraint on crop production. Irrigation practices have been introduced in arid regions and supplemental irrigation has been introduced in more humid areas to offset this constraint. Availability of optimum supplies of moisture for plant growth will probably rank high among the factors affecting agricultural productivity in the future, and additional emphasis will likely be given to the adoption and expansion of irrigation activities in humid and subhumid areas.

Availability of suitable land is a problem for some individual operators. For the moment though, total land supplies are more than adequate in Canada and the United States to take care of our agricultural production needs. Both nations can care for their domestic food needs and also supply the large exportable surpluses that make them the world's top breadbasket areas. Farmers in both nations could reclaim old farmlands and bring large additional areas into use if the relationship between product prices and costs made such developments economically feasible.

But while we have enough farmland to care for our current and expected future needs, no one can be certain about the extent of our future demands for cropland resources. Given this uncertainty, wise resource management calls for the protection and prudent management of the more productive agricultural lands. Science may provide the key for handling future production needs from fewer acres; but whether it does so or not, the technical know-how we apply can be expected to yield a higher return if applied on high-grade soils as opposed to lands of lower inherent productive potential. The diversion of prime agricultural lands to other uses, particularly when lower grades of land would suffice, represents an emerging constraint on food and fiber production. The adverse potential of this constraint for society should be clearly recognized by farmers and consumers alike and should receive priority emphasis in the devising of appropriate public policies.

Other natural resource inputs. Agricultural production is affected by a wide gamut of natural resources other than land and water. Important among these are our supplies of mineral fuels, minerals used as production aids, biological resources, agricultural soils, and certain man-made resources. Of these factors, soils have always rated high in importance, but most attention in recent months has been given to the availability of energy resources.

Mineral fuels—natural gas, petroleum, coal, and uranium—now account for the great majority of the energy resources consumed in Canada and the United States. The relatively low costs associated with past production of electricity, heat, and gasoline from these sources has led to a tremendous expansion of per capita demands for energy resources. These demands in combination with supply limitations and rising prices have made energy resources a critical and limiting factor for millions of consumers.

With agriculture in the two countries largely mechanized, shortages of petroleum products can be a potent constraint for agricultural production. In practice, our worries on this score may be overworked as agricultural operations will probably enjoy allocation priorities long after many competing uses are curtailed or subjected to rationing programs. More significant than this institutional priority are two other facts: (1) While energy resource prices rise with the impact of market demands on limited supplies, it is unlikely that we will ever run out of these resources. Prices will simply rise as supplies become more scarce and harder to capture from nature. (2) Farm operators are in an excellent position to lead the parade in adopting technologies that will use biological products and wind and solar power as substitute sources of energy.

In addition to the mineral fuels used to produce energy, minerals are needed in agricultural production to provide machinery, building materials, commercial fertilizers, needed trace elements for soils, and farm chemicals and pesticides. With possible mineral shortages in prospect, operators can expect higher operating costs over time. They may take comfort though in the knowledge that higher prices create (1) incentives for discovering and developing new sources of minerals, (2) opportunities for the profitable processing of lower grades of ores, and (3) pressures for shifting to substitute resources than can compete with the minerals in question (1).

Biological resources are important to farmers because agriculture is primarily concerned with the production of plants and animals. Farmers work with biological constraints when they operate with unproductive or only moderately productive herds, or with less than the most productive crop species. They use biological inputs, such as hay, silage, feed grains, and animal wastes, in their operations. They also can fall back on the use of animal power or the distilling of alcohol as they seek viable alternatives to energy constraints.

Soil resources and man-made resources, such as irrigation reservoirs, farm ponds, drainage systems, and farm buildings, also are important to farm production. Deficiencies in these resources can pose major production constraints. Farmers who are suffering inordinate soil losses, who have worn out soils that need rebuilding, who have inadequate moisture for farming, or who have water-logged soils have real problems. Fortunately, many of these problems can be readily diagnosed and can be handled with appropriate investment and management measures.

Economic, technological, and institutional constraints. Favorable economic conditions and relationships are a major ingredient of successful farming operations. Farmers prosper when they have a crop and prices are high relative to costs. They suffer when the reverse situation applies. With some economic constraints, farmers are either the beneficiaries or the victims of factors affecting the national economy. There is little they can do as individuals to raise product prices or lower production costs. With other economic constraints, however, individual operators can often take major steps to improve their competitive positions by moving to more profitable locations, shifting to other enterprises, using better inputs, devising improved input-output combinations and strategies, and by seeking lower cost credit or more efficient marketing facilities.

Technological change is probably the most important single factor affecting the prospects for future food and fiber production. With discoveries of new technological know-how comparable to those of the last 50 to 100 years, many of today's production problems will likely fade into insignificance. Unfortunately, there are more uncertainties with new technology than with the other factors. We can be confident that new breakthroughs and developments are ahead; but no one can predict what, how much, or when the new technology will come.

Most new agricultural technology of the past has involved mechanical, biological, and chemical developments. Labor-saving machines have made it possible for farmers to operate large acreages more efficiently. Biological developments have brought the breeding of improved livestock and plant species. Chemical developments have brought progress in pest control, seed treatment, commercial fertilization, and the use of feed additives.

Logical questions about the future of agricultural technology can be raised with each of these types of development. The high energy consumption requirements associated with much farm mechanization suggest a needed reorientation of new mechanical developments. Some geneticists fear that, without new breakthroughs, they have pushed breed and variety improvements about as far as they can. In view of the emphasis given to environmental concerns, the future also seems to promise more limitations than opportunities for the adoption of new chemical developments.

Institutional factors can operate as constraints if they prevent farmers from operating in ways they otherwise would. In this respect, it may be noted that public policies can operate as a double-edged sword. Land use regulations can prevent some owners from using land as they wish while preserving land for future agricultural use. Similarly they can restrict farming operations while trying to enhance local environments or favor the taxation of land out of farming while applying a uniformity rule to property taxation. Farmers have less to say about the devising of public policies than they had when they represented a larger portion of the electorate. They still have popular sentiment on their side, however, if care is taken to educate the public concerning the impacts of potential institutional constraints on farm production.

Implications for future action

What are the policy implications of resource constraints for future production? Is there something we can do about them? In addressing these questions, it should first be noted that we will always face the problem of resource constraints. As soon as we remove one constraint, we can expect other factors to become the limiting and strategic items that prevent further increases in production. If we had no resource constraints, we could produce enough food from a single flowerpot to feed the world. This reality of life, however, should not deter us in working to modify and remove existing constraints.

From the standpoint of treatment in action programs, our major resource constraints fall into four principal groups. Some constraints, such as the length of growing seasons, are not subject to change. They must be accepted as givens. A second group represents changes in practices or organization that individual operators can accept to improve their productivity. The third group involves the role technological change and scientific developments can play in modifying existing constraints and opening up new horizons for production. A final group concerns the use of public policies to achieve better production conditions.

Public programs can logically be used to deal headlong with the last three groups of constraints. Education, demonstration, and extension programs can and should be used to help individual operators modify and avoid those constraints that are subject to their control. Continued support of research is greatly needed to keep the flow of scientific developments coming and hopefully to facilitate the unlocking of new secrets that can help farmers to better feed the world.

Public policies are needed not only for the promotion and stimulation of education and research but also to give direction to the workings of our economic system and to our resource utilization practices. Most of us want to retain a maximum of personal freedom and individual self-agency. Yet in a world of increasing competition and conflicts of interest, it is obvious that strong public policies are needed to make certain that farmers receive a fair return for their productive efforts, that farmlands and other vital resources be protected for future use, and that good stewardship policies be pursued in the development and use of our natural resources.

REFERENCES

1. Barlowe, Raleigh. 1978. *Land resource economics* (third edition). Prentice-Hall, Inc., Englewood Cliffs, New Jersey. p. 113.
2. Bunce, Arthur C. 1945. *The economics of soil conservation.* Iowa State University Press, Ames.
3. Holman, Eugene. 1952. *Our inexhaustible resources.* Atlantic Monthly 189(6): 29-32.
4. Marsh, George Perkins. 1864. *Man and nature, physical geography as modified by human action.* Scribners, New York, New York.
5. Schultz, Theodore W. 1956. *The declining importance of land.* The Economic Journal 61: 740.
6. Schultz, Theodore W. 1953. *The economic organization of agriculture.* McGraw-Hill Book Company, New York, New York.
7. Social Science Research Council and Resources for the Future, Inc. 1960. *Natural resources and economic growth.* Ann Arbor, Michigan.
8. Turner, Frederick Jackson. 1893. *The significance of the frontier in American history.* American History Association, U.S. Government Printing Office, Washington, D.C. p. 187.

9. U.S. Bureau of Mines. 1976. *Minerals in the U.S. economy: Ten-year supply-demand profiles for mineral and fuel commodities (1965-74).* Washington, D.C.
10. Zimmerman, Erich W. 1951. *World resources and industries.* Harper & Row, New York, New York.

11
Agricultural productivity: Technology potential

Carl W. Carlson

How to adequately feed the world continues to plague leaders of the major governments. Even though global per capita consumption now averages 108 percent of the minimum nutritional requirements, the average daily intake in the developing countries falls short of the minimum requirements. Therefore, leaders in developing countries have to worry first about feeding their population.

We in the United States are among the fortunate. In fact, our food and fiber reserves have been so adequate that over the past four decades production constraints have been part of our agricultural program. As a result, it is difficult for us to accept that the percentage of undernourished people in the world is the same as it was 20 years ago. We do know, however, that we cannot expect to always have adequate food reserves when people in the developing countries of the world are hungry.

History tells us that the relationships between population pressures and soils have always been fragile. The Tigris-Euphrates Valley, once known as the Fertile Crescent, supported more people in pre-Biblical times than it does today. When good land is scarce, the production of adequate food and fiber is a serious problem. Studies of land around the world that has been cultivated for thousands of years show that when the soils of a nation are destroyed the freedoms of citizens are also destroyed (*10*). Destruction of

Carl W. Carlson, former acting assistant deputy director, Agricultural Research, Science and Education Administration, U.S. Department of Agriculture, Beltsville, Maryland, is now retired.

the soil tends to condemn citizens to privation.

The increase in world population from 2.5 billion in 1950 to 4.0 billion in 1975 placed tremendous pressure on the cropland base. One result of placing great production pressure on fragile lands was dramatically demonstrated in Africa when drought in the 1970s triggered widespread famine in Ethiopia and the Sahelian Zone. But drought only brought into sharp focus the fundamental problem of growing pressure on local land resources (*14*).

As world leaders look to the future, most agree that the United States will continue to be a major exporter of food and fiber. There is a disagreement among these leaders, however, as to whether the United States can continue to supply 85 percent of the soybeans, 60 percent of the feed grains, 45 percent of the wheat, 30 percent of the cotton, and 24 percent of the rice to

Table 1. Land with potential for conversion to cropland, by regions (*11*).

Region	High Potential (million acres)	Medium Potential (million acres)
Northeast	1.2	4.6
Lake states	2.5	6.8
Corn Belt	5.6	9.9
Northern plains	5.4	13.0
Appalachian	5.1	10.1
Southeast	5.3	11.6
Delta states	3.4	7.2
Southern plains	5.5	15.0
Mountain	4.0	11.7
Pacific	1.9	4.7
Hawaii, Puerto Rico, Virgin Islands	0.1	0.2
Total	40.0	94.8

world markets. There is growing evidence that such an attempt to meet the food and fiber obligations of growing populations will put natural resources in the United States under stress.

Land available for food production

Additional food can be produced only by adding to the cropland base or by increasing production per unit of land. Increased population and economic activity in any country increases the competition for land resources. In the United States there is land available for conversion to cropland. The National Resource Inventory recently completed by the Soil Conservation Service shows that we have about 135 million acres of land with a high or medium potential for conversion to cropland (Table 1).

These projected acreages are based on numerous assumptions about new technology, water availability for agriculture, energy constraints, and farm prices. These data suggest that 40 million acres, of which half is prime farmland in small parcels, have high potential for future cropland use. These conversions undoubtedly would require conservation measures to ensure adequate protection of the land.

Conversion of medium-potential land would require significant investments. Inflation and energy shortages will impact heavily on the feasibility of farming these acres. Because most of the potential lands for conversion to cropland are currently being used for pasture, range, and forest, appreciable tradeoffs would be involved.

In the United States there is a significant shift of cropland to urban uses. Between 1967 and 1977, urban land increased by 30 million acres—a threefold increase over that of the previous 10 years. Statistics show that most of the acres converted were Class II and III lands. Changing land use patterns in Canada show that half of the farmland being lost to urban development is the best one-twentieth of its cropland.

Limitations to crop production

In the United States the problems of meeting our required production with our soil and water resources and limited fossil fuel can best be described by looking at our production of wheat, corn, and soybeans. These three crops occupy nearly half of our cropland acres. They are important both to our domestic food supply and for our export commitments and our balance of payments. At the present time, these three crops are produced on some of our best soils by using a high level of technology.

Wheat.   Winter wheat is produced in the southern and central Great Plains and hard red spring wheat in the northern Great Plains. The Palouse in the northwest also produces significant amounts of winter wheat.

As we examine the prospects of maintaining wheat production on a sustained basis, we recognize that drought frequently limits wheat production. History tells us that severe droughts have occurred in our wheat-producing areas long before the area was plowed from sod. The most severe drought in my time occurred in the 1930s. Soils data and tree ring observation give us evidence that droughts more severe than the one occurring in the 1930s have occurred and will occur again. Therefore, we must be prepared to meet droughts more severe than Great Plains farmers have experienced to date if we are to maintain current levels of wheat production.

Long-term studies of dryland agriculture by the U.S. Department of Agriculture (USDA), starting early in this century have shown that as much as 40 percent of the soil nitrogen was lost during the first years of cultivation (5). Legumes could not be used to supply the needed nitrogen because these crops exhaust soil moisture reserves needed for the next wheat crop. Therefore, the nitrogen needs of the crop must be met with chemical fertilizers.

These studies also showed that summer fallow was an effective method of stabilizing wheat production. The water stored under a fallow system was generally sufficient to assure a crop the following season. However, soil losses from wind and water erosion were always higher under fallow (*5, 7, 9*). Probably the most serious soil erosion in this country today occurs under fallow systems in the Palouse. Only by maintaining crop residues on the soil surface can soil loss be reduced to a tolerable level. Precise, well-timed tillage is required to keep these residues on the soil surface. Large equipment, powered by big tractors, makes the fossil fuel requirements high for these farming systems.

But in spite of the problems that farmers have to contend with, national wheat yields have about doubled over the last three decades (Table 2). These

Table 2. *Wheat and corn yields in the United States, 1945 to 1975.*

Year	Wheat	Corn
	— *bushels/acre* —	
1945	17	33
1950	16	38
1955	19	42
1960	26	55
1965	27	74
1970	31	73
1975	31	86

increased yields do not necessarily come about from more productive soils. Rather, these increases come from fertilizer, improved varieties, weed control, and tillage methods. These inputs are dependent on fossil fuels.

Probably as important, these yield increases have resulted from the long-term field research studies conducted over the last 60 years. Data from these studies provided the input needed for today's agricultural technology. Also, these data provide the grist for the mills of the present-day computer modelers. Today's climate for funding agricultural research is not conducive to the kind of long-term studies that gave us the past improvements in wheat production.

Corn and soybeans. Corn and soybean production systems have also undergone a revolution since 1940. Low-population stands of check-row planted corn, which were dependent on legumes and manure for their nitrogen, have been replaced by high-plant populations and supplied nitrogen by commercial fertilizer. Pesticides are essential in these high population systems to assure high yields.

Soil organic matter and nitrogen have also declined in the soils producing corn and soybeans. Studies conducted over the last 100 years of various cropping systems at the University of Illinois show that chemical fertilizer used under proper management will sustain the productivity of the soil. However, even with the use of nitrogen fertilizer and returning the crop residues to the soil, the soil organic matter continues to decline. The declining organic matter may account in part for the increased soil erosion experienced in the Corn Belt.

Recent studies by the Soil Conservation Service (SCS) show the erosion in the Corn Belt exceeds the amount considered tolerable for protecting the soil resources (12). Most soils in the Corn Belt are deep and are underlaid by parent materials with good physical properties. Therefore, the impact of soil erosion is often on reservoir sedimentation or streamwater quality rather than decreased yields.

Table 3. Annual soil loss under four cropping systems on two land slopes (9).

Cropping System	Soil Loss	
	3% Slope	6% Slope
	tons/acre	
Fallow	35.0	67.0
Corn - corn - soybeans	13.0	24.0
Corn - oats - meadow	02.0	04.0
Continuous grass - alfalfa	00.1	

The soils in the northeastern and southeastern United States are different. These soils are shallow and are underlain by subsoils or parent materials that deter deep rooting. Therefore, soil losses (1, 2, 6, 7, 10) in these areas can seriously affect soil properties and crop yields.

In the 1930s, erosion in row crops was controlled by sod-based rotation, contouring, and terracing (1). In recent years, the use of larger equipment, fertilizer, and chemicals for weed control has led to the abandonment of the erosion control practices considered effective (Table 3).

Today, we are depending on managing crop residues and limited tillage for erosion control. Limited measurements of erosion from these practices indicate that they are effective. However, the data needed to assess these practices are not compatible with today's agricultural research funding climate. Further, these systems depend on pesticides.

There is good evidence that the record corn yields in 1978 were not due to increased soil productivity. Rather, a mixture of such inputs as better hybrids, fertilizer, timely tillage, good pest control, and irrigation account for these high yields.

In examining the question of what the future acreages and yields of corn and soybeans might be, it becomes evident that we can maintain production if we continue to use our present technology. However, this technology is highly dependent on fossil fuels. If the costs of fossil fuels continue to soar, the farmer will look for alternatives. A recent study made in Iowa suggests that a return to the legume and sod-based rotations could be made with little or no decline in per acre corn yields. However, to accomplish this, 6 million acres of corn land would have to be shifted to legumes and sod crops.

Scientists who were once optimistic about increasing our major crop yields by new technologies have become more conservative. The dramatic increases in U.S. wheat yields that began in the mid-1930s are levelling off (8). There is good evidence that a slowing of technological development, coupled with the health, safety, environmental, and energy constraints that today's farmer is faced with, will result in ceilings on the yields of our major crops in the years ahead.

Impact of government programs on soil erosion

Land use in the United States is determined in part by the various government grain production control programs. These programs include the Conservation Reserve Program, Acreage Reserve Program, Cropland Conversion Program, and Crop Adjustment Program. The greatest impact of those programs is on the wheat-producing areas of the Great Plains and the northwest.

For example, in North Dakota, more than 11 million acres were planted to wheat in 1949. Control programs were begun in the early 1950s, and by 1957 the acreage had been reduced to about 5.5 million acres. About 4 million of the acres taken out of wheat were summer fallowed. The acreage stayed at about that level over the next 7 years. In the early 1970s the wheat acreage climbed back to 11 million acres. However, in 1977 and 1978 setaside programs caused the acreage to again decline.

Haas and Boatwright showed that soil losses from wind and water erosion on fallowed land were substantially higher than from continuously cropped land (4). They pointed out that use of fertilizer and weed control chemicals could eliminate summer fallow from cropping systems in most of the states. Further, they suggested that erosion losses in the Great Plains could be reduced by eliminating summer fallow.

Soil erosion surveys by Verle Kaiser (private communication) over the last 39 years in Whitman County, Washington, show that yearly soil losses have ranged up to 10.6 tons per acre per year. Losses increased during the years when large acreages of summer fallow were used to comply with wheat acreage control programs. Kaiser estimates the soil loss from fallow land to be 25 tons per acre per year as compared to less than 8 tons under wheat. These data suggest that the increased use of summer fallow brought on by grain production control programs has increased soil erosion in the United States.

Policy changes in USDA, which are reflected in government programs, hamper conservation. The recent plowing out and planting of land enrolled in the Great Plains Conservation Program, to comply with the wheat setaside program, is an example of government programs that work at cross-purposes. These several-million-dollar conservation practices, paid for by the Great Plains Program, were put in place to protect land vulnerable to excessive erosion.

A recent article (12) assessing the history of USDA soil conservation programs emphasizes that soil erosion control has been only one of a number of different competing goals in these programs. The programs, which have been fractionized and poorly coordinated, have given conflicting advice to landowners and distributed funds to many landowners rather than provide financial support for erosion control on lands with high soil losses. Further, the program failed to recognize that to be effective erosion control practices have to be site unique.

The impact of man on soils

Most of those writing about the impact of modern agriculture on soil erosion and future world food prospects are pessimistic (3, 6, 7, 10). However, many of the land resource areas in the United States are producing more today than when first put into production. For example, farmers in Florida, by using a combination of drainage, irrigation, and fertilizer have been able to make very sandy soils some of the most productive in the nation. Also, several thousands of acres of swamplands in the southeastern states have been made productive by proper drainage. Use of fertilizer and irrigation has made it possible to obtain a good economic return from lands once considered too poor to crop. While some farmers have damaged the soil resource, most have been good stewards of the land.

Conclusions

Present levels of crop production in the United States are in delicate balance with the soil resource base. Declining resources for research make it unlikely that new technology can continue to give rise to additional productivity. The high dependence of present production technology on fossil fuels makes it unlikely that agriculture can reduce this dependence without cutting current producing levels.

Agricultural land use policies in the United States are resulting in less available cropland. Modern farming systems are leading to increased soil erosion. Although the impact of soil loss on crop productivity is not well defined, present-day production systems do lead to soil losses that conservationists consider excessive. Even though the principles of erosion control are well understood, there is a real problem of getting control practices applied. Therefore, we need to reexamine recommended conservation practices to determine why the landowner is reluctant to accept them.

There is general agreement that any erosion represents a potential loss of an essential resource, but there is no generally accepted standard for determining how much erosion should be tolerated. It is important that the tolerable erosion level be attainable at a reasonable cost to the landowner.

Today's farmer must be conscious of the payoff from any practice he undertakes. The farmer cannot pass his costs on to the consumer, like other businessmen. Furthermore, he has to accept what the government pays him for conservation practices. Short-term financial benefits from conservation practices continue to be difficult to obtain. Unless there is financial assistance for cost-sharing of the recommended conservation practices, implementation is not likely to be rapid. Further, these practices have to fit modern farming systems.

The estimates made of the conservation practices needed on the land to control erosion indicate that implementation will be costly. Although the principles of erosion are understood, we lack technology for developing production systems with adequate erosion control that are acceptable to the farmer. With better methods for estimating soil erosion and determining acceptable erosion tolerances, the effectiveness and costs of farming systems required to assure maximum productivity with minimal soil erosion can be assessed for farmer acceptance.

These accomplishments must be made with limited manpower and dollars. Therefore, a balanced effort between research and development directed squarely at the goal must be maintained. If we are to ensure adequate production and tolerable soil erosion losses on our farmland, agriculturists must have the assistance of the rest of society. However, the public will not give their support unless they are assured that the policies and objectives of state and federal conservation programs are directed to a common goal.

REFERENCES

1. Bennett, H. H. 1939. *Soil conservation.* McGraw-Hill Book Company, New York, New York.
2. Carlson, C. W., D. L. Grunes, J. Alessi, and G. A. Reichman. 1961. *Corn gardena growth on surface and subsoil as affected by application of fertilizer and manure.* Soil Science Society of America Proceedings 25: 44-47.
3. Eckholm, E. P. 1976. *Losing ground.* W. W. Norton & Co., Inc., New York, New York.
4. Haas, H. J., and G. O. Boatwright. 1960. *Let's take another look at summer fallow in the northern plains.* Journal of Soil and Water Conservation 15(4): 174.
5. Haas, H. J., C. E. Evans, and E. F. Miles. 1957. *Nitrogen and carbon changes in great plains soils as influenced by cropping and soil treatment.* Technical Bulletin 1164. U.S. Department of Agriculture, Washington, D.C.
6. Hilgard, E. W. 1880. *Report on cotton production in the United States.* Census Bureau, Washington, D.C.
7. Jacks, G. V., and R. O. Whyte. 1939. *Vanishing lands: A world survey of soil erosion.* Reprint Edition, 1972. Arno Press, Inc., New York, New York.
8. Jensen, Neal. 1978. *Limits to growth in world food production.* Science, July 28, 1978.
9. Laflen, J. M., and W. C. Moldenhauer. 1971. *Soil conservation on agricultural lands.* Journal of Soil and Water Conservation 26(6): 225.
10. Lowdermilk, W. C. 1953. *Conquest of the land through 7,000 years.* Agricultural Information Bulletin 99. U.S. Department of Agriculture, Washington, D.C.
11. National Association of Conservation Districts. 1979. *Tuesday Letter* (June 19).

12. U.S. Department of Agriculture, Soil Conservation Service. 1977. *Cropland erosion.* Washington, D.C.
13. Williams, Craig L. *Soil conservation and water pollution control: The muddy record of the U.S. Department of Agricuture.* Environmental Affairs Law Review 7(3): 365.
14. Wortman, Sterling, and Ralph W. Cummings, Jr. 1978. *To feed this world—the challenge and the strategy.* John Hopkins University Press, Baltimore, Maryland.

12
Alternatives to energy-intensive agriculture

Roger Blobaum

A growing number of alternatives is being considered in American agriculture in an attempt to deal with rapidly rising prices of purchased energy and to reduce the vulnerability of producers to energy shortages and price increases. This is a remarkable change for a production system that has increasingly substituted fossil fuel energy for labor and land over the past 35 years.

Recent responses range from consideration of approaches like solar heating and crop drying to an overwhelming interest in on-farm production of alcohol for use in tractors, trucks, and other equipment. Even such controversial alternatives as organic farming, which emphasizes crop rotations that include nitrogen-fixing legumes, are being considered seriously for the first time.

Agriculture's immediate challenge is to choose and demonstrate proven technologies, both energy-conserving and energy-producing, that reduce dependence on nonrenewable energy sources without cutting yields or overall productivity. Unfortunately some energy-conserving approaches entail higher production costs, lower output, or higher labor requirements. Tests of both practicality and economic feasibility must therefore be applied to all the alternatives considered.

These recent developments are of considerable importance in assessing the ongoing debate between proponents of conventional agriculture, who

---

Roger Blobaum is president of Roger Blobaum & Associates, West Des Moines, Iowa.

insist that specialization and applications of large amounts of fossil fuel energy are essential to production efficiency, and ecologists, who contend this kind of system is too costly in terms of environmental deterioration, soil depletion and erosion, and the growing scarcity of petroleum-based inputs.

There is growing evidence that wide adoption of these alternatives will help agriculture become a producer of energy as well as food and move it closer to becoming a sustainable system that can be highly productive, economically viable, and environmentally sound in an era of resource scarcity. There also is evidence that adopting alternative systems, particularly those that emphasize crop rotations and recycling of organic materials, will enhance soil and water conservation efforts. It may well be that these changes will help shape an agricultural system that proponents of both high productivity and environmental quality can embrace.

Impact of energy use on farms

There is general agreement on the need to take a close look at energy use in agriculture. In adopting labor-saving practices over the last 35 years, producers have become increasingly dependent on a reliable supply of commercial fertilizer and of electricity, propane, gasoline, diesel fuel, and other forms of energy. Projected increases in energy prices over the next few years suggest how vulnerable they are likely to become.

Energy use and other records maintained for 48 diversified farms in northeastern Nebraska the last three years by the Small Farm Energy Project show that fertilizer, fuel, and other purchased energy inputs accounted for 13 percent of the average gross sales of $35,600 per farm (1). This outlay, which covered both farm and household use, exceeded the average net income of these farms.

Projections based on estimates provided by the U.S. Department of Energy indicate energy expenses on these family-sized farms will double by 1984. (This assumes a 10 percent inflation rate plus specific price increases estimated by the U.S. Department of Energy for the various kinds of energy used in agriculture.) These increases would more than wipe out the equivalent of all net income on these farms at the present time. A comparison of average energy consumption by type of operation suggests that diversified, general livestock farms are less vulnerable than dairy or hog farms of comparable size, mainly because of differences in consumption of electricity.

The impact of price increases on larger or more specialized farms may well be different. Little information is available on the relationship between farm size and energy intensiveness, and little is known about the relationship between size and energy-related production costs, or about how the effects of energy price increases would differ between small and large farms. Clearly, though, controlling energy expenses will be an increasingly important farm management challenge; and it is becoming a critical factor in encouraging producers to adopt a wide range of energy-conserving and energy-producing alternatives.

Energy-related innovations on small farms

Work with the Small Farm Energy Project, a national research and demonstration project that emphasizes on-farm applications, suggests that the interest farmers have in solar and other renewable energy sources is underestimated. The response from project cooperators since 1976 suggests that agricultural producers would be willing to adopt alternatives if they had easy access to technical information and assistance, if they were encouraged with some economic incentives, and if their efforts were not hampered by institutional or administrative barriers.

Experience thus far shows that commercial farmers with no previous knowledge of energy alternatives are able to use their skills and ingenuity in designing and building a variety of projects that save both energy and money. Completed projects include solar water heaters on dairy barns, an attached solar greenhouse, three types of solar grain dryers, several types of solar vertical wall collectors, a portable solar collector used for grain drying and home heating, solar food dryers, and a roof-mounted collector on a farrowing house.

The work completed so far suggests that full-time farmers would be willing to build low-cost systems that are reasonably reliable, that are not too complicated, that have relatively short payback periods, that can be retrofitted to existing buildings, that are made from materials obtained locally, and that require a minimum of attention. This work suggests an interest in low-technology systems that are economically viable, and that farmers can build, maintain, and fix themselves.

Several state agricultural experiment stations and universities are cooperating with the federal government in a solar agricultural program that was authorized in 1974 and is aimed at developing systems for reducing fossil fuel consumed in drying grain and other crops, heating livestock and poultry buildings, and heating and cooling greenhouses (8). These systems, which would be mass produced after on-farm testing is completed, are designed for larger producers who are able to invest in manufactured alternative energy systems and are less likely to design or build their own.

A look at organic farming

An energy-saving alternative that is likely to become important is organic farming. Little reliable data is available even though organic methods are being used on thousands of commercial-size farms. Given the small amount of research devoted to this alternative so far, particularly for research conducted over any length of time on farms that use organic methods, it is not surprising that organic farming remains a controversial subject.

The results of a study of commercial-size organic farms in the Corn Belt suggests that they are an economically viable alternative for mixed crop-livestock operations in that region (6). This project, initiated by Washington University and funded over a five-year period by the National Science Foundation, studied the economic performance of these farms, their energy use patterns, and the impact of organic methods on soil quality and erosion. The conclusions were based on a comparison of 14 pairs of matched commercial-size organic and conventional farms in five states.

The study concluded that organic farms used only about 40 percent as much energy as conventional farms, mainly because organic farmers did not use herbicides, insecticides, or manufactured fertilizers. It concluded that organic farms produced about 10 percent less in gross market value per acre of cropland, mainly because they had fewer acres in high-value crops, such as corn and soybeans, and more in rotation hay. They also required about 10 percent more labor, although this was usually provided by the family. In terms of net returns, however, the two groups were roughly comparable, mainly because the production expenses of the organic farms were lower.

Although corn uses more nitrogen (N) fertilizer than any other crop, organic farmers had corn yields that averaged only nine percent below those of their conventional neighbors. Under highly favorable conditions, when corn benefits the most from fertilizer applications, the conventional farmers did considerably better. In dry years, however, organic farmers did as well and in some cases better than conventional farmers. The larger portion of land in rotation on the organic farms produced a one-third reduction in soil loss, an important agronomic benefit that is difficult to document in terms of dollars and cents.

Use of manure on cropland

Another alternative, which is not new by any means, is applying manure and other organic materials to cropland as a supplement to or a substitute for manufactured fertilizers. Consumption of inorganic fertilizers in the United States has doubled since 1960, reaching a record level of 22 million tons for the year that ended in mid-1977. Total energy consumption for fertilizer in 1977 was 594 trillion British termal units, which was roughly 0.8 percent of the national energy budget.

Opportunities to increase the effective use of organic wastes as a source of energy include improving the handling of manures to decrease loss of N, applying manures that are now wasted, applying crop residues that are not being fully utilized, increasing the percentage of sewage sludge currently applied, and increasing the use of the organic fraction of municipal waste.

A recent study of organic waste recycling in agriculture in China, sponsored by the Food and Agriculture Organization of the United Nations, concluded that about two-thirds of the total nutrient intake is derived from a variety of natural manures (4). These include animal and poultry wastes, human habitation wastes, crop wastes, fish wastes, green manures and aquatic plants, biofertilizers, silt, bone meal, and ashes. They are applied to the 130 million hectares of land under arable and permanent crops. The study also noted that the Chinese match up different wastes with different soils and attempt to keep livestock numbers in balance with the area of cultivated land so the optimum requirement for organic manures can be met.

Increased use of organic wastes on cropland in the United States could not eliminate the need for commercial fertilizers as a source of nutrients. However, a task force sponsored by the U.S. Department of Agriculture estimated that the nitrogen in organic wastes not currently applied to the land amounts to 4.5 million tons, nearly half the current annual demand of 10.6 million tons of commercial fertilizer N (1). The task force also concluded that the phosphorus (P) and potassium (K) present in organic wastes not currently used on land could supply 69 percent of the current purchases of P and 57 percent of the current purchases of K.

Potential for areawide land applications of waste

An assessment of the potential for applying urban wastes to agricultural land in a three-county Midwest region showed that nearly all the fertilizer needed on more than 80,000 acres of cropland could be met by the year 2000 by applying all the sludge, paunch manure, and livestock manure available from urban sources in the region (2). This study, undertaken in the Omaha-Council Bluffs Standard Metropolitan Statistical Area, treated the entire region as a waste recycling system that included close-in, privately-owned farms as an essential component. It was futuristic in the sense that it attempted to show what would happen between now and the year 2000 if all suitable urban wastes in a region were applied at agronomic levels to close-in agricultural land. Instead of asking how many acres would be required to dispose of organic urban wastes, it asked how many acres could be supplemented with these wastes to help meet the fertilizer requirements of commonly grown crops.

When urban wastes were composted and applied at the rate of 12 dry tons per acre, for example, they provided all the nutrients needed in five of every six years under a six-year rotation of corn, oats, alfalfa, alfalfa, corn,. and soybeans. Some N fertilizer would be required for the second planting of corn in the fifth year. For sludge application alone, this study concluded that a land application system started this year in the region could deliver anywhere from $105,000 to $127,000 the first year in fertilizer equivalent. By the year 2000, with increasing waste volumes and rising fertilizer prices, benefits to the region's farmers in terms of supplying nutrients for crop production could exceed $1 million annually.

The study concluded that the total regional impact of a well-managed land application program, involving cooperating farmers in terms of N, P, and K supplied, would range from $11 million to $14 million by the year 2000. Included in this estimate is anywhere from 17 million to 29 million pounds of N, which could be delivered for crop production under several different management programs.

Although the heavy metals content of sludge was not a problem in the Omaha-Council Bluffs region, it does limit land application in many areas. This suggests the need for both prohibitions against certain manufacturing and fabrication operations and pretreatment at the source for wastes released into municipal sewers.

Clearly, areawide land application systems would save substantial amounts of both money and energy, particularly if enough agricultural land were available close in. These systems also provide substantial soil-improving and other agronomic benefits. For example, composted sludge can improve soil physical properties in a number of ways: (1) addition of sludge compost to sandy soils will increase their water-retention capacity and provide more water to plants during periods of drought; (2) in heavy-textured clay soils the added organic matter will increase permeability to water and air and increase water infiltration, which minimizes surface runoff; and (3) adding compost to clay soils will reduce compaction and crusting, lower the bulk density, improve soil structure, and provide increased rooting depth (3). It is possible, therefore, that agronomic benefits would exceed those derived from the nutrient content of the waste materials involved.

Production of methane from animal wastes

Production of methane gas from manure and other organic wastes, a process widely used in small-scale systems by farmers in developing countries, such as India and China, appears to be an energy-producing alternative for feedlots and for larger agricultural producers. It is receiving increasing attention in the United States because it is technically suited for use on individual farms and it offers an organic waste recycling alternative that provides methane gas while avoiding disposal problems and producing usable products, such as fertilizer and animal feed.

The present economics of producing biogas from animal wastes suggest that it will be difficult at the farm level to capture the economies of scale necessary to produce methane at competitive prices. The best approach from an economic standpoint would appear to be using the gas to generate electricity on a year-around basis. A technical study completed by the Small Farm Energy Project concluded that this probably is not feasible at this time for small diversified farms in the Midwest. As prices of natural gas and other agricultural energy inputs increase, however, production of methane will become economically feasible in a wider range of locations.

Renewed interest in windpower

One of the oldest alternative energy sources is windpower, which has been harnessed throughout the world to pump water and grind grain. Using windmills to pump water has been largely abandoned in areas served by rural electric systems, although they are still used in remote areas. Submerged electric pumps, which operate whether the wind blows or not, are used by most agricultural producers in the United States to pump water for live-stock, household, and other uses.

Wind electric generators, which were widely used on farms and ranches prior to rural electrification, are an energy alternative with considerable future potential. The state of the art has not changed much since the 1940s because cheap electricity has discouraged the development of wind technology. Larger and much-improved systems are needed now because the amount of electricity used by producers is much higher.

The main improvement in recent years is development of the synchronous inverter, which makes it possible to hook farm wind systems into electric lines. This approach eliminates the cost, maintenance, and electric compatibility problems associated with battery storage systems.

Preliminary monitoring of a four-kilowatt system installed by a Small Farm Energy Project cooperator suggests that wind generators now available for farm use are not nearly large enough to meet the electrical demands of a modern farm. The monitoring records have established, however, that the availability of the wind and the electrical demand of the farm are closely matched. This suggests that wind energy can become an important power source if reasonably-priced systems become available that will meet the higher demands of modern farms or if farm electric demand can be cut back.

Use of alcohol for motor fuels

The energy alternative attracting the greatest attention at this time in the United States is the production of alcohol for use as a motor fuel. Public interest has been stimulated by the promotion of "gasohol," a blend of 10 percent industrial-grade alcohol with 90 percent regular gasoline, that is being marketed through more than 800 service stations around the nation. The federal government has waived the 4-cent-a-gallon federal excise tax on gasohol, and several states have made similar tax concessions.

Reports that Brazil is moving decisively in the direction of producing its own fuel from agricultural sources also have stimulated this interest (5). The Brazilian government has launched a program to replace must of that country's imported oil with ethyl alcohol produced from sugarcane and other crops. An initial target is to produce enough alcohol to replace 20 percent of the country's gasoline by 1980. It is estimated that less than two percent of the land area of Brazil could produce enough fuel to replace all of its imported petroleum.

Production and use of gasohol was viewed initially as a price-support approach. It has had strong support from corn promotion and similar groups that work for expanded industrial uses of grain. The recent shortage of diesel fuel and uncertainty over future prices and supplies, however, have focused increasing attention on alcohol production on farms and in local communities as an important energy alternative.

The successful demonstration of ethanol production and use on working farms has focused a tremendous amount of attention the last few months on on-farm and community-wide systems. The best-known on-farm system was built by Archie and Alan Zeithamer on their diversified farm near Alexandria, Minnesota. Their system, which includes a 4,000-gallon cooker and a 22-foot-high distilling column, has a capacity of 750 gallons a week. The 160-proof alcohol produced is being used in a tractor, a combine, trucks, and other vehicles. The Zeithamers also plan to use it this coming winter to heat their home.

The Bureau of Alcohol, Tobacco, and Firearms, a U.S. Treasury Department agency that regulates alcohol production, has been overwhelmed with requests from farmers for temporary permits. The bureau has issued more than 800 permits so far this year, mostly to individual farmers, compared with only 18 in 1978. Even so, the main federal emphasis is still on huge multimillion dollar plants that would produce industrial grade alcohol for blending. No studies are being funded for renewable agricultural residue conversion to liquid fuels on a farm scale or rural community scale so that farmers can use locally produced liquid fuels to produce food and energy crops.

Small-scale production appears to have several advantages that would give it a favorable energy balance and enable it to overcome the probability that it would not be able to capture all of the economies of scale of centralized commercial systems. One of the most important is that the distillers grain from a small-scale facility can be stored on the farm and fed wet to livestock, eliminating the considerable energy input and equipment needed to dry them so they can be transported and marketed. Local production also eliminates the need to transport grain long distances from farm to distillery and makes it possible to use wood or crop residues for process heat needed to make alcohol. Farmers also could reduce labor costs by providing some of the labor for building a small system and by making alcohol in the off-season.

Perhaps the central consideration for farmers is their ability to control their fuel supply through their own farm production systems. They appear to be attracted by the idea of avoiding the political problems of competing for centrally controlled energy allocations.

Energy production effects on soil and water

The wide range of energy alternatives becoming available make sense for agricultural producers, both large and small, and provide substantial public benefits at the same time. They will make it possible for producers to substantially reduce their consumption of purchased energy without disrupting their operations or reducing overall productivity. They will allow those who are willing to make substantial changes in their operations to exercise the option of producing their own energy and becoming energy self-sufficient.

Almost without exception these alternatives either have no impact one way or another on soil and water resources or return some agronomic benefits. These benefits are particularly important for alternatives that emphasize crop rotations or involve recycling of organic wastes. The main exception is alcohol production, which could result in removal of too much crop residue from the land.

The main public benefit is slowing the substitution of petroleum and other nonrenewable energy for labor and land and bringing closer the time when agriculture can become a net energy producer. Eventually agriculture will have to stop converting petroleum to food and become a sustainable system that produces food from energy sources that are renewable. The alternatives available now make it possible to begin making that transition and to begin doing those things that are necessary to operate in the coming era of resource scarcity.

REFERENCES

1. Blobaum, Roger, Dennis Demmel, Ron Krupicka, and Rob Aiken. 1979. *The impact of various energy innovations on energy consumption and net income for 48 small farms.* Center for Rural Affairs, Walthill, Nebraska.
2. Blobaum, Roger, S. Fast, L. Holcomb, and L. Swanson. 1979. *An assessment of the potential for applying urban wastes to agricultural lands.* A report prepared for the National Science Foundation, Grant No. AER77-08280. Roger Blobaum and Associates, West Des Moines, Iowa.
3. Epstein, E., and J. Parr. 1977. *Utilization of compost as a fertilizer and soil conditioner.* In Proceedings, National Conference on Composting of Municipal Residues and Sludges. Information Transfer, Inc., Silver Spring, Maryland.
4. Food and Agriculture Organization and the United Nations. 1977. *China: Recycling of organic wastes in agriculture.* Soils Bulletin No. 40. Rome.
5. Hammond, A. L. 1977. *Alcohol: A Brazilian answer to the energy crisis.* Science 195: 564-566.
6. Klepper, R., W. Lockeretz, B. Commoner, M. Gertler, S. Fast, D. O'Leary, and R. Blobaum. 1977. *Economic performance and energy intensiveness on organic and conventional farms in the Corn Belt: A preliminary comparison.* American Journal Agricultural Economics 59: 1-12.
7. U.S. Department of Agriculture. 1978. *Improving soils with organic wastes.* Washington, D.C.
8. U.S. Department of Energy. 1978. *Solar energy for agricultural and industrial process heat.* Report No. CS-0053. Washington, D.C.

13
Economic and social realities of soil and water conservation

Lawrence W. Libby

The federal government is reassessing its 40-year commitment to soil and water conservation programs. The major issue is not if we need conservation, but how much, where, and by whom. Impetus for the current scrutiny began with an appraisal by the U.S. General Accounting Office (GAO) in 1976 and an oversight directive from the Senate Agriculture Committee in that same year. The GAO concluded that society should expect more from the millions of dollars invested each year in the 34 conservation programs in five agencies of the U.S. Department of Agriculture (*14*). The Senate Agriculture Committee sought more detailed evidence of the performance of those programs.[1] The biggest push for analysis is from the Soil and Water Resources Conservation Act of 1977 (RCA) (*7, 15*).

New conservation policy will emerge in a setting of informed support. People agree that conservation is important, but so are other things government might do with those dollars. People also demand efficiency in government, accomplishing valid objectives at the least possible cost. In this context, cost is more than dollars. It includes loss of things that people value.

In my view, we are not choosing between economic and social concerns,

[1]Oversight correspondence from Senators Dole and Talmadge to John Knebel, assistant secretary of agriculture, December 1, 1976.

Lawrence W. Libby, formerly coordinator for land, air, water and solid waste, U.S. Department of Agriculture, Washington, D.C., is now an associate professor, Department of Agricultural Economics, Michigan State University, East Lansing.

but are building ways in which social judgments can guide development of economically viable policies. The prevailing social and economic reality is that we must build conservation programs on more than the general agreement among ourselves that it is good.

The evolution of institutions

Governments exist primarily to enact various rules that influence how people go about their business. These rules define the rights and obligations that people have relative to each other. Each person has judgments as to which rules are appropriate and which are not. A new institution indicates that people, usually in groups, exerted enough pressure at the right points to bring about a change that they favor. Institutions change over time. It seems to me that there are five distinct stages for any particular rule or area of concern: (1) Initial alarm—a problem is apparent, new laws are needed. There is urgency. The problem must be solved at any cost. (2) Join the club—the new institution attracts friends who see that there is money and political support involved. Other interest groups, agencies, and governments see the virtue of cooperation. (3) Solid respectability—the institution now has its own establishment. Seeds of complacency are sown. Everyone is comfortable with things as they are. The institution has a life of its own, beyond the problem that started it all. (4) Competition among the goods— other rules have been set up to solve other problems. People like them all, but there are choices and not enough money to keep all the establishments going. There is competition. (5) Agonizing reappraisal—some people and groups go after a more attractive interest. People ask what has been done to solve the problem that got this all started. The problem is still there, but we need better ways to solve it so we can get more of something else that we also want.

There is attrition as we move from stage to stage. Only the most robust and adaptable institutions survive. Those that do, however, develop real staying power. Some recycle, taking on new purpose, new sources of support. Several variables determine rate of movement from stage to stage.

We are in stage 1 of efforts to protect endangered species and historic or cultural resources. There is strong sentiment that we should protect them at all costs. The real struggles for institutional survival are ahead. We are somewhere between stages 3 and 4 with water quality. We have had a tough environmental target, basically zero pollution, built on early enthusiasm. Now the establishment is in place and the real sacrifices necessary to meet the goals are increasingly apparent.

Soil and water conservation is definitely in stage 5. Some groups have abandoned ship for the flashier aspects of the environmental movement. Budget cutters are circling hungrily. Even long-time members of the conservation establishment are wondering if we cannot find a better way to do the job. This is a healthy sign, demonstrating that institutionalized concern for conservation has matured gracefully. It is a critical juncture, however. If soil and water conservation programs are to survive, they must recycle back to stage 2, attracting new sources of political support.

We know from recent studies that people are leaving metropolitan areas and moving back to rural areas (2). These new rural residents have a stake in conservation practices that enhance water quality and support the economic health of the community. They have a stake, but they may not know it. Most of them do not farm, so benefits they derive are less direct than might have been true for earlier conservationists. Further, their interests are likely to be more diverse than in the past, placing greater emphasis on documented payoff from public investment in conservation. They have more substitutes for conservation practices.

Most of our success in maintaining the vitality of conservation programs, thus continuing the evolutionary process and avoiding extinction, depends upon a more careful statement of the rationale for conservation. We must contribute to better understanding of why we conserve soil and water. We must have a modern conservation ethic.

Toward a modern conservation ethic

Conservation is concerned with retaining resources and, therefore, choices about their use for future generations. Government tries to correct the discrepancy between what is rational for the individual farm or resource user and for society over the long haul. Current use is modified. Options are shifted toward future users. Obviously, current actions that enhance future resource choices also entail distribution of risk among generations. For example, a decision rule assuming that the technology of food production will increasingly permit substitutions of new varieties and chemical fertilizers for soil and water may be fairly risky for future users. The costs of being wrong can be enormous. By the same token, overly cautious conservation policies may deprive current consumers unnecesarily by failing to take account of technological substitutions. To define today choices for future generations of farmers and consumers is a difficult and hazardous task, not to be taken lightly. But neither can it be avoided.

Discounting. The degree to which we shift risk from future to present and resource choices from present to future is a critical social decision. Economists refer to a discount rate as an expression of the trade-off between present and future. The basic concept is that future benefits are worth less to us than present ones in decisions regarding resource use. On the face of it, that may seem illogical to many people. But we know that needs exist today and are uncertain about the extent and nature of future needs. The problem is to establish the appropriate expression of social time preference. Public funds spent for conservation programs will not be available for other purposes. The public has the right to expect that benefits returned, including future benefits appropriately discounted, exceed returns from those dollars in other uses. Some argue that public funds invested in conservation or any other public purpose should return at least as much as the market yield on private investment to be a rational use of those public funds. After all, if those funds were in fact invested, the interest could be available for future soil and water users to make their own decisions. The market rate evolves in transactons between individual buyers and sellers. It indicates risk preference of individuals. Obviously this approach implies a fairly high rate for discounting future benefits from conservation expenditures.

Supporters of conservation programs argue that a much lower discount rate is appropriate to reflect various uncertainties about the long-run quality of our productive base. To consume these soil and water resources today, through wasteful use or conversion to nonagricultural purposes, may lead to real scarcity in the future. The nonmarket rate acknowledges a social responsibility for future users, beyond the motives of the individual farmer facing his own management needs. A low discount rate means more public investment in that purpose. Those resource investments with large amounts of initial expense, like dams, for example, are actually helped more by this lower discount rate than are projects with small initial cost and high annual expenses, like conservation cost-sharing. Even if society agrees on a lower discount rate for conservation, decisions must be made as to the best types of conservation expenditure.

Societal support for conservation. As noted, the scale and character of our investments in soil and water conservation are reflections of the implicit intertemporal preferences of society. These preferences have changed over time. My purpose is to identify some of the threads of current thinking on natural resource conditions. These are the supporting structure for a contemporary conservation ethic.

The conservation movement in this country was founded on the fundamental belief that the five basic and essential materials of civilization—wood, water, coal, iron, and agricultural products—must be used sparingly today to preserve enough for future generations (*11*). We know some resources are renewable. In many cases they can be substituted for nonrenewable resources and managed for the benefit of present as well as future generations. That was the central theme of work by Barnett and Morse who questioned the basis of resource scarcity (*1*). The concepts of materials balance and sustainable flow replaced the Malthusian fixed resource stock concepts of the earlier era.

But a new sense of caution replaced the resource optimism articulated by Barnett and Morse. Boulding coined the phrase "spaceship earth," connoting definite limits to our capacity to expand, increase, and develop (*4*). Mishan went so far as to suggest that economic growth may, in some cases, be a net loser—costing us more than we get out of it (*8*). Others expanded on this theme of the constraints or even disutility of economic development.

Another main theme concerns the health effects of the residue of development—the toxic chemical wastes and air pollution that endanger human health. The single work that best focused this whole concern was an essay by Heilbroner (6). He speaks of the real limits to rationality as a mode of thought for social change in coping with inevitable resource depletion and environmental destruction. Individual, incremental, rational choices may lead us in very logical fashion to societal dead ends. He doubts the capacity of democratic, pluralistic societies to avert disaster as population pressures confront worldwide resource limits. We have no alternative, he says, to authoritarianism to bring about the drastic social changes that are needed. He does not advocate authoritarian action; he simply observes that as other instruments of change fail, like tax adjustments and economic incentives, people will demand a massive shift of authority to a single force that can direct the course of change. The life-style changes, birth rate reductions, and other changes needed are too drastic to be accomplished by our weak, mushy, consensus-oriented public institutions. As things get tight, the social order dissolves.

I need not belabor that point. I am not suggesting that Heilbroner's work is representative, or precise. He intended neither. I view this book and some others like it as the *Silent Spring* of resource scarcity—the two-by-four between the eyes to get our attention.

There is ample evidence (9) that people are at least uneasy about the apparent limits to our natural resources and are willing to pay, in dollars or in foregone opportunities of some kind, to do something about it. Television and other mass media bring the pain and inconvenience of resource problems directly into our living rooms. In Michigan, we live with the horror of misplaced fire retardant chemical poisoning and eventual destruction of a major part of the state's dairy industry. We have all witnessed Love Canal and Three Mile Island. Many of us sat in gas lines, firsthand experience with the foolishness of our gas expensive lifestyle.

There is no such thing as the social discount rate that captures our national mood on the appropriate balance between present and future. But the weight of evidence suggests increasing popular sensitivity to resource limits and support for conservation.

The motive for conservation. While people are aware of and concerned about resource and environmental limits, it does not necessarily follow that people are willing as individuals to forego current consumption on behalf of future. The free rider phenomenon is rampant in conservation. The benefits of resource conservation for future generations are available to all current resource users. Since benefits cannot be withheld from those who refuse to conserve, there is no clear economic incentive for the individual to bear any cost on behalf of saving for future generations when he can enjoy the benefits without doing so. The assumption of self-interest is the basic tenet of standard economic theory and, incidentally, a fairly useful assumption when predicting behavior in our political economy.

Self-interest may be stretched a bit in ways that are instructive for our case at hand (5). I may exercise enlightened self-interest that is sensitive to future generations in hopes that future generations will be nice to me in turn. That is why parents take care of their children. There is an implicit bargain struck. Fear is the other side of that bargain. If I don't do well by others, the others will do me in. Perhaps some are motivated by the desire to be known as someone who considers the needs of others. By being a good citizen, he gets a good reputation that yields satisfaction on its own (4).

A further variation of economic rationality and the self-interest assumption simply expands the decision horizon to include future uncertain benefits. Using the preservation of endangered species as the case, Smith and Krutilla discussed optimal public investment strategy to maximize net discounted social benefits available from a natural asset (3, 13). This means a change in resource use behavior today to account for future values. It also means government action to assure that future benefits enter the arena of current choice. There are measurement problems in determining future value of a natural asset, or the potential for current decisions that may irreversably sacrifice future options, as in loss of an endangered species or paving of farmland. Estimating and discounting future benefits also permits consideration of technological changes that can affect output. We are not bound by present technology or preferences. When measurement problems are particularly severe, Smith and Krutilla suggest that the benefit of the doubt be given to the future. In a sense, this is the insurance policy approach to conservation. We pay today to be covered in case something goes wrong with our anticipated resource use pattern.

What of conservation just because it is right? We know that if future voters could express their opinions and vote, current decisions would reflect the future needs for soil and water resources. We cannot alter the facts of time and generations, but perhaps we should act as if we could.

Contemporary philosopher Rawls developed a social contract theory as the foundation of ethical positions on such matters (12). He posits a situation in which all affected parties get together to determine the rules of the game. He imposes an initial "veil of ignorance" in which no one knows his status, his natural assets, or even his self-interest. Further, no one knows his position in time—some of our participants are from future generations. There are no coalitions, no interest groups, no lobbyists, just an assembly of individuals seeking to structure a decision process that is fair. Consensus will be reached, and it will be fair.

Page has observed that this Rawlsian original condition is not totally different from the actual conditions facing the framers of our constitution. The future was not discounted at that convention (10).

Once the basic conditions for survival of generations have been established, we can turn over the short-run allocation problems to a market of some kind. Philosophers seldom suggest ways to accomplish ethical adjustments, or change patterns of human behavior accordingly. They describe a state of mind and leave it at that. But I think Rawls is on the right track when it comes to an ethical foundation for soil and water conservation. It speaks to a collective sense of responsibility to those who come after us. It is not a land ethic, as such, but an ethic of human interrelationship.

Conclusions

After all of this, what may we conclude about the social and economic realities of soil and water conservation?

The first reality is that with a few poorly documented exceptions conservation apparently does not pay for the individual users. There is little incentive for them to make dramatic changes in use for a conservation purpose of some kind. The stakes go far beyond those to the individual user, both in space and time. Thus government is involved. Effective conservation can only be accomplished through the process and institutions of public choice.

Reality number two is that conservation is important only because people say it is important. Human perception of importance is key. There is nothing superhuman about it. Rhetoric about physical imperatives is useless if not designed to influence people. The constituency for soil and water conservation is changing, partly because the population in rural America is changing, but also because mass communication brings this and other issues directly to American families. Proximity is no longer requisite to support. I suspect that the support for conservation is fairly broad, but shallow.

Whatever the conceptual rationale for conservation as a general activity, we must be increasingly concerned with getting more conservation per public dollar. The system demands evidence of pay-off from dollars spent to compare against other valid uses for those funds. There is an element of cyclical economics ("Proposition 13," for example), but more compelling is the evolving nature of institutions.

The next fact of life is that we will make all sorts of decisions that imply a trade-off between present and future generations. We do not need to vote on a social discount rate—time preferences evolve in various public actions and expressions of political support. There is no optimum social discount rate, and I find efforts to force conservation policy into the intertemporal investment optimization mode of traditional economic theory to be particularly uninstructive. I have not pulled together the evidence on the matter, but suspect that the balance of support favors policies sensitive to the possibility of soil and water scarcity for future production.

There is considerable thought and empirical evidence in all scientific disciplines that short-run exploitation of resources produces various social costs, unaccounted for by the private investor. Further, the costs of development may shift significant burdens to future generations. Thus, there is some validity to a growing social mood for caution today on behalf of future users.

Reality six is that it is far easier for some to be good conservationists than for others. One's preference for retaining resources for future generations is partly conditioned by how much it costs him today. We should not expect otherwise. Any set of rules for conservation implies a distribution of im-

156   LAWRENCE W. LIBBY

pacts, distribution that will shape overall political support. Policy development is a comparison of these impact distributions. We should not force people to choose between ethical support for conservation and immediate economic impact that seems out of line. We should instead reinforce the ethical dimension with policies sensitive to cost distribution.

REFERENCES

1. Barnett, Harold, and Chandler Morse. 1963. *Scarcity and growth: The economics of natural resource availability.* Johns Hopkins Press, Baltimore, Maryland.
2. Beale, Calvin. *The recent shift in U.S. population to non-metropolitan areas, 1970-75.* International Regional Science Review, 2(2): 113-122.
3. Bishop, Richard. 1978. *Endangered species and uncertainty: The economics of a safe minimum standard.* American Journal of Agricultural Economics 57: 10-18.
4. Boulding, Kenneth. 1975. *ECON is a four letter word.* In *Understanding Public Policy.* The Farm Foundation, Chicago, Illinois.
5. Collard, David. 1978. *Altruism and economy.* Oxford University Press, New York, New York.
6. Heilbroner, Robert. 1974. *An inquiry into the human prospect.* W. W. Norton and Company, New York, New York.
7. Libby, Lawrence W., and John Okay. 1979. *National soil and water conservation policy: An economic perspective.* Journal of the Northeastern Agricultural Economics Council, 8(2): 61-65.
8. Mishan, E. J. 1967. *The costs of economic growth.* Frederick A. Praeger, Inc., Washington, D.C.
9. Mitchell, Robert. 1978. *The public speaks again: A new environmental survey.* Resources (September-November). Resources for the Future, Inc., Washington, D.C.
10. Page, Talbot. 1977. *Conservation and economic efficiency.* Johns Hopkins Press, Baltimore, Maryland.
11. Pinchot, Gifford. 1910. *The fight for conservation.* Doubleday, New York, New York.
12. Rawls, John. 1971. *A theory of justice.* Harvard University Press, Cambridge, Massachusetts.
13. Smith, V. Kerry, and John Krutilla. 1970. *Endangered species, irreversibilities and uncertainity: A comment.* American Journal of Agricultural Economics 61: 371-375.
14. U.S. General Accounting Office. 1977. *To protect tomorrow's food supply soil conservation needs priority attention.* Washington, D.C.
15. Unger, David G. 1979. *Resource conservation act: A new approach to conservation policies and programs.* In Soil Conservation Policies: An Assessment. Soil Conservation Society of America, Ankeny, Iowa.

VI. LAND ISSUES IN RESOURCE-CONSTRAINED ECONOMIES

14
Important farmlands: Public policy to reduce pressures for their continuing conversion

Norman A. Berg

In 1976 I said, "Demands on the resource base have never been higher and continue to escalate, while limits on resource supplies are coming closer to reality. The inescapable collision of unlimited demands on limited resources will test our will and our skill in making critical choices" (*2*). I am convinced that our world's important farmlands and their continued conversion to other uses are key issues.

During the 1970s, world population increased an average of 72 million people a year. For the United States, it was more than 1.7 million; for Canada more than 250,000. Meanwhile, the total land area in the United States is still 916 million hectares (2.26 billion acres) and in Canada 920 million hectares (2.28 billion acares). These totals have not changed.

I would like to discuss some new and valuable data about rural land use issues; review policy and actions of the United States Department of Agriculture (USDA) and others in aiding farmland retention; and then suggest some questions that need answering for the future.

National resource inventories

The Soil Conservation Service (SCS) started the National Resource Inventories (NRI) in March 1977 (*9*). The inventories were needed to provide

Norman A. Berg, former associate administrator, Soil Conservation Service, U.S. Department of Agriculture, Washington, D.C., is now administrator of SCS.

current resource data to update the 10-year-old Conservation Needs Inventory and soil erosion estimates; update the 1975 Potential Cropland Study; answer U.S. Senate Committee on Agriculture, Nutrition and Forestry requests for oversight information; answer the General Accounting Office's questions related to an audit of conservation operations; respond to findings of an SCS task force on Adequacy of Conservation Systems on Cropland; and aid in the appraisal of natural resource status, condition, and trends called for in the Soil and Water Resources Conservation Act (RCA).

The NRI data are being used for state long-range soil and water conservation programming and planning. Decision makers in other agencies as well as private industry, groups, and organizations that need current resource information will also find the NRI data useful in selecting resource-oriented research, activities, and evaluations.

The inventories were designed to provide statistical data for nonfederal lands in each state (except Alaska) and in the Caribbean area. The inventories used about one-third of the randomly selected sample areas that were used in the 1967 national inventory of soil and water conservation needs (8). NRI data were collected in the field at 70,000 primary sample units and more than 200,000 sample points.

The first phase of the inventories has been completed. It includes data on land capability classes (soil quality), land use and use of small water areas, conservation needs, floodprone areas, wetland types 3 to 20, sheet and rill erosion, wind erosion in the 10 Great Plains States, potential for new cropland, irrigation, and prime farmlands.

Soil quality

Rural land available for agricultural, forestry, and other uses in the United States declined by nearly 15 million hectares (37.05 million acres) in the 1967 to 1977 period. Yet the percentage of good, fair, and poor land remained about the same. That is, 44 percent of the rural land (248 million hectares or 612.56 million acres) is in land capability classes I-III, 13 percent is in class IV (76 million hectares or 187.72 million acres), and 43 percent is in classes V-VIII (242 million hectares or 597.74 million acres).

Of the total rural, nonfederal land, nearly 168 million hectares (41.5 million acres) occurs on level to nearly level slopes. Over 400 million hectares (988 million acres) occurs on gentle to very steep slopes. At least 110 million hectares (271.70 million acres) is naturally wet, while nearly 163 million hectares (402.61 million acres) is droughty or lacks sufficient water to grow crops. Some lands are sloping and wet, while others are level and droughty. Many of these conditions limit the use of land.

Land use

Cropland. There is a continuing decline in the acres of nonfederal land used for cropland in the United States. During the 10-year period from 1967 to 1977, cropland decreased by 7 million hectares (17.29 million acres), from 174 million hectares (429.78 million acres) to 167 million hectares (412.49 million acres). This represents a decrease of 730,000 hectares (1.80 million acres) a year. The rate is considerably less than the decline of the 1950s, but about the same as the decline of the 1960s. The 1977 NRI data shows that landowners and operators retained the better land for cropland. Since 1950, there has been a 3 percent increase in the use of good land (capability classes I-III) for cropland and a 4 percent decrease in cropping of poor land. Use of fair (marginal) lands increased by 1 percent.

Potential for new cropland. A 1975 inventory estimated how much pastureland, rangeland, forestland, and land in other uses could be converted to cropland and created much interest and debate. New data were collected for the 1977 NRI, based on 1976 prices and costs. Although the total cropland acreage with a high or medium potential for conversion was estimated at 54.6 million hectares (134.86 million acres) in 1977, compared with 45 million hectares (111.15 million acres) in 1975, the acreage with high potential was down nearly 50 percent. The acreage of land with medium potential for conversion was up to 38 million hectares (93.86 million acres), suggesting that conversion problems were thought to be more complex in 1977 than in 1975, and/or the cost to produce a crop versus the price received was such that more lands with conservation problems might be brought into production in 1977.

Grassland and forestland. Land available for grazing increased greatly, accounting for 219 million hectares (540.93 million acres) in 1977. Now, over half of the nonfederal agricultural land is used for native pasture, pastureland, and rangeland. The NRI data show an overall decline in nonfederal forestland. In 1967, there were 180 million hectares (444.60 million acres) of nonfederal forestland. The total decreased to 150 million hectares (370.50 million acres) in 1977, a change of 30 million hectares (74.10 million acres).

Floodprone areas. The 1977 NRI data specifically identified the acreage of floodprone areas and furnished new information on the use and quality of this fragile resource. There are 71 million hectares (175.37 million acres) of floodprone areas on nonfederal land in the United States (excluding Alaska). About 31 percent (22 million hectares or 54.34 million acres) is pastureland, native pasture, and rangeland. Another 29 percent (23 million hectares or 56.81 million acres) is forestland. Another 28 percent (19 million hectares or 46.93 million acres) is cropland. The remaining 12 percent is in other uses. About 46 percent of the floodprone area is land of good quality (capability classes I-III); 54 percent is fair to poor land (classes IV-VIII).

Wetlands. New data are available on the use, composition, and potential of wet soils and wetland types 3 to 20 (as defined in Circular 39, U.S. Fish and Wildlife Service). There are 17 million hectares (41.99 million acres) of wetlands, of which 16 million hectares (40.73 million acres or 97 percent) are in noncropland uses. Forested wetlands account for 50 percent of the acreage. None of the wetlands has potential or is available for conversion to cropland. In contrast, the United States (except Alaska) has almost 110 million hectares (271.70 million acres) of wet soils on nonfederal lands. Nearly 43 million hectares (106.21 million acres) are now cropped. Another 67 million hectares (165.49 million acres) of land have some wetness conditon, yet only 12.5 million hectares (30.87 million acres) of this reserve have potential for conversion to new cropland.

Urban and built-up. The 1977 data confirmed previous SCS estimates that homes, factories, roads, and other similar uses are absorbing rural land at a rapid pace. Some 39 million hectares (96.33 million acres) are now in these uses or committed to these uses. Another 1.6 million hectares (3.95 million acres) are in small built-up areas and are considered part of other rural land uses. Nearly 95 percent of the rural land shifted from agricultural, forestry, and other uses is related to urban development. The remaining 5 percent of land is changed to small water areas. This suggests that land is converted to these irreversible uses at a rate of more than a million hectares a year. About 10 percent of the land converted to small water areas and 30 percent of the urban and built-up areas come from land formerly used for cropland.

Prime farmlands

More current data are available on the amount and use of prime farmlands in the United States and Caribbean area. The 1975 estimates showed 155 million hectares (382.85 million acres) while the 1977 NRI data showed 140 million hectares (345.80 million acres). The 1977 acreage figure is a more accurate measure of these important farmlands. Three states have more than 8 million hectares (19.76 million acres) each of prime farmland, four states have 6 to 8 million hectares (14.87 to 19.76 million acres) each, seven states have 4 to 6 million hectares (9.88 to 14.87 million acres) each, and nine states have 2 to 4 million hectares (4.94 to 9.88 million acres) each.

Most of the prime farmland (67 percent) already is being used for cropland. Only about 47 million hectares (116.09 million acres) of prime farmland are in other uses. Of these, the 1977 NRI data showed that about 45 percent (21 million hectares or 51.87 million acres) could be shifted to cropland production under certain conditions. A multiagency group chaired by SCS determined for each sample point the potential for conversion to cropland within 10 to 15 years. They used a detailed set of guidelines for their decisions. The result represents the reserve of prime farmland in the United States.

Prime farmland is defined by USDA as that land having the best combination of physical and chemical characteristics for producing food, feed, forage, fiber, and oilseed crops. In order to be classified as prime farmland by USDA, the land must meet technical criteria and also be available for agriculture (not already committed to a nonagricultural use). Two-thirds of the land that meets the USDA criteria for prime farmland was being cropped in 1977 (Table 1).

Most of the prime farmland acreage lies in a broad belt reaching from the Great Lakes to the Gulf of Mexico. The Corn Belt contains 20 percent of the nation's total supply of prime farmland, with the Northern Plains close behind at 19 percent and the Southern Plains at 18 percent.

Of the rural land converted to urban and water uses between 1967 and 1975, SCS has estimated that about one-third was prime farmland. With the addition of 12 million hectares (29.64 million acres) of urban, built-up, and

Table 1. Land use, 1977.

Land Use	Hectares (millions)	Percent
Cropland	93.5	67
Pasture	15.8	11
Rangeland	9.3	7
Forestland	17.0	12
Other land	4.5	3
Total	140.1	100

transportation land between 1967 and 1977, almost half a million hectares (1.23 million acres) of prime farmland is converted to other uses each year.

To aid local and state governments as well as federal agencies in many kinds of program decisions that may affect farmlands, SCS has been preparing countywide and statewide maps showing the location of prime and unique farmlands as well as other farmlands that may be of statewide or local importance. It has completed about 400 of these maps and should have them available by the end of 1980 for about 1,600 counties that have the most pressure on farmlands.

In Canada, based on 1976 and 1977 data, there are more than 44 million hectares (108.68 million acres) of prime land (capability classes I-III) (5). This is 4.8 percent of the land area of 930 million hectares (2.29 billion acres). Some 17,400 hectares (42,978 acres) of rural land are converted to urban land uses each year. Of this, almost 11,000 hectares (27,170 acres) are prime land.

Implications of land use shifts

The NRI shows that the use of the nonfederal land in the United States continues to change, especially as it relates to agricultural production.

These shifts, particularly from agriculture to nonagricultural uses, have serious implications for the continued production of food and fiber products needed to meet uses at home and abroad.

Changes in the use of our nation's lands result from efforts to stimulate economic development, sustain agricultural and forest production capabilities, produce and conserve energy, provide community services and living space, maintain open space, and preserve the natural environment—our natural life-support system. Each of these uses provides public benefits. They also are interrelated; some compete for the limited supply of suitable and available land while others are complementary.

Well-managed farm and forest lands often play environmentally beneficial roles by assimilating the residues resulting from other economic activities, by serving as buffer zones, and by offering relative environmental stability when compared with some other land uses. They also provide open space, relative freedom from air pollutants, and recreational opportunities, thus enhancing the quality of living for many persons. Maintaining existing farm and forest lands provides a stable economic base in rural communities. At the same time, retention of productive farm and forest lands for assuring adequate supplies of food, fiber, wood, and water means that other natural systems, such as forests, grasslands, wetlands, and floodplains, can be preserved and improved as natural areas.

Yet United States public policy to hold the best land for agriculture is either absent or not working. It is traditional to say that land use conversion out of agriculture is the result of market forces. This generalization holds no one responsible and is too simple an answer. Questions need to be raised in the policy arena: How serious is the problem? What is the proper role for the various levels of government? What changes are needed and where?

Many people have long shared an assumption that the earth is infinitely generous. The perception of scarcity, now rearing its head, is an unwelcome one; it is transforming relationships among nations, among regions within countries, and among classes of people.

The notion of growth that began in the United States "New Deal" era, rooted in Keynesian economic theories, is being replaced by the feeling that we have come to the end of the frontier. The realization finally is dawning that there is a short supply of land, water, energy, capital, even air. How do we convey a sense of realism without totally depressing the nation's citizens weaned on the myth of abundance?

The idea of irremediable systemic worldwide scarcity (1) is so revolutionary in its political and social implications that we cannot fully grasp its significance. We even note and experience disbelief in our own disciplines. Land as a constrained resource, including prime land, is clearly one factor in continued agricultural production, an indispensable factor for most of agriculture. There is general acceptance that land is important and that the most important farmlands should be retained to the extent feasible for agriculture. Or is there?

The issue, as expected, is much more complex: What are the definitions?

Isn't it a dynamic ever-changing situation? Don't inputs change the classifications? And so on.

USDA policy for land use

There are essentially two schools of thought within USDA regarding the status of agricultural land. They cause conflicting signals to emerge.

The conservation point of view holds that farmland, particularly prime farmland, is a national resource asset to be protected. On this basis, observations about the continued loss of agricultural land are made and serious concerns expressed.

The economic point of view looks at land as one factor in production, evaluates the productive capability of United States agriculture, estimates probable supply and demand, and comes forth with assurances that America has an abundance of good land for the foreseeable future.

Within USDA, differences also exist in the estimates of how much land is being converted to urban and transportation uses. For example, the Economics, Statistics and Cooperatives Service (ESCS) estimates that 384,000 hectares (948,480 acres) of rural land were converted to urban and transportation uses annually between 1959 and 1974—less than half the annual acreage loss estimated by the SCS. Differences in data collection methods and in the definition of urban transportation uses may account for these varying estimates.

Otte (7) estimated that during the 1960s about 287,000 hectares (708,890 acres) of land were converted to urban uses a year in Standard Metropolitan Statistical Areas and that between 49 and 76 percent of this land had previously been in crops, depending on the region. Based on these estimates and on information about changes in agricultural productivity and additions to the cropland base, Otte concluded that urbanization does not pose a serious immediate threat to the nation's supply of agricultural land.

Otte's conclusions have been reexamined several times since their publication in 1974. For example, Hart (6) analyzed data from the 1958 and 1967 Conservation Needs Inventories and found that relatively little land had been urbanized during the 10 years between the surveys. He concluded, "Little more than 4 percent of the nation's land area will be urbanized by the year 2000 and that urban encroachment will not remove significant acreages of land from agricultural production within the foreseeable future."

It has been suggested that a possible solution to this confusion is to seek more direct case study data of land conversion, but even here there is substantial variation among investigators as to the severity of the land loss problem.

What seems to be overlooked in this dialogue is that each day, each year, individually and on a national scale, the conversions of cropland to non-agricultural uses may not be large in proportion to the total national landscape. However, collectively and cumulatively, these land use shifts are seriously reducing the world's supply of important farmlands. Moreover, while these continued losses are significant or rather serious on a global scale, they may already be critical for individual, local, or regional areas.

USDA has wrestled with this dilemma for more than a decade. I chaired a land use committee, established in 1972, that wrote the secretary's first land use policy, published in February, 1973 (*13*).

Late in 1974, attention of the USDA land use committee shifted to the issue of retaining agricultural lands in production. A task force of the committee planned and conducted a national seminar on the retention of prime lands in July 1975. Both the background papers for that seminar and the findings and recommendations of the seminar were published and widely disseminated (*14, 15*).

The seminar brought together representatives of the many points of view and asked that they settle on some conclusions and recommendations. The 80 participants, representing experts from across the nation in many professional disciplines, worked hard for two days. At the end a clear consensus emerged: "The continued conversion of prime production lands to other land uses is a matter of growing concern that will require a great deal of attention in the future."

Although couched in the careful language of bureaucrats and experts, the summary of findings and conclusions from the seminar contained the following statement that represented a sharp turn in USDA policy thinking: "The demand for food, fiber, and timber from United States production lands is expected to increase to the point where the production capability of the nation will be tested, although it is not certain when or with what degree of urgency this will occur" (*15*).

To implement what they suggested was a national policy issue, the participants recommended: "Public interest will be served by maintaining a maximum flexibility of options with respect to future land use needs in a changing and uncertain world. Extreme caution should be exercised in approving actions that result in irreversible conversions of prime farmland to other uses. In some states, problems must be faced now or significant options for the future will be closed. USDA should be concerned with any actions that will diminish the nation's ability to produce food, fiber, and timber" (*15*).

The recommendations of the seminar were not USDA policy—yet. But the die was cast. Agricultural land became a national policy issue in a new sense, and USDA embarked on a new venture in national land use policy leadership.

Several actions were begun by the USDA land use committee in response to the seminar. A specific policy statement on prime lands was published in June 1976, as Supplement No. 1 to the secretary's policy statement on land use (*16*). It called for every USDA agency to make special provisions in its programs and services for the recognition and retention of prime lands.

Meetings between USDA and the Council on Environmental Quality (CEQ) followed. In August 1976, the chairman of CEQ sent a memorandum to the heads of all federal agencies calling for them to include an analysis of the impact of their actions on prime agricultural land in the preparation of any environmental impact statement called for under the National Environmental Policy Act of 1969.

The CEQ memorandum directed federal agencies to seek assistance from USDA in the definition and delineation of prime agricultural lands. USDA was developing a nationally consistent definition at the time and, following substantial local, state, and interest-group input, published its final definition in the January 1, 1978, *Federal Register* (4).

To date, not much attention has been given the CEQ memorandum. Recent studies have shown that few environmental impact statements contained any recognition of the proposed action on agricultural lands, and even fewer, if any, actions were modified because of their impact on agricultural lands.

An intensive effort also was started to complete workable definitions of prime and unique farmland and to begin a mapping program so that local, state, and federal decision makers could have a better understanding of the facts. Prime lands seminar participants complained: "A frustrating lack of data prevents a clear picture of either the current situation or the probable future amount of land available or needed for agricultural production." As a result, SCS issued Land Inventory and Monitoring Memorandum No. 3 on October 15, 1975. This memorandum defined prime and unique farmland and established additional categories of important farmlands that could be defined at the state and local levels because of concerns that might exist there. It inaugurated the program of county and state mapping of these lands. Most importantly, it provided a working definition of prime farmland that could be used in conjunction with other monitoring efforts in order to begin the process of inventorying the national supply of good farmland, identifying some of the trends in its use, and beginning to fill the frustrating lack of information.

One of the payoffs of this effort occurred during the legislative consideration of the Surface Mining Control and Reclamation Act of 1977. Concerns about the impact of surface mining on the prime farmlands of Illinois and surrounding states led the secretary of the interior to tell Congress that he did not "want to replace an energy crisis with a food crisis." SCS advocated special soil reconstruction standards for prime farmlands, and the Carter Administration supported that position. Ultimately, the new act set forth special standards for soil reconstruction after mining on prime farmlands, to the end that agricultural productivity would be as completely restored as technically possible. That focus would not have occurred without the definition of prime farmlands and the newly acquired information on their account and use.

USDA further revised its policies on land use in December 1977, when Secretary's Memorandum No. 1807 created the current USDA Committee on Land Use (*17*), and in October 1978, when an updated Secretary's Memorandum No. 1827 was issued (*3, 18*). This latter statement codifies USDA's responsibilities that evolved since 1972. For example, with respect to prime farmlands, it deals explicitly with departmental policy in fulfilling requirements under the CEQ letter of August 30, 1976.

The statement used by the secretary with the news media said: "The policy established by this statement is a reflection of my concern and this Administration's concern with the land use issue.

"The document is designed to emphasize and clarify the department's role in encouraging the retention of important agricultural land. It will assist agency personnel in responding to policy priorities emerging at the state and local levels.

"This policy reinforces efforts by the department to advocate the retention of important agricultural lands and work with local and state governmental and other federal agencies through establishing procedures for environmental and administrative review. There is no additional authority to intervene in decisions of other governmental entities.

"This policy requires that USDA agencies adjust their technical and financial programs to minimize the adverse effects of their actions on important agricultural lands, wetlands, and flood plains.

"With Supplement 1, the revised memorandum constitutes departmental response to the executive orders on floodplain management and wetlands protection. The statement provides the opportunity for the department and this administration to demonstrate leadership and concern on these issues.

"The statement continues the department's recognition of the rights and responsibilities of state and local governments for developing public policies and for planning and regulating private land use.

"This department has recently acquired authority under the Surface Mining Control and Reclamation Act (P.L. 95-87) with respect to planning for the surface mining of coal and other minerals. This act requires the federal government to assist in planning for the extraction of coal and other nonrenewable resources to facilitate restoration of the land's productive capacity. In addition, the department has responsibility under the same legislation for reclamation of abandoned surface mined lands. The department's role in this area is also incorporated in this statement.

"This statement contains no major new authority or responsibility for the department. There is added emphasis to actions listed in the 1973 and 1976 land use policy memoranda.

"This statement does not:

• Permit, facilitate or imply federal control of land use decisions of state and local governments, beyond actions required already under NEPA. The department will, however, provide information and assistance useful in generating decisions sensitive to impacts on agricultural lands, and will encourage attention to these matters.

• Stop or discourage development. It simply seeks to help guide the pattern of development consistent with important agricultural lands.

• Deprive any individual of property rights.

"My office and the Land Use Committee have worked hard over a period of nearly 18 months to formulate the statement I am signing today. In the process we have involved more than 600 members of the department's field staff leadership from ten agencies in face-to-face discussions. These professionals operate and stand accountable for programs delivering direct assistance to more than 50 million local citizens in over 3,000 counties of the United States.

"By establishing this policy, I am pledging this department philosophically and substantively on this important issue."

The revised land use statement reflects the recommendations of over 600 workshop participants at five multi-state meetings who interact daily with local and state governing officials; environmental, conservation, commodity, wildlife, and sportsmen's groups; energy producers; other land user organizations at the state and local levels; and with individual farmers, businessmen, industrialists, homeowners, and other landholders.

Beyond USDA

USDA leadership in articulating and establishing national policy in the United States for important farmlands has had limited but significant outside support.

First, a few other federal departments—CEQ, Environmental Protection Agency, and Housing and Urban Development, and several state agencies—now have developed strong policy positions on land use.

Second, the prime land issue has become a concern and a timely topic on the agenda of many organizations. I have my first letter ever from a major national consumer advocacy group that wants to help protect prime farmlands. The Soil Conservation Society of America, National Association of Conservation Districts, and related groups have surfaced the issues in several ways.

Third, efforts to retain important farmlands for agriculture have been accelerated through legislative action by many states and local jurisdictions. Funding for testing varied activities, such as purchase of development rights, already has been provided in a few states. Several forms of differential tax assessment are being tried.

Fourth, Congress has increasingly had legislation under consideration "to establish internal federal policy concerning protection of certain agricultural land; to establish a Study Committee on the Protection of Agricultural Land; to establish a demonstration program relating to methods of protecting certain agricultural land from being used for nonagrcultural purposes; and for other purposes."

Fifth, the secretary of agriculture and the chairman of the CEQ on June 14, 1979, signed an agreement to jointly provide leadership in a national study that will (a) determine the nature, rate, extent, and causes of farmland losses; (b) evaluate the economic, environmental, and social impacts of these losses on rural and urban areas; and (c) recommend administrative and legislative initiatives necessary to minimize these losses. The report on the findings is to be made to the president by January 1, 1981.

Heads of eight other federal departments or agencies—including the secretaries of the interior, housing and urban development, transportation, energy, commerce, and defense; the administrator of the Environmental Protection Agency; and the director of the Office of Management and Budget are being asked to cooperate in staffing and funding this activity.

At the press conference kicking off the availability of agricultural land study, Secretary of Agriculture Bob Bergland said, "We need to examine very carefully the fundamental question—private rights versus public interest—how do we join the two?"

This, of course, brings us back full circle to the frustrations of all the earlier actions in USDA dating back at least 40 years. Now, as then, the challenge remains: to determine if states and local governments, in conjunction with the federal government, can put into place a program to slow down, if not stop, the rate at which we are converting our best agricultural land, short of enacting some type of a national land use law.

USDA convened the first National Conference of Land Utilization in 1931. The 1938 USDA Yearbook, *Soils and Man* (*10*), discussed the nation and its soil. Chapters on the "Remedies—Policies for Public and Private Lands" dealt with rural zoning and land use regulations.

The 1940 USDA Yearbook, *Farmers in a Changing World* (*11*), had a section by Milton S. Eisenhower, who was land use coordinator in the Office of Land Use Coordination, USDA. The yearbook raised a number of important questions: How far should planning go in a democracy? How much territory should the planning take in? What is the proper balance between central authority and decisions by the mass of our citizens?

Net results of this early venture into national land use planning, especially the agricultural phases of land use, were mixed. It became apparent that water and land use are ultimately inseparable. Public attitudes were partially shifted away from heedless and unplanned land exploitation. The point of view emerged that public policy should aim at assuring ownership and use of land that will best subserve general welfare rather than merely private advantage. Knowledge of good land use practices was the key.

Unfortunately, the ideas that land use policy resting upon individual private choice was inadequate and that public decisions should result from a careful planning process were viewed as a threat to private property rights. The whole scheme was terminated in the late 1940s.

In the foreword of the 1958 Yearbook of Agriculture (*12*), the secretary of agriculture said, "This book will stimulate thought about our land and its use. This is as it should be, for discussion often strikes the spark to ignite inspired thoughts that guide us into a better future."

The preface states, "We present no ready program, no easy solution, and no definite policy. This is not our intention or our province; policies and programs are made by the people and their elected representatives."

In light of USDA's extensive history it was unbelievable that as land use legislation was debated in Congress in the late 1960s and early 1970s, USDA was not involved. A long history of land use experience by USDA and land grant universities was simply ignored.

Under the early Nixon reorganization plan, USDA was to be eliminated and the Department of the Interior was to be the nucleus for a proposed Department of Natural Resources. Thus, Interior became the focal point for land use legislation.

Interior saw the issue of land use as one of inadequate federal, state, and local regulation. Misuse of land could be cured by better regulation, often meaning regulation by a larger unit of government. Local government, historically the only level involved in land use controls, would be replaced or supplemented by state controls, operating under federal guidelines.

Agriculture's constituency—the owners and users of most of America's land—found this to be the wrong conception of the issue and the wrong prescription for curing the nation's land use problems. As a result, they mounted heavy opposition to land use bills.

The concept is essentially one of informed citizen input into decisions that involve conflicting social goals and require complex trade-offs between values. Land use questions are seldom absolute. It is not a matter of whether or not you can build the subdivision on the prime farmland, or whether or not you can fill in the swamp for an airport, but whether or not you should do these things. Such issues become the major battleground where citizens determine the entire direction of growth and change in our society. Land use decisions are not so much rational designs as social and political expressions of what people perceive is good or bad for the future.

USDA has seen the proper federal role in this process as a limited but vital one. Major federal investments in roads, schools, airports, or power plants often are the growth shapers that guide or overpower all local determinations. Federal lands make up one-third of the nation, and their management affects surrounding communities and ecosystems. Federal guidelines and regulations on everything from air and water pollution control to airport safety either limit or demand local actions. Many federal programs, functional in nature, often have unintended side effects that pave over prime lands, limit productive land uses or encourage destructive growth patterns. A key federal responsibility should be to improve this process and reduce the harmful effects of major federal actions. USDA, particularly in regard to prime farmlands, has been working to see that this was done.

In 1974, regional workshops were held for USDA state-level officials, followed by a request that each state establish a land use committee to help local and state officials deal with land use questions. Committees have been established in every state, with varying organizational structures and ties to existing USDA mechanisms, such as rural development committees. In most states, the USDA State Land Use Committee quickly established itself as the best source of technical assistance available to state and local agencies and officials concerned with land use questions or programs.

Yet the land use issue, by itself, still was not a particularly attractive one for the department's focus. There were several reasons:

• If the problem was land use, then what was to be the solution? The Jackson-Udall land use bill was under active consideration, and much of

USDA's clientele felt it was not the way to go. If USDA, with its expertise and field delivery system was to do something constructive, it would have to be on a more clearly focused issue.

• Politically, the term "land use" was becoming inextricably tied to regulation and specifically federal regulation. The longer the Jackson-Udall bill debate continued, the more politically damaging it became to be associated with anything that could be labeled "land use." (That problem exists to this day, prompting at least one observer to suggest that the Interior bill set back the cause of proper land management and conservation by 10 years or more.)

• There were too many issues in land use that were outside USDA's main focus of interest. Urban growth problems, inner city decay, facility siting, and similar issues concerned USDA because they affected agricultural land, but they were not issues that were primarily within USDA's scope. The one issue that clearly is within USDA's purview and that shows clear promise of becoming an issue of national concern is agricultural land.

• The agricultural lands issue has not been without its problems in USDA. When the major agricultural policy problem for two decades was crop surpluses and the major farm program efforts were toward land retirement, it was hard to interest anyone in believing that farmland is a valuable resource that should be protected or preserved. When the major problem became one of plowing fence-row to fence-row to meet domestic and international needs, it was hard to convince anyone that it mattered what lands you plowed or for how long.

A look toward the future

Land use problems and issues have not been very attractive ones for anybody. Yet the United States does need to improve the use of its land to meet ever more pressing demands. The land base, particularly that part of the land base that is highly suited for agricultural use, is a serious constraint on the economy and the society for all of North America.

As Canada and the United States have realized through a six-year cooperative study in the Great Lakes Basin, there is a very direct tie between land use activities and water quality. Thus, land use problems and issues will not go away.

Three years ago, I thought that we didn't need to cry wolf on the prime farmland issue. As we enter the 1980s, perhaps we had better at least whisper skunk.

I am not an advocate of any local or state agency taking quick, desperate action on farmland issues that may set us back 10 years. Neither am I an advocate of delaying all land use action until the outcome of any study, no matter how pervasive or thorough. There is little use in being sure of the solution for a problem that has become insoluble.

We are making some gains:

• We have better definitions.

• We have come a long way in getting internal USDA and state agency attention, as well as the support of a number of environmental groups.

• States and local governments are moving ahead with many programs that deserve to be supported, followed closely, and talked about often.

• Under the Soil and Water Resources Conservation Act, we have beefed up the whole process for refining USDA conservation programs to do a better job on prime farmland retention.

• The newest farmland retention study that began in June 1979 with the signing by Secretary Bergland and chairman of CEQ means that the farmland issue is elevated to a government-wide concern. There still is disagreement within the Executive Branch and the Congress as to what the issue is and how important it is, but we have the attention. They may be our greatest achievement to date.

America is spending millions of dollars on preservation of parks, refuges, and other important areas, yet USDA and others are told they cannot spend a dime on retention of important farmlands. America is spending billions of dollars for community services made necessary by scattered or leapfrog urban development, yet with the Proposition 13 movements as successful as they are in limiting tax money available for services, the result is an easing of some pressure for future conversion but a nightmare for the lands already converted.

In some areas, including several counties in Maryland where I live, it is difficult to awaken much public interest in the fact that the last few farms may become residential subdivisions. People have been led to believe that we can always import food and fiber from the next county or the next state. Will energy constraints permit that luxury?

In the end, the farmland issue will have to be related back to our ability to feed ourselves and our neighbors. Where shall we jeopardize that ability? Or what other values shall we jeopardize in order to retain or regain that ability? Or what flexibility shall we lose in future options for resource use?

The time for careful review of impacts and alternatives in many areas of public policy that touch land use is right now. The time for more informed land use decisions also is right now. Ten years from now, Americans could be as concerned over the nation's loss of prime and important farmlands as they are today over shortages of oil and gasoline.

REFERENCES

1. Barnet, Richard J. *The meaning of scarcity.* Council for Educational Development and Research. Washington, D.C.
2. Berg, Norman A. 1976. *The best uses of America's natural resources: Issues and options.* In *Critical Conservation Choices: A Bicentennial Look.* Soil Conservation Society of America, Ankeny, Iowa.
3. Bergland, Bob. 1978. *Secretary's Memorandum No. 1827.* Issued October 30. Washington, D.C.
4. Federal Register. 1978. *Part 657, Subpart A, Sec. 657.5.* Washington, D.C.
5. Fisheries and Environment Canada, Lands Directorate. 1976. *Canada land inventory: Land capability for agriculture.* Ottawa, Ontario.

6. Hart, John Fraser. 1976. *Urban encroachment on rural areas.* The Geographical Review 66(1): 3-17.

7. Otte, Robert C. 1974. *Farming in the city's shadow.* Agricultural Economic Report No. 250. Economic Research Service, U.S. Department of Agriculture, Washington, D.C.

8. Soil Conservation Service, U.S. Department of Agriculture. 1971. *Basic statistics—national inventory of soil and water conservation needs, 1967.* Statistical Bulletin No. 461. Washington, D.C.

9. Soil Conservation Service, U.S. Department of Agriculture. 1979. *National resource inventories.* Washington, D.C.

10. U.S. Department of Agriculture. 1938. *Soils and Man.* Yearbook of Agriculture. Washington, D.C.

11. U.S. Department of Agriculture. 1940. *Farmers in a changing world.* Yearbook of Agriculture. Washington, D.C.

12. U.S. Department of Agriculture. 1958. *Land.* Yearbook of Agriculture. Washington, D.C.

13. U.S. Department of Agriculture. 1973. *Secretary's Memorandum No. 1827.* Issued October 26. Washington, D.C.

14. U.S. Department of Agriculture. 1975. *Perspectives on prime lands: Background papers for Seminar on Retention of Prime Lands.* July 16-17. Washington, D.C.

15. U.S. Department of Agriculture. 1975. *Recommendations on prime lands: From the Seminar on Retention of Prime Lands.* July 16-17. Washington, D.C.

16. U.S. Department of Agriculture. 1976. *Secretary's Memorandum No. 1827. Supplement No. 1.* Issued June 21. Washington, D.C.

17. U.S. Department of Agriculture. 1977. *Secretary's Memorandum No. 1807,* Issued December 17. Washington, D.C.

18. U.S. Department of Agriculture. 1978. *Secretary's Memorandum No. 1827.* Issued October 30. Washington, D.C.

15
Reconciling competing demands for land resources in the urbanizing environment

Bill Thomson

The physical world around us is dynamic and ever-evolving. Man's intrusion into this world was inevitable, and one of the major roles of planners and other professionals working in the field of the environment is to fit man into his natural surroundings in such a manner that all organisms can live in harmony. This can only be accomplished by creating a number of restraints for natural resources and for man, then developing a series of trade-offs for both. The trick is to make sure the trade-offs are acceptable to both sides.

To accomplish restraints and create reasonable trade-offs, firm, clear, politically committed policies are required, as well as a decision-making process that is credible to citizens, the development industry, and various organizations concerned with conservation of soil and the environment.

Planning for the Waterloo setting

The Regional Municipality of Waterloo covers 519 square miles in the rich agricultural interior of southwestern Ontario, including the cities of Waterloo, Kitchener, and Cambridge and the townships of North Dumfries, Wellesley, Wilmot, and Woolwich. Provincial legislation required the region to prepare, for ministerial approval, an official master plan for "the

---

Bill Thomson is commissioner of planning and development, Regional Municipality of Waterloo, Waterloo, Ontario.

economic, physical and social development" of its area within three years of its January 1, 1973, formation. According to the Canada Land Inventory (3), Class 1, 2, 3 and 4 food producing soils surround two cities and part of the third and makes up the vast majority of the four rural townships.

Beneath much of the Class 1, 2, 3 and 4 soils lies a vast storehouse of prime sands and gravels, another valuable and sought after resource.

Last, but not least, are many environmentally sensitive areas in the region, remnants of earlier abundant natural resources, yet still the home of rare plants, birds, insects, animals, prime woodlots, and aquatic life.

Urban uses and farmers alike are competing for quality soils. The construction industry in Ontario needs the rich gravel deposits beneath the soil. Urban uses and, in some cases, expanding farm operations, together with major utility corridors are continually infringing upon the slowly disappearing environmentally sensitive areas.

The dilemma that faced us in 1973 was to first establish the priority for the utilization of the land. Then we had to make the policy decisions that would help us sort out the competing demands of society on the land and, at the same time, retain the nonrenewable natural resources for their best uses. The exercise was first one of gaining knowledge and insight into the consequences of any one of the many strategies concerning the use of the natural resources in the region and then educating the citizens as to what was involved. To help us in this area we created advisory teams with expertise in specific resource areas and investigated the various methods for trade-offs, and compromises. Finally, with the help of the advisory teams, we presented logical and understandable criteria and policy options to the people and the elected councils for discussion and decision.

During this tedious, but ultimately rewarding exercise, we were constantly confronted with the whole spectrum of society that includes the pure, unbending academic resource-oriented professional to the practical, pragmatic builder of urban structures. Between these extremes were farmers, urban residents, gravel operators, politicians, environmentalists, lawyers, engineers, students, foresters, agriculturalists, naturalists, realtors, and a host of other individuals and organizations with differing points of view, biases, wants, and demands. Throughout the debate ran a common thread of understanding and willingness to learn and to help use and/or to retain, in the wisest manner possible, the natural resources of our region.

Open houses and specific policy papers circulated to all who wished to participate in the planning of our region helped us arrive at two major priorities for land use: land for people to live on—including those yet to come—and the preservation of the best crop lands in our region. Included as part of the preservation priority were the environmentally sensitive areas.

Compromise in developing policies

Our settlement policies created the framework and trade-offs for denoting land for urban growth and the preservation of good food land. The Agricultural Policies created more detailed preservation policies, the framework, and specific regulations necessary to permit good food growing lands to be used for other uses deemed more important for public good or to be temporarily disturbed for less permanent uses.

Using all the available population data and professional expertise we could muster, we projected the trends for urban development to a time beyond 2001. The urban envelope that we developed around our major urban centers took into account the necessity for increasing the density of people living on the land and the intensity of various urban uses. We recognized that increased densities and a greater intensity of land use must be a major long-term goal in order to eventually halt the sprawling urban march onto the good soils. The first major compromise was to give up some of our prime soils on the edge of our cities to permit growth in the next century. The second compromise was to increase urban densities and urban uses to slow and eventually stop the growth of our cities onto the remaining good soils and create new urban areas on poorer food producing soils. Increasing energy costs and the soaring price of single family houses is helping us reach that goal earlier than expected.

It is not just the spread of cities and towns onto good agricultural lands that is depleting these better food growing soils, but also the severed lots from farmsteads for urban escapers, farmers' relatives, and other nonfarm related uses. Almost as many residential lots are created in Ontario by farm severance as by registered subdivisions, at least up to 1976. We felt a two-step process could halt such severances. The first step is now being implemented. Commencing in January 1973, only a bonafide farmer would be permitted a retirement lot if there was no previous severance on that farm.

This simple policy eliminated many severances and thus influenced the growth of small established rural settlements where infilling would not cause a problem. We now have a draft report ready that recommends the elimination of all severances from farms in the prime food growing areas, as of a certain time. This is the last step.

We encourage mobile homes for retiring farmers instead of permanent houses on the farm, farm retirement settlements, and duplexing the existing farmhouse to permit flexibility and choice for the retiring farmers. These options have been slow to catch on. We are also considering the possibility of limiting the minimum size of farms to keep the farm size economically viable and thus discourage small farms that invariably become large estate-type lots when they no longer are viable farm operations. This will be difficult. But instead of talking about the problem, we will attempt a practical solution for staged implementation.

We are also prohibiting the location of new rural nonfarm houses within prime woodlots in order to preserve another natural resource, for economic management purposes and for environmental and conservation purposes as well.

The region's official plan created the catalyst for continued discussion and education concerning our natural resources as well as becoming the

main source of major region-wide policy guidelines that have gained political commitment, regionally and provincially.

After encouraging and helping us and then monitoring our policies for
several years, the Provincial Ministry of Agriculture and Food recently published a "Foodland Guidelines Policy" for the entire province that is similar
to our official policies on foodlands. This is a tremendous step forward for
the province and a long-awaited recognition of our pioneering.

The third major compromise we made was in the prime agricultural soil
areas. While the Canada Land Inventory categorizes the first four classes of
soil as the prime food producing soils, we created a policy for only the first
three classes, leaving Class 4 as an area that could, with proper studies, be
used for purposes other than agriculture.

The trade-offs in these ventures have become acceptable, but they had to
be phased in over a period of time. To be successful and gain the respect of
those involved, you must not only know exactly what you are doing, but
you must also tell everyone exactly what you are doing. Monitor the trade-
offs you develop constantly so you can learn firsthand what should be done
the next time around. Do not be afraid to experiment and take chances. You
will never learn by doing another study to study the studies that have been
done. We are not in this business to create a retirement plan for consultants
or a Ph.D. topic for students.

Factors affecting policy formulation

Overall region-wide policies are established in the regional official policies plan. Every municipal official plan must be in conformity with the regional plan according to legislation. Until this is done, the region's plan is
the only legal and operative one. No severance of land, subdivision, zone
change, or any bylaw can be passed or instituted unless it is in conformity
with the regional and municipal official plan.

All applications that might affect agricultural land are submitted to the
region and area municipality for checking against policy and in the region's
case for approval. Applications for a change in land use are sent to agencies who might be affected or involved, such as the Federation of Agriculture, Ministry of Agriculture and Food, Conservation Authority, and
others, for their comments, advice and/or recommendations. The Regional
Council has authority to approve all municipal development applications
that are in conformity to the official plans. Appeals to final council decisions can be heard by the Ontario Municipal Board at public hearings.[1]
Again, the board must be cognizant of council and provincial policies.

We spend a great deal of time monitoring our policies, particularly when

---

[1]The Ontario Municipal Board is appointed by the Provincial Government to hear and
make decisions on appeals against municipal decisions on changes in the legal use of land,
among other matters, that are conducted in a semi-judicial manner before the public. Appeals
of decisions of the Ontario Municipal Board may be heard by the cabinet of the provincial
government.

processing various plans, in order to be aware of problems, inconsistencies, and hardships so that we can bring solutions and recommendations before the council to further implement our policies and commit ourselves to preserving the better soils. We are now working on specific zoning categories whereby farming will be the only use permitted on the best soils and other uses, such as golf courses, schools, etc., will only be permitted on poorer soils by a zone change.

Policies cannot be created in a logical and practical manner with full and consistent implementation unless good reliable natural resource data and complimentary economic, physical, and social data as they relate to farm size, viability, operations, production, and the social and cultural backgrounds of the people involved in farming, are readily available. These factors must be understood if any practical policies are to be formulated. There is not much point in having farms at a maximum size of 100 or 150 acres if a broiler operation needs only 25 acres. Exceptions to the rule must be carefully considered because when the broiler farm ceases, the farm uses for 25 acres are minimal. Then comes the push for the estate developments.

Creating a data base

The Canada Land Inventory and the Waterloo County Soils Report (1), where land was classified as to capability, slope, drainage, etc., were our main sources of physical agricultural data. Statistics Canada was the main source of the remaining data, but sometimes this was not detailed enough and we found we had to supplement it through our own research and field work. Graduate students at our universities produced various research papers. One student divided our region into four acre sites and recorded various soil, topographical, and environmental data on each site and then computerized the results (2). We can make print-outs of this material for various parts of the region to aid us in creating policy and practical implementing tools. We have been attempting to keep this particular work up-to-date. Without all of this data, we could not have developed a successful policy for our agricultural lands.

As data becomes available on other aspects of our resource policies, we assess the implications and amend policy where required. It is a constant process because our physical region is dynamic and ever-evolving. As we understand it better and gain an insight into potential future influences, we will create and re-create policy and regulations to fit.

Controlling gravel developments

Under the best soils in the region is a prime sand and gravel resource. Work by one of our associates (4) helped us map these prime deposits and create policies to preserve them until needed. Urban structures are not permitted on such deposits until the sand and gravel have been extracted. As a further measure, at the time of development, a study of nearby alternative sites for development must be explored and a calculation of the remaining unused resource considered before urban development will be considered on the resource area.

Policies in our plan indicate how an extractive operation should commence, how it is to be regulated and licensed once it gets underway, and how the topsoil is to be stored. The pit or quarry is to be restored on a rolling basis and the end use implemented as per the plan approved prior to a license being granted. The major after use in most cases will be agricultural. Some, of course, will be used for recreational uses and perhaps housing. Fortunately, there are a number of examples of rehabilitated pits near our area that are now growing economic crops, proving the feasibility of this use.

We have also studied all abandoned pits in the region in cooperation with the province (5) and developed a restoration plan. We are now formulating policies and funding arrangements for restoration, hopefully to take effect once the new Pits and Quarries Act comes into force in our province.

Again the official plan creates the policies with zoning and licensing being the major implementing and regulating tools. As with agricultural soils, we have detailed studies and analysis of where the best sand and gravel deposits are located and their potential viability.

The trade-offs between good agricultural soil and the extractive industry are difficult ones. Since soils have a higher priority than the extractive industry, most extractive sites have now been located on less valuable soils. Thus, the majority of pits are congregating in one of our southern townships that may cause other and different problems.

To encourage new pits to continue locating on poorer soils, we recommended that municipal official plans should create the policies, guidelines, and criteria for the development of a new extractive industry, while the implementing tool be a development agreement, thus circumventing the traditional zoning bylaw. It is an innovative idea and as such will take a while to implement. We have yet to gain experience with this idea that offers good control, yet moves the process more quickly and at less cost to all concerned, particularly where poorer soils are encountered.

Policies to control flooding and runoff

With the help of the Provincial Ministry of Natural Resources, the Grand River Conservation Authority, and our own participation in the International Joint Commission studies on pollution along and into our Great Lakes, we collected and analyzed a considerable amount of data concerning storm water runoff. Within that phrase, storm water runoff, lies countless tons of lost soil that could have been used for food growing but instead is contributing to water pollution during heavy runoff periods and to siltation problems downstream. Policies in our plan addressed both urban and rural runoff problems.

It took a long time through discussion, education, and actual site visits besides being aware of the cost to cure floods. We now have more detailed policies and regulations inserted into area municipal official plans and implementing subdivision agreements. Storm water management plans are required for all community plans and plans of subdivision to create and implement the zero runoff concept.

In rural areas, our task has been frustrating. Contour plowing, grassed areas or berms at the field edges where they abut streams, storm ditches to help slow runoff, newer methods of tillage that slow runoff and soil erosion, storm drainage and siltation ponds, all of which are practical and sound solutions, are rarely implemented or even encouraged financially by our province.

We have tried to encourage those agencies in control, such as our Provincial Ministries of Natural Resources and Agriculture and Food, to seriously implement storm water runoff policies in rural areas. Instead of working jointly toward the same goal, they appear to have two different philosophies. One attempts to control runoff and mitigate flooding while the other offers grants to drain farm fields as fast as the water drops. However, our province is about to implement a new grant program to encourage farmers to reduce soil erosion.

The pioneering work in our region, together with the work of many individuals and agencies, stemming from policies in the regional official policies plan is finally being rewarded. One thing we have learned in all of this is patience.

Protecting environmentally sensitive areas

The last resource I want to touch upon is one called environmentally sensitive policy areas. These are the remnants of once huge land tracts containing woodlots, marshes, and swamps in the region. Many of these areas are located in rural parts of the region where urban growth is minimal. A few are within the expanding suburban areas of our cities and thus create a challenge for preservation.

To help locate, document, map, and formulate an environmental policy for our regional plan, we formed an Ecological and Environmental Advisory Committee. This committee advises the regional council and offers input and advice to my department. It is made up of environmentalists from three universities in our area; environmental consultants; the building and development industry; the Ministries of Agriculture and Food, Environment, and Natural Resources; semi-private organizations, such as the Field Naturalists and Pollution Probe; a citizen; and myself.

This committee mapped and documented every major environmentally sensitive area in our region and devised criteria that created a hierarchy of significance to the region and our part of Ontario. From this the first trade-offs began.

Any sensitive area that was zoned or had been committed to urban development by a municipality was eliminated unless there was a stream or body of water involved. Small areas within the urban envelopes were eliminated from the regional plan and local municipalities were encouraged to fit them into their own, more detailed planning.

Every sensitive area and its documentation was discussed in the field with the landowners and those living adjacent to these sites. The reasons for preserving the natural areas and methods that would be employed to do so were explained in detail.

All of this work for 69 environmentally sensitive areas paid off because, in the end, not one owner made a major objection to the Regional Council or the provincial minister of housing, who had to approve our plan before the policies became legal. We are now working with the province to create a financial incentive for those who own the environmentally sensitive areas whereby no land taxes would be charged if the land is preserved in its natural state.

Our official plan lists the process one must go through to develop in the vicinity of a sensitive area or to actually encroach into one. The development industry must prepare an environmental impact statement and submit the relevant assessment studies to the Ecological and Environmental Advisory Committee and to my department at the same time they are submitting a development proposal near or impacting one of the sensitive areas.

With minor trade-offs, we have managed to preserve those sensitive areas lying in the path of urban development so far. Studies by environmental consultants defined the exact edge of the sensitive areas and usually devised methods of preservation even when we permitted some back yards and park edges to intrude into the less sensitive parts of these areas. We permitted a gravel pit adjacent to one site to commence by amending the pit's license to preserve the sensitive area. We shifted proposed alignments for major highways and a major provincial gas line away from affected sensitive areas. In several instances, we built extra storm water ditches, culverts, and berms as part of a highway construction program to protect the sensitive areas from road and nearby urban runoff.

There have been trade-offs to be sure, but throughout, the environment has been the major winner and in the end the development industry has, by and large, been proud of their contribution.

In many cases, growing knowledge of the natural resources in our region permits us to work out problems in the field in a practical manner. Common to all field examinations has been the "as it was, as it is, and as it will be" philosophy. This entails a knowledge of what forces of nature and activities of man brought us to the present state. It is important to understand the current state of affairs relative to what is taking place on the environmentally affected site that provides information about the forces of nature that play a part in the future and realize that those natural forces also change over time regardless of whether there is urban development nearby or not.

Finally, we attempt to look into the future of that particular site in terms of what might happen naturally, what might happen if we permit man to do exactly what he wishes in terms of development, and what might happen if we do something different in the way of development or preservation. By taking a few early precautions and considering a few restraints for both sides, perhaps we can create an environment that man can fit into without dominating or ruining and thus grow to enjoy his environment and gain further respect for it.

The road ahead

We still have a long way to go in preserving good farmland, in implementing sound water management programs, and protecting environmentally sensitive areas. But if we are to accomplish anything we cannot be too academic or "motherhoody" in our approach. Policies must be clear, concise, firm, and practical. Regulations must be clear, workable, and flexible to a degree, depending upon the specific circumstances, but never inconsistent and never ignored when the tough sledding invariably comes. Above all, the provincial, federal, and other farm related agencies must work together and help the municipalities and farmers retain good farmland for food production without forcing farmers into bankruptcy while trying to save land. Most of these other types of help are far outside the jurisdiction of a municipality and thus are of major concern to us.

What we accomplished with our official plan for the natural resources I've discussed has not been accomplished before in Ontario, not even by the province. The way we are implementing our policies and creating compromises and trade-offs is new to all of us. Our educational program is continuous. Credibility is gained and eventually proven once you start accomplishing what you said you would at the public meetings prior to the approval of the official plan.

In our region, the Regional Council is the final decision-making body unless there is an appeal lodged against one of its decisions. Then the Ontario Municipal Board, the province, and/or the courts are the next and final steps in the process. If we take care, the last three steps may never take place.

Conclusion

Implementing tools, such as subdivision agreements or zoning bylaws, are often used by individuals or companies seeking a legal change in the use of land. Depending upon the nature of the application and its influence on a natural resource recognized in our plan, we would seek the advice of the involved provincial ministry, Federation of Agriculture, Ecological and Environmental Advisory Committee, or some other interested party, with a request that replies must be returned within 30 days. Citizens are usually involved in public meetings during the process so we can get input, as well as for the citizen to become more informed. Recommendations are made directly to a Regional Council Committee, and the following week, to the Regional Council itself. At any of these two steps, the public can be heard.

Once commitments are made in official plans and when elected people are the only ones on the Regional Planning Committee and on the Council, decisions are made quickly, and for the majority of cases, in favor of the retention of good soils and the preservation of the environment.

The system is not perfect. It is fraught with problems. Trade-offs might be too much for the environment. Financial restraints may force giving up or delaying purchase of land that is to be preserved for an environmental reason and thus letting some development intrude into sensitive areas causing irreparable damage. Again, the policy may not be strong enough or clear enough in the beginning. Forcing through an amending, tougher policy too quickly may lose the whole policy.

Sure, it is not perfect academically nor perfect in a practical sense depending on which side you are on, but the philosophy of preservation of the natural resources in the region is retained. We are slowly but surely preserving more and more good soils and the sensitive remnants of the environment each day. As we gain practical experience and expertise, and as people gain more knowledge of the benefits of our policies, we will perhaps be able to retain all of our natural resources for future generations.

REFERENCES

1. Canadian Department of Agriculture. Research Branch. 1971. *Soils of Waterloo County.* Report No. 44. Department of Agriculture, Ottawa, Ontario.
2. Coleman, Derek J. 1975. *An ecological input to regional planning.* University of Waterloo, Waterloo, Ontario.
3. Environment Canada. Lands Directorate. 1972. *Soil capability classificaton for agriculture.* Report No. 2. Canada Land Inventory, Ottawa, Ontario.
4. McLellan, A. G., and C. R. Bryant. 1973. *The aggregate resources of Waterloo-Wellington Counties: Towards effective planning for the aggregate industry.* Open File Report 5100. Ontario Division of Mines, Geological Branch, Toronto.
5. Ontario Ministry of Natural Resources. 1979. *Abandoned pits and quarries in Ontario.* Miscellaneous Paper 79. Ontario Geological Survey, Toronto.

16
Resource-constrained economies: Implications for land use law and policy

Mark B. Lapping

In a provocative essay Geographer Warren Johnson argues that growing resource scarcities will, after a period of initial dislocation, move us toward a leaner, more productive social environment as we muddle toward frugality. "As mobility is reduced," Johnson writes, "the traditional basis for responsibility to one's community and environment will be reestablished; people will have to live with the consequences of their actions rather than escape the effects by moving away.... The timeless virtues of loyalty, cooperation and selflessness—all thinly observed now—will once again be functional, as will the simple pleasures of family and friends, the knowledge of a trade and the comforts of a well-known environment" (4). Such a society, though it smacks of something of a pastoral Luddite landscape, is an articulation of values, both traditional and fundamental; and as we became more urbanized and industrialized, our hunger for these preindustrial values has also become greater.

Yet the road to such a society is likely to be a difficult one with lots of sharp curves, plenty of bumps and potholes, many bridges in need of repair, and a reduced speed limit which will make the trip seem twice as long. It is during the transition period—a "swing era" in the current parlance of

Mark B. Lapping is associate director of the Environmental Program; chairman of the Natural Resources Planning Program; and associate professor in the School of Natural Resources, University of Vermont, Burlington.

energy policy—that we will most need rigorous systems of land use guidance. If the era of frugality is to have meaning and wholeness, then the one preceding it must preserve our options.

The assault on regulation

In the short term there is little reason for optimism. The gap between those who have access to resources and those who do not will sharpen social and political conflict. The pressures created by resource scarcities are likely to fracture society along various lines (sunbelt versus snowbelt, urban versus rural, haves versus have-nots) with the result that ever more special interest groups will emerge, making it exceedingly difficult for any political leader to develop the consensus necessary to implement difficult policies. Our historic reliance upon the price system to allocate scarce resources will further exacerbate our situation. In sum, the potential clearly exists for the disintegration of the democratic polity. If this occurs, then the scarcest resource will not be oil or water or land, but the ability of people to find common ground, the necessary calculus of consent for government (7).

Complicating things still further is the widely held belief that there are, in reality, few resource scarcities. This assessment sees the multinational corporations, especially the oil companies, at the center of a "devil theory." Once prices rise and other restraints are eliminated, the flow of resources and our historic levels of consumption will once again resume according to this view. Such an ideology does not see conservation as the center of resource policy. On the contrary, emphasis will be placed upon invalidating or withdrawing barriers to further resource development and exploitation.

The implications for resource policy are several, but in terms of land use policy there will be a drive to scuttle several pieces of federal environmental policy. Fundamental to this move will be the easing of restrictions under the 1977 Amendments to the Clean Air Act, which limit sulphur dioxide emissions and require the desulfurization of all new coal-fired power plants. Additionally, changes in the 1977 Surface Mining Control and Reclamation Act are possible. Currently, a suit seeking revisions in this law is pending between several major coal companies, the National Coal Association, and the American Mining Congress on the one side and the U.S. Department of the Interior on the other. Again in the realm of energy versus land use related problems, it is highly probable that moves against the National Environmental Policy Act (NEPA) will continue unabated. Oil companies have been particularly vocal in this area as they have attempted to speed up the granting of offshore oil licenses. Clearly, many of the efforts to resolve coastal zone conflicts and to develop comprehensive multiple-use strategies for these areas hang in the balance as pressures mount to erode or end-run NEPA altogether.

The current demand for the establishment of major synthetic fuel installations also raises critical land use concerns. For not only will land be mined and soils disturbed, but significant amounts of water, which simply do not exist in the West, will have to be used in the process. A weakening in exist-ing laws in the wake of growing demands for synfuels is likely to have pro-foundly disastrous consequences, not only in terms of land but in water re-sources as well. Yet again the mind-set is such that production and an in-crease in supplies is to be preferred over those strategies that see conserva-tion and a turn to solar investments as being central. Though President Carter has promised specific aid to local communities that undergo rapid change due to energy-related activities, dislocations in community struc-ture, especially in those rural areas where coal capable of being easily sur-face mined exists, will increase. Perhaps this is simply one more trade-off cost that must be absorbed.

Other resources are likewise in some danger of rapid and unplanned ex-ploitation. The escalating price for housing has seen a federal response that will result in an increase in the harvesting of timber from national forest lands. What this activity will mean in light of existing laws and planning programs, especially the Resources Planning Act and the National Forest Management Act, is open to some debate. Nevertheless, it is apparent that efforts are being directed to expand the supply sector so as to fulfill much of the demand that has surfaced within the marketplace.

What will happen to water resource planning may evolve into the most serious long-term issue to face the resource community. Demands for water are increasing, and new initiatives in energy development will surely exacer-bate the situation. It is fundamental to any understanding of the water resources problem that this is no longer just a western problem, if it ever was. More than one eastern river basin currently faces rigid regulation and control. While many had hoped that the president's water message of June 1978 would usher in a new era in water resource planning, the fragmenta-tion and polarization that often accompanies congressional debate has focused attention almost solely on water projects to the exclusion of the other important elements of this key policy statement (10). The result is like-ly to be another disjointed response to resource scarcity.

It would seem, then, that the immediate future will see sentiment for the erosion in existing federal land use and environmental programs. Two criti-cal variables that cannot be overlooked must be noted, however.

First, while we can expect numerous demands to end the "red tape bureaucracy" that many believe keeps us from a greater availability of fuel, land, and water, there is just so much that the federal government can do unless it wishes to reshape radically its relationship with the states. It is one thing to talk about developing synthetic fuels and quite another to blow away half of Colorado or Wyoming. The role of the states, particularly those with environmental policy acts and systems of land use control, then becomes critical. And while one must grant that state legislatures have not been any more immune to lobbyists and special interest groups than the Congress, the issues of further energy development, water withdrawals, land conversion, timber harvesting, and the like have an intimacy to state legislatures that does not exist for the federal government. The state legislatures will have to live with the consequences of their actions.

Second, it must be noted that one man's red tape is another man's protection. The hard-fought-for advances that have been made in the past are likely to be defended even more vigorously, witness the recent decision upholding the California coastal zone program [*American Petroleum Institute v. Knelt* 456 Fed. Sup. 889 (U.S.D.C., Aug. 31, 1978)] and the National Flood Insurance Program [*Texas Landowners Rights Association v. Harris* (U.S.D.C., May 31, 1978)].

Land use futures and scarcity

Regulation of land use takes new forms as new problems emerge. The coming age of scarcities is likely to see major efforts dealing with the retention of agricultural land, the interface of energy and land use, and the disposal of toxic and hazardous wastes. Equally important will be a reemergence in importance of multiple-use resource policy.

As I suggested in a recent article, the retention of agricultural land has become something of a motherhood issue (6). Any number of federal agencies are now working to bring their programs into synchronization with the need to preserve agricultural lands. A number of bills are now pending in Congress to do likewise. And the states and localities are also working in this area. Perhaps the best indicator of the newfound importance of agricultural land policy is that the U.S. Department of Agriculture no longer talks about prime agricultural land. Now, significantly, the emphasis is upon important farmland. Americans have sufficiently awakened to the need to protect their agricultural resources, not only for future food production but just as importantly to keep the balance-of-trade deficit in reasonable view.

What makes the current discussion on agricultural land retention so refreshing is that we are joining the issue on realistic levels. First, the problem is national in nature. This is being reflected in the policy options being raised and the support that is coming forward for such efforts.

Second, we are beginning to introduce justice and equity considerations into these discussions. The result has been a movement toward the public purchase of development rights. In a sense we have matured to the point that we recognize that the retention of farmland is a social good with the broadest possible base. This has enabled us to realize too that the farmer's ox can no longer be gored and that society as a whole must pay to retain such lands.

Third, the preservation of the small family farm—broadly defined—is also of fundamental consequence. Policies to aid this unit of production may help to guarantee that there will be farmers to farm the land we move to retain. How strong the commitment to agricultural land retention is may be tested by the competing demands for energy from surface coal exploitation in the West, where waters used for agriculture are at stake as well as the very land itself.

Most importantly in terms of scarcities we are on the threshold of an era when the energy problem will translate itself into new programs that will impact on the planning process (2). Let me suggest several areas where this is likely to occur.

First, new efforts to revitalize urban areas through downtown revitalization, neighborhood renewal efforts, and the development of new, mass, rapid-transit systems uniting whole metropolitan regions are going to be developed.

Second, we are likely to see a reintroduction of the concept of multiplicity of uses in our communities. Gradually, the energy crunch will work to end the formal opposition of workplace and residence. Business, industry, and residence will be brought together. Doubtless, this will represent a total horror to those Euclidean planners among us, but the efficiencies to be derived from the mixing of land uses will be better realized in the future.

Third, zoning and subdivision ordinances and building codes will be reevaluated and redeveloped so as to encourage energy savings in land usage. Presently, the Argonne National Laboratory of the U.S. Department of Energy is engaged in a pilot program to encourage communities to move in this direction.

Fourth, as solar technologies become more sophisticated and more economically viable, solar access regulations will become part of the baggage of local land use planning, assuming the argument can successfully be made to extend the local police power to solar accesses (3).

Fifth, the sheer price of energy as reflected in space conditioning, transportation, and other factors may conspire to make clustering, planned unit developments, and certain forms of subdivision exactions—long the "pets" of planners—possible. What this means is that the realities of the housing market may develop to the point where these types of land use solutions, and not the single-family detached dwelling, may become commonplace.

Sixth, the desire to control growth, as reflected in communities as diverse as Petaluma, Boca Raton, and Ramapo, may find allies in both the energy situation and the "Proposition 13" trend moving through the country. The fiscal constraints that have been placed upon local governments are likely to make them less hospitable and amenable to new development because of the expense of infrastructure investments—schools, sewers, police and fire protection, etc. (8). Thus, there will be an important movement to avoid the hopscotch land use patterns so typical of suburbia because they are so inherently expensive to service and are energy inefficient. At least in terms of our communities, energy and its price is likely to become a potent driving force in land use guidance and allocation in the near future.

One of the potentially most significant pieces of land use legislation to emerge in recent years has been the Resource Conservation and Recovery Act of 1976 (RCRA). Section 1008 of the act specifies that the Environmental Protection Agency will develop guidelines that provide for "(A) protection of public health and welfare; (B) protection of the quality of groundwaters and surface waters from leachates; (C) protection of the quality of surface waters from runoff through compliance with effluent limitations under the Federal Water Pollution Control Act, as amended; (D) protection of ambient air quality through compliance with new source performance standards or requirements of air quality implementation plans under the Clean Air Act, as amended; (E) disease and vector control; (F) safety; and (G) aesthetics." Additionally, RCRA also provides for the regulation and management of hazardous wastes.

While any element of this law has some importance, that dealing with the protection of groundwater resources may be the most powerful. Areas identified as "sole aquifers" are likely to fall under a large degree of protection from waste disposal because of the threat of groundwater pollution and recharge areas in general will have new protection. Clearly, this section of the law can have large-scale implications in terms of land use. Governments throughout the nation will attempt to avoid potential Love Canal disasters through the monitoring of waste disposal sites and the implementation of other mitigation measures. Alabama, for example, has just passed such a regulation, vesting the State Board of Health with far-reaching authority in this area. Yet it is in the limitation of what industries, including power plants, will be located where that this law may have its greatest impact. Waste disposal, one of the externalities of a highly chemical dependent, throwaway society, will emerge as one of the key future land use uses.

Finally, as resources of all sorts become less available and more expensive, the reemergence of a multiple-use theory of resource use is necessary. Single-purpose projects and policies simply cannot be afforded. Water, energy, and land will be thought of in terms of their eventual reuse or recycling potential. The accent will be on achieving sustainable returns and the delivery of a multiplicity of goods and services from a given resource mix.

The role of the courts

No discussion of land use can ignore the role of the courts. The courts have been activists in the land use planning process and are among its most sophisticated elements. Though this is not the place to assess where the courts have been and where they may be going, recent decisions defining the "general welfare" merit some examination (1, 9).

Courts traditionally have demanded that the exercise of the police power has some relationship to the public's welfare and security. Historically, the definition of general welfare was applied to the community that created the ordinance being reviewed. Through an evolutionary process, the courts have come to see the region as the arena for determining the general welfare. In other words, without defining the boundaries of the region, the judiciary has substituted the concept of region in place of that of community. The movement toward a regional definition of welfare has signaled the abandonment of the idea that communities and their land use configuration were "islands" somehow swimming in but not part of the region or the ocean.

Starting in the early 1970s in Pennsylvania [*Appeal of Kit-Mar Builders, Inc.*, 439 Pa. 460, 268 A.2d 765, (1970)] and Michigan [*Green v. Town of Lima*, 40 Mich. App. 655, 199 N.W. 2d 243, (1972), and *Knopf v. City of Sterling*, 391 Mich. 139, 215 N.W. 2d 179, (1974)], the expanded impact area doctrine was articulated. The key case was in New Jersey in *Southern Burlington County NAACP v. Township of Mount Laurel* [67 N.J. 151, 336 A.2d 713, (1975)]. Here the issue became housing for all income groups within the Philadelphia-Trenton region. The court ordered that Mount Laurel must provide areas within its borders where low- and moderate-income housing might be built in accordance with Mount Laurel's "fair share" of the region's low- and moderate-income inhabitants (5).

More recently this doctrine has been extended further in *SAVE v. City of Bothell* [576 P. 2d 401, (1978)] where a Washington municipality amended its zoning ordinance to permit the development of a large shopping center on agricultural land. SAVE, an environmental organization, argued that Bothell should have been compelled to review the impact of a reduction of agricultural land on the total Puget Sound region. The court noted that "where the potential exists that a zoning acton will cause a serious environmental effect outside jurisdictional borders, the zoning body must serve the welfare of the entire affected community. If it does not do so, it acts in an arbitrary and capricious manner...."

While the courts have been moving in this direction, so have several states. Minnesota, for example, has a law dealing with the Twin Cities region that states "[a] local governmental unit shall not adopt any official control or fiscal device which is in conflict with its comprehensive plan or which permits activities in conflict with metropolitan system plans..." [Minn. Stat. Ann. §473. 865(2), 1977]. The result of this litigation and legislation is that communities within a regional system are seen as being tied one to the other. It is likely that the externalities a community does not wish to live with can no longer be visited upon a neighbor. It will become increasingly more difficult, then, for communities to declare "not on my block you don't" when it comes to bearing its share of the burden to fulfill its obligations under the expanded concept of "general welfare." Likewise, this may be just the incentive to create true regional planning efforts at the expense of parochial and highly localistic planning efforts.

Conclusion

Initially, the impact of resource scarcities upon land use will be growing resistance to planning and regulation. Perhaps this can be seen as something of a cultural lag or the last roundup for the cowboy mentality. The potential does exist, however, for significant environmental deterioration until things get turned around. Eventually, though, efforts to live within our scarcities will create an atmosphere in which agricultural lands are likely to find real protection, energy considerations will create less wasteful forms of community structure, and conservation will be of primacy in design and planning. A major obstacle to be surmounted will be that of waste disposal for hazardous wastes and substances. Scarcities among resources will also see a resurrection of multiple use resource theory; not to do so would be too wasteful and wanton. Finally, the courts are moving toward a position that expands the concept of general welfare in such ways as to create a real potential for regionalism.

The goals of land use planning and control will essentially remain the same as we move into an era of resource scarcities. The need to find mutually acceptable levels of coercion in terms of land use will become more poignant and immediate. Failure to do so can only lead us farther away from an eventuality which is best confronted quickly and in a forthright manner.

REFERENCES

1. Brower, D. 1979. *Courts move toward redefinition of general welfare.* Land Use Law and Zoning Digest 31(5): 5-10.
2. Burchell, R. W., and D. Listokin. 1975. *Future land use: Energy, environment and legal constraints.* Rutgers University Center for Urban Policy Research, New Brunswick, New Jersey.
3. Jaffe, M. 1978. *Some comments on drafting solar access regulations.* Land Use Law and Zoning Digest 30(8): 4-7.
4. Johnson, W. 1978. *Muddling toward frugality.* Sierra Club Books, San Francisco, California.
5. Lapping, M. B. 1978. *Exclusionary land use controls in suburbia: Current judicial review.* State and Local Government Review 10(1): 16-19.
6. Lapping, M. B. 1979. *Agricultural land retention strategies: Some underpinnings.* Journal of Soil and Water Conservation 34(3): 124-126.
7. Lowi, T. 1969. *The end of liberalism: Ideology, policy and the crisis of public authority.* W. W. Norton, New York, New York.
8. Odell, R., editor. 1979. *Proposition 13 triggers various land use shifts.* Conservation Foundation Letter April: 1-8.
9. Williams, N. 1976. *On from Mount Laurel: Guidelines on the "regional general welfare."* Vermont Law Review 1(1): 23-50.

17
Land ownership and tenure patterns as a constraint: The farmer's perspective

Marjorie Bursa

Canada has 922 million hectares of land. The land in farms accounts for 67 million hectares, or about 7.3 percent of the country's land area. All of this farmland is in southern Canada.

Nearly all of Canada's farmland exists in two great belts. The western prairies account for 81 percent; the Windsor-Quebec corridor, extending east into the Maritimes, accounts for 16 percent; and the remaining 3 percent is in British Columbia's river valleys, mountain basins, and the Peace River district.

The extent of Canada's agricultural land resources is restricted by the physical limitations of the Canadian Shield to the north, the Rocky Mountains to the west, and the boundary between Canada and the United States on the south. Northern regions also face a climatic limitation in the number of frost-free days.

The amount of land therefore constitutes the primary constraint on Canadian agriculture.

According to two federal departments, Agriculture Canada and Environment Canada, land with a capability for agriculture amounts to 119 million hectares. The idea of a "reserve" of land is misleading, however. Almost all reserve land is located on the northern limit of cultivation, where the climatic limitation prevails, and is class 5 or 6 land comprised of soils with

Marjorie Bursa is senior economist with the Canadian Federation of Agriculture, Ottawa.

severe limitations for producing anything but perennial forage crops.

Almost all fertile soils are either farmed already or under urban development. A small acreage of fertile soils in the Maritimes is not in agricultural production because the soils are widely dispersed and/or remote from markets, making their use for agricultural purposes unprofitable.

Tenure and ownership characteristics

Basic farmland ownership and tenure patterns in Canada are not a constraint to the nation's agricultural economy. According to the 1976 census, there were 300,118 farms in Canada with gross sales of $1,200 or more. Sixty-three percent of these farms were owner operated; 6 percent were operated by tenant farmers; and 31 percent were farmed by part owner/part tenants.

The family farm prevails everywhere. The family farm and the maintenance of the family farm is a fundamental tradition and the bedrock of agricultural organization on which the rest of the agricultural industry is built. Whether totally owned, rented, or partly owned/partly rented, it is primarily a family unit enterprise. This is by no means to be considered as a constraint. It is rather quite the opposite: the family farm has facilitated the development of Canadian agriculture by farmers who do their own thing and make their own decisions. Farmers are well content with this pattern of family farm ownership and, as was seen in British Columbia, were adamently opposed to even the suspicion of a possibility of impending change.

Ninety-one percent of all farms are owned by individual proprietors; 4 percent of farms are in partnerships; another 4 percent are in family farm corporations. Nonfamily farm corporations, institutionally owned units, and common pastures account for only 1 percent of Canada's farms. The farms owned by nonfamily corporations, 0.6 percent of the total number of farms, account for but 1.4 percent of Canada's farmland.

Land market problems

But all is not well for Canada's farmers. The price of farmland is rising rapidly, 77 percent between 1961 and 1971, 165 percent between 1971 and 1978. The farmer is having to compete in the land market with an invasion of speculators, investors, developers, commuters, and hobby farmers, most of whom have greater financial resources to draw on than do farmers. Price and availability of land is therefore a constraint to farmers who wish to buy land or consolidate their holdings.

The impact of this on farmers is multifaceted:

• Farmers are receiving offers to purchase their land for much more than other farmers are able to pay.

• Farmers are faced with the decision to accept such an offer and retire in comfort, or sell their farms to sons or daughters at a much lower price and accept a much smaller monthly retirement payment as a result.

• Farmers are looking for class 1 or 2 land to enlarge their units and are unable to find the land at a price they can afford.

• Farmland is disappearing around cities, first into disuse, then under buildings. Jesus Island (now Laval City) in Quebec, the Niagara fruit belt in Ontario, and the Fraser Delta in British Columbia exemplify this situation.

• Farmland is being expropriated, willy nilly, for highways and pipelines.

• Farmland is being disadvantaged for cultivation, though not expropriated, in the vicinity of highways and pipelines.

• Farmers are receiving complaints about odor problems and are even being obliged to restrict or move their beef, hog, and poultry enterprises to leave the air sweet for newly arrived ex-urbanites.

• Farmland is being acquired for city dwellers' secondary homes in scenic areas, then left disused, if only temporarily, facilitating the spread of weeds.

• Processors of agricultural commodities are buying farmland and extending their operations back into primary production.

The climatic constraint

Simultaneously there is growing concern throughout Canada about climatic variability. At least some climatologists expect greater climatic variability during the remainder of this century than was the case over the past 30 years. Canadian agriculture thus becomes especially vulnerable because it is on the continent's northern limits for crop production. The growing season in terms of frost-free days is crucial. Climate is a constraint.

Farmers may be experiencing a squeeze on farmland. There is a possibility that while urban encroachment takes the best land in the south, climatic variability or deterioration may be reducing the possibility of substituting land in the north, which is in any case less fertile and more demanding to operate.

The Canadian government expressed concern about these trends at the opening of Parliament in February 1974: "In the long term the continuity of domestic supply must take into account optimum overall land use in Canada and especially the trend to diversion of productive land for non-agricultural purposes. The government intends to enter into discussions with the provinces since they are vitally involved in this question."

In Canada the provinces have jurisdiction over land use and planning. The federal government's influence is limited and exercised via the transfer payments made by the federal government to the provinces and in land owned by the Crown through its Canadian federal government in numerous locations across the country.

The federal government initially approached the provinces on the matter of an intergovernmental land use policy in 1976. However, two or three provinces were not interested in a combined federal-provincial approach to land use policy; and the discussions went no further.

For its part, the federal government has since developed a set of policy guidelines relating to land use. These guidelines are intended to be used by federal departments when decisions are made that in one way or another affect land use. The guidelines, or incipient federal land use policy, had reached the Cabinet committee stage but had not gone to the Cabinet earlier this year when the change of government occurred.

It appears that the new government is ready to continue in the same direction and give early Cabinet consideration to this incipient federal land use policy.

Role of the Canadian Federation of Agriculture

Much of the Canadian Federation of Agriculture effort has gone into analyzing farm-related statistics, asking its members to identify particular problems, and examining the priority problems in each province.

Statistically the number of Canadian farms, which declined from 387,000 in 1951, to 339,000 in 1961, and 300,000 in 1971, has, for the moment at least, stabilized around the 300,000 mark. Average farm size continues on an upward trend, from 146 hectares in 1951, to 176 hectares in 1961, 217 hectares in 1971, and 224 hectares in 1976. Total farmland likewise remains on an upward trend, from 56 million hectares in 1951, to 62 million hectares in 1961, 65 million hectares in 1971, and 67 million hectares in 1976.

However, this slow upward trend in the amount of farmland nationwide is comprised of striking decreases in eastern Canada and southern British Columbia, which have been compensated for by the farming of additional, but usually less fertile, land in the prairie provinces and in northern British Columbia.

The amount of rented farmland is increasing, particularly in the east. Renting of land has been well established for some time in western Canada.

Identification of land-related issues

The Canadian Federation of Agriculture asked its members to identify land-related problems or issues from the farmer's perspective. Topping the list was the need for comprehensive planning to give full weight to agriculture. Thereafter, four issues were identified and rated on a nearly equal basis: (1) the loss of agricultural land to nonagricultural uses, (2) the farmer's right to compensation in the event of imputed loss due to government restrictions on the sale of land, (3) land ownership, (4) and the provision of farmland to new generations of producers with the associated need of retiring farmers for retirement income.

Next on the list was the problem of regulations restricting the operation of beef, hog, and poultry enterprises. Receiving occasional mention were the problems of agricultural land in disuse, soil deterioration and erosion, tax relief, grazing rights, long-range planning for housing development, vertical integration, and the structure of farm units that are too small or poorly located.

In general, land-related problems were judged very important in eastern Canada and British Columbia and moderately important in the prairie provinces.

All provinces are experiencing the same types of problems, but in varying degree. It is the amount of land that is a constraint in eastern Canada and in southern British Columbia. In the prairie provinces the constraints are land ownership, meaning foreign ownership; the high price of land; and the intergenerational transfer of land.

Some provincial actions

At the time the Canadian Federation of Agriculture began to look at farmland problems, there existed no integrated analysis of the national situation concerning changes in farmland ownership. Access to data was difficult. Most was buried in registry offices. The Federation therefore examined the priority issues in each province. This involved a review of legislation, policies, programs, and literature relating to each issue in each province.

British Columbia. British Columbia has a little less than one-half hectare of farmland per person, a situation similar to that in eastern Canada. The province was the first to take positive steps to deal with the problem of preserving agricultural land.

Prime farmland is being lost especially in the Fraser Valley, Vancouver Island, and Okanagan Valley. A study made for the British Columbia Land Commission estimated an annual loss over the last 20 years of 3,940 hectares of prime agricultural land. All class 1, 2 and 3 soils are in use, and sales of these lands are in 2-hectare and 4-hectare lots when they are sold.

It is reported that the New Democratic Party came to power in 1972 in British Columbia on a platform that included a promise to the British Columbia Federation of Agriculture to preserve agricultural land for farmers. If so, the party fulfilled its promise.

First, an Order-in-Council in 1972 prohibited "all subdivisions of farmland including all land deemed by the Committee to be suitable for cultivation of agricultural crops...." This in effect made sales of farmland to developers pointless.

It appeared to farmers that the provincial government was encroaching on farmers' rights to do what they liked with their land. Remotely, there appeared to be a threat to the family farm. Reaction was immediate and uncompromising. The Federation of Agriculture embarked on what is probably its most forceful period of active opposition to the provincial government. In December 1972 the Federation went to the limit, saying the farmland freeze must be lifted. There were noisy meetings up and down the province, culminating in an orderly demonstration on the front lawn of the provincial legislative building in Victoria. This is all the more remarkable for the fact that by late 1974 the opposition had disappeared. The package of legislation passed is producing more expressions of satisfaction from farmers than one hears in the other provinces.

The freeze was not lifted. In early 1973 the British Columbia government introduced the Land Commission Act. The act established a Provincial Land Commission that had as its first objective to preserve agricultural land for farm use by designating agricultural reserves.

The objectives of the Commission were said to be: (a) preservation of agricultural land for farm use; (b) encouragement of the establishment and maintenance of family farms, and land in an agricultural land reserve, for a use compatible with the preservation of family farms and farm use of the land.

The act provided that "...no person shall occupy or use agricultural land designated as an agricultural land reserve for any purpose other than farm use except as permitted by the act or the regulations...."

The violent opposition from farmers throughout the province, focused in the activities of the Federaton of Agriculture and its executive, was directed against two main points: (1) there was no mention of compensation to those farmers who would lose the opportunity to sell their farmland for urban development; (2) it appeared in the wording of the bill that the Commission would have the right to expropriate farmers' land.

The bill was modified to exclude the powers of expropriation and passed. No commitment to individual compensation for the imputed lost opportunity to sell was given, and it is important to note that individual compensation for selling rights is not part of the British Columbia solution.

The British Columbia government turned the state of farmer discontent into one of considerable satisfaction by following up with other pieces of legislation. The most important of these is the Farm Income Assurance Act, a voluntary farm income assurance program organized on a commodity basis.

There remains speculation in land, however.

Saskatchewan. With 28 hectares of farmland per person in Saskatchewan, concern for the preservation of agricultural land is subordinate to concern for the preservation of the family farm. This is expressed in relation to problems of rentals, foreign ownership, and intergenerational transfer.

In 1971, 39 percent of Saskatchewan's farmers were part owners/part tenants. They controlled 54 percent of the farmland.

The Saskatchewan Royal Commission on Agriculture and Rural Life in its "Fifth Report on Land Tenure of 1955" compared the three forms of farm holdings, namely ownership, tenancy, and a combination of ownership and tenancy. The report concluded: "A combination of ownership and tenancy avoids many of the deficiencies found in each form of tenure when considered individually. Although insecurity of tenure applies to the rented portion, social consequences are minimized by ownership of the home portion. Income factors, particularly size adjustment, make owner-tenants the most advantaged of the three tenure groups. Proper land use, while it may be adversely affected where insecurity of tenure exists with respect to the rented portion, may also be encouraged by the superior economic position of the owner-tenant."

Much of the rented farmland in Saskatchewan is on a sharecrop basis, with one-third of the crop going to the owner. Cash leases have become more common in recent years. Leases of farmland tend to be for periods of one to three years. About one-third of the leases are unwritten.

Renting is frequently between relatives or persons socially acquainted, and there is greater reliance on custom and tradition and confidence in one's neighbor than inclination to be bothered by the written word.

Non-Canadian ownership of farmland in Saskatchewan was mentioned in the final report of the Special Committee on the Ownership of Agricultural Land in 1973 as accounting for 0.97 percent of the province's agricultural land. American ownership in the part of Saskatchewan within 54 miles of the border averaged 2.34 percent of the land area in December 1970. Canadians living outside Saskatchewan were reported by the special committee as owning 560,000 hectares.

In Saskatchewan, farmers' concern is their inability, in terms of personal assets, to compete with wealthier purchasers. The Saskatchewan Federation of Agriculture submitted a brief to the Special Legislative Committee on the Foreign Ownership of Farmland and expressed the view that it was necessary to consider restrictive legislation.

In 1974 the Saskatchewan government responded with an Act to Regulate the Ownership and Control of Agricultural Land in the province. Subject to various exceptions, no nonresident person may have or acquire an aggregate land holding with an assessed value for municipal taxation purposes in excess of $15,000. A nonresident for this purpose is a person who lives less than 6 months of the year within the province of Saskatchewan.

The intergenerational transfer is the transfer of a farm property from father to son or from a retiring farmer to any young person who succeeds him in owning and farming the property. The problem arises when a young man has to pay his father for the farm, which is also something fairly new. Earlier generations did not have to deal with it. A man customarily inherited the farm from his father, and the older man stayed on, frequently in the same house, in his retirement. The problem of expanding the farm has always existed, but the process of getting started was looked after by the customs and/or laws of inheritance.

Nowadays some Canadian farmers can sell their farms for cash to nonagricultural users. Moreover, our general level of affluence and expectations is higher than it was at, say, the beginning of the century. All farmers, whether located on the urban fringe or not, have come to expect to convert their farm asset into a retirement plan that will bring them an income and independence.

Saskatchewan has responded to this need by forming the Saskatchewan Land Bank Commission. The Commission now intervenes to bridge this difficult transaction between the retiring seller and young purchaser by itself buying the farm and leasing it to the young farmer with an option for future purchase.

Conclusions

The problem of preserving agricultural land will continue to be acute in eastern Canada and British Columbia, where the acreage of farmland per capita is low.

Provincial governments will not be strong enough to resist pressure of urban developers to encroach on agricultural land.

The federal government will refrain from direct intervention in land use planning because planning is a provincial jurisdiction.

The trend of farmers to be part owners/part tenants will continue to increase in the East and probably remain about the same in the priairie provinces.

The family farm will continue to be the dominant form of ownership.

Any hope of deceleration of encroachment of urbanization on the most fertile agricultural land in the country, in the south around Canada's major cities, will be based on slower growth of population and/or the invention of the self-contained, pipeless, dwelling house by about 2000 A.D.

VII. ENERGY ISSUES IN RESOURCE-CONSTRAINED ECONOMIES

18
Energy issues in resource-constrained economies

J. M. Ramirez

The mighty American economy, strongest in the world, is running out of gas. That statement may be literal, but it is painfully factual. And we are not running out of gas alone. We are running out of oil and will be running out of coal. These fossil fuel reserves provide over 95 percent of the total energy needs of the American economy, and soon, probably sooner than we anticipated, may well vanish. Man faces a most serious challenge—that of survival in a technological world fed by dwindling supplies of fuel.

Three basic reasons may be cited for the energy crisis: (1) our ever-expanding appetite for energy; (2) our often profligate and inefficient use of the supplies available to us now; and (3) our yet insufficient efforts to develop new alternate sources of fuel.

Among these reasons, the third is most critical. Even if our appetite for energy remains the same, or even if it is substantially reduced, we will still run out. As the most intelligent creatures on earth, we must learn how to use our available supplies most efficiently.

Food and the energy crisis

It is generally accepted that over the next several decades a rising share of the growth of food production, in North America and Third World countries as well, will come more from increasing crop yields than from bringing

---

J. M. Ramirez is a commodity research meteorologist, Mars, Inc., Randolph, New Jersey.

new land under cultivation. The essential condition for increasing yields is
that farmers increase their use of nonland inputs per unit of land, principally fertilizer, pesticides, improved seeds, water, and often machinery. That
spells energy.

Twenty-two percent (3) of the total energy used in 1974 was related to the
production, processing, marketing, and consumption of food, natural
fibers, and forest products. Of this 22 percent, 16.5 percent is spent in the
chain from production through consumption. Only 3 percent is generally attributed to the farm production of the food that is eventually processed,
marketed, transported, and prepared for home consumption. Three percent
may be a small fraction of our total energy use, but it is the availability and

Table 1. Distribution of direct energy use in farm production.

Use	Amount (Percent)
Fertilizer	31
Irrigation	13
Farm vehicles	13
Pre-harvest field operations	12
Harvest operations	10
Grain/feed handling	8
Livestock care	6
Pesticides	5
Other	2

Table 2. Amount of fertilizer used versus energy stored in
corn crop.

Amount (Pounds of Nitrogen)	Return
The first 70	10 to 1
Next 70	9 to 1
Next 70	4 to 1
Final 70	1.5 to 1

cost of this three percent which starts the chain. That is, if farm production
is curtailed or becomes too costly, the rest of the chain all the way to consumer prices suffers.

Though food processing, marketing, and transportation consumes 13.5
percent of our total energy use and, as such, is quite relevant, let us explore
our energy use in farm production.

Nearly 90 percent of the energy used in farm production is to grow, harvest, and cure crops. About 10 percent goes to livestock production. It is interesting that our four major export crops—corn, wheat, cotton, and soybeans—consume over half of the energy use. We, in the global commodity
market, then have to be concerned about the consequent implications to our

day-to-day and long-term decision making. It used to be that our daily advisories to traders were primarily guided only by a constant monitor of crop/weather developments in key areas. Now we have to worry about the availability of oil and prices for fertilizers, irrigation, pesticides, and other materials. These prices may well decide potential acres, yields, and ultimately, stocks and future prices.

According to the Economic Statistics and Cooperative Service (ESCS), fertilizers consume the largest single component of energy in agricultural production (Table 1).

Table 2 shows, however, that at least for corn, an all-important export crop, the energy stored in the crop grossly exceeds that embodied in the fertilizers. The trade-off becomes critical when energy becomes too costly, or worse, when it simply becomes unavailable.

These figures may be revealing, but their relevance to our current energy crisis is further punctuated by the fact that the energy inputs to farming have increased enormously since the start of the century (3) and are continuing to rise. While our energy input to the food systems increased and shows no apparent sign of leveling off, the ratio of the farm output to each energy input apparently is tending to level off (4). Looking much like the exponential growth curve, the relationship suggests that, while there was nearly an exponential increase in farm output from each unit of energy input, it is quite likely that further increases in farm production from increasing energy inputs will be harder and harder to come by.

But while that may be so in a highly technological agriculture such as ours, it is not the case in the Third World nations or lesser developed countries, where about 85 percent of the world population resides. The greatest return per increment of fertilizer input would probably be achieved in most deficient areas, such as in lesser developed countries. While 30 to 40 percent of the increased productivity in the United States may be attributed to fertilizer usage, a comparable figure is 50 percent for the Third World nations (2).

World food problems developed with disturbing suddenness in 1972 (1, 6). World grain shortfalls in 1972 were repeated in 1974, and a world food crisis became a much talked-about political, social, and economic issue. In the background, climatic change, variability, and ominous signs of climatic instability worsened the fears of pessimists. The voice of the optimists, on the other hand, were somewhat echoed by the United Nations' own assessment for the World Food Conference in 1974 (1, 5). That conference recognized that the problems were serious, but that over the next decade, more food could be produced and that the conditions could be corrected.

Relief from world food problems is generally agreed to rely upon increased crop yields from limited agronomic lands. Realists recognize that this solution is beset by problems of its own: energy. In the late 1960s and early 1970s, euphoria about the "Green Revolution" cheered optimists. The period, interestingly, was also a period of re-emergence of world grain surpluses. But one must be reminded that "the revolution" depended primarily on high-yielding wheat and rice seeds that prosper only on the concomitant use of high-energy inputs, such as fertilizer and irrigation.

The question is worth reconsidering: Can we effectively export energy-intensive agricultural methods to Third World countries? Energy for fertilizers, irrigation, herbicides, pesticides, and machinery are needed for a green revolution in these countries, and yet many of these nations with the most serious food problems are also those with scant supplies of fossil fuel reserves.

What are the alternatives?

So what are the alternatives? Several alternative solutions and combinations of approaches have been suggested, tried, and many will still be proposed. These solutions may be generally classed into two basic approaches: save energy by more efficient use or seek alternate energy sources. A large number of studies, reports, and other discourses in the scientific journals and popular media have already been in circulation regarding these two alternatives.

It is a painful fact that the question of trade-offs will remain a thorny issue in energy development. Anti-nuclear power advocates continue to exhort the danger of "nukes." Environmentalists question the environmental impacts of coal development. Both point to solar energy as a more acceptable recourse. But the economic and the technical feasibility of solar power development are still in question.

The sad fact is that the technological world, as we have designed it, survives only because we still have some precious fossil fuel reserves remaining. This fact and the worsening of the world food problem suggest that the trade-off is not just energy development versus quality of life anymore. It may well be energy development versus the existence of life itself.

REFERENCES

1. Economic Research Service. 1974. *The world food situation and prospects to 1985.* Foreign Agricultural Economics Report No. 98. U.S. Department of Agriculture, Washington, D.C.
2. Ewell, R. 1974. *Testimony before the House of Representatives, Committee on Foreign Affairs, Subcommittees on International Organizatons and Movements and on Foreign Economic Policy, 93rd Congress, U.S. Policy and World Food Needs.* U.S. Government Printing Office, Washington, D.C.
3. Pimental, D., L. E. Huud, A. C. Bellotti, M. J. Forster, F. N. Oka, and O. D. Scholes. 1977. *Current energy use in the food and fiber system.* Beltsville Agricultural Research Center, Beltsville, Maryland.
4. Steinhart, J. S., and C. E. Steinhart. 1974. *Energy use in the U.S. food system.* Science 184: 307-316.
5. University of California Food Task Force. 1974. *A hungry world: The challenge to agriculture.* Berkeley.
6. Walters, H. 1975. *Difficult issues underlying food problems.* Science 188: 524-530.

19
Forest biomass energy potential

Thomas Anthony John Keefer

During this century, petroleum has become the dominant energy source, supplying about 45 percent of total world energy consumption. With a major fraction of proven oil reserves in the Organization of Petroleum Exporting (OPEC) countries, the ability of this group to escalate prices dramatically has been clearly demonstrated in recent years. Regardless of future OPEC production and pricing policies, however, it is apparent that petroleum supply will fall substantially short of anticipated demand by the turn of the century. Some analysts are predicting this shortfall to begin by as early as 1985, with sharp increases in prices and decreasing availability. Natural gas supplies and prices are expected to follow a similar pattern.

Canada will not be isolated from international oil scarcities and escalating costs. Oil and natural gas currently make up about 65 percent of total Canadian energy consumption and will continue to be the most important energy sources for the next 10 to 15 years (2). Canada is highly dependent on imported crude oil and recently moved from being a net exporter of oil to a net importer. Latest National Energy Board forecasts are for a shortfall of domestic oil supply relative to requirements of 650,000 barrels per day in 1985. At the Tokyo Summit, Prime Minister Joe Clark committed Canada to a target for net oil imports of a maximum of 600,000 barrels per day in 1985. Achieving this target will require continued conservation to keep a

Thomas Anthony John Keefer is director of Economic Studies and Program Development, Department of the Environment, Ottawa, Ontario, Canada. The opinions expressed in this paper are those of the author, and do not necessarily represent those of the Government of Canada or the Department of the Environment.

low growth of energy demand. In addition, expectations of new supplies from frontier areas and increased production of synthetic crude oil from tar sands and heavy oil deposits must materialize.

A requirement to import this amount of oil has continuing implications for Canada's strategic security of supply, balance of payments, and domestic inflation, all of which are matters of considerable concern. To illustrate: The expected annual import liability for 600,000 barrels per day in 1985 would be $4 billion to $6 billion (in 1977 Canadian dollars), depending upon future world oil prices. This import liability is comparable to the export earnings of the forest products industry, Canada's largest export sector. Steadily increasing world oil prices and the lower value of the Canadian dollar are likely to make the oil import account even worse. It is unclear how exports can be increased dramatically to pay for such imports, as other countries are also trying to do the same, and as more energy is needed in industrial expansion. Import substitution thus becomes important for both economic and strategic reasons.

Fortunately, Canada is well endowed with alternative energy sources. As world oil prices escalate, conservation, interfuel substitution, and increased efficiency in fuel use become increasingly attractive, as do development of alternative energy sources, such as tar sands, heavy oil, and frontier reserves. In addition, fuels derived from nonpetroleum feedstocks can become economically justifiable; coal, nuclear energy, and renewable resources in particular are receiving increasing attention. Recognizing that all of these courses of action need to be pursued to a greater or lesser extent in Canadian energy policy, I will focus on the potential contribution that forests can make to Canada's energy future.

Biomass energy

Biomass energy is the energy from the sun that has been captured through photosynthesis and stored in trees, plants, and animal matter. Biomass includes agricultural and forestry crops and residues as well as the wastes and by-products of all living things. Biomass represents a tremendous renewable source of energy. In Canada the annual capture and storage of solar energy by biomass far exceeds our energy demand.

Biomass can be used in direct combustion, or it can be converted by biological or chemical means into gaseous or liquid fuels or into electricity. Biomass can also be used to produce substitutes for high-energy products, such as fertilizers. Highly efficient wood stoves and wood-burning furnaces are currently being developed and marketed. Surplus field crops and residues are being used as fuel to dry grain and supply hot water, but on a limited scale. Canadians are experimenting with anaerobic hog manure digesters, which produce methane gas with effluents that can be used as fertilizer. Consideration is being given to various energy crops. Also, municipal solid waste is used to fire steam boilers in several Canadian municipalities, saving the costs of disposal of trash by landfill or incineration. While all of these approaches to using biomass for energy are of considerable interest, they are dwarfed by the current and potential energy use of the forest resource in Canada (3).

Increased interest in energy uses of forest biomass

A hundred years ago wood was North America's principal source of energy, but it was displaced by low-cost oil and natural gas. As the prices of these energy sources have risen, interest has returned to the use of forest biomass for energy, with the following factors being important (5):

• Forest biomass could provide perpetually renewable fuels in large quantities.

• Much forest biomass is available at reasonable cost.

• Wood as fuel causes little air pollution.

• Ashes can be returned to the forest area as fertilizer, maintaining soil fertility.

• Biomass fuel does not alter the heat balance or carbon dioxide balance of the earth.

• Hazards such as oil spills, gas leaks, or radiation are avoided.

• When forest biomass is grown, there are parallel benefits of recreation, wildlife, and soil and water conservation.

• Energy harvests from forests, representing years of growth, offer economic and security advantages over annual crops.

• Energy demand can be decreased through using wood in manufacturing

Table 1. Levels of forest biomass energy potential.

| | | Estimated Primary Energy | |
| | | EJ (10^{18} Joules) | Fraction of Present (percent) |
Time	Extent		
Present	Domestic wood heating, charcoal, mill wastes, kraft liquor	0.3	3.5
Medium term	Forest industry energy self-sufficiency, and electricity co-generation	0.6	7
Longer term	Replacement of transportation fuels and other petroleum products	2	20

Table 2. Programs to encourage forest biomass energy development.

	1978-1984 Amount
Forest Industry Renewable Energy (FIRE) program	$143 million
Biomass energy loan guarantees	$150 million
Energy from the Forest (ENFOR) program	$ 30 million
Large-scale prototype demonstrations (federal share)	$ 11 million (approximate)

and construction to replace higher energy-content synthetics.

While forest biomass is not generally regarded as playing a major role in Canada's energy picture, domestic wood heating, fuel wood and charcoal, kraft mill liquor, and mill wastes even now contribute about 3½ percent of Canada's primary energy supply of some 9.5 EJ annually (6) (1 EJ = 10^{18} Joule = 0.945×10^{15} BTU = 0.945 quad.). The potential contributions by biomass to Canada's energy picture can be conveniently expressed in terms of the two general levels of increased energy substitution shown in table 1.

Forest industry self-sufficiency and electricity co-generation

The forest industry is a major user of fuel oil and natural gas, accounting for 7.5 percent of Canada's total consumption of these. At the same time, the industry generates large unused quantities of combustible biomass and leaves larger amounts unrecovered in the woods. Canadian lumber and pulp and paper mills now burn hog fuel (bark, sawdust, and waste wood) to provide heat, process steam, and electricity. Extending the forest industry's woodlands operations could, by 1985, supply up to 0.6 EJ. This would involve the sustitution of mill residues, which in some localities constitute a pollution and disposal problem; logging residuals presently left at harvesting sites; surplus stands of unused species; and degraded, diseased, or overmature stands of timber. Forest industry self-sufficiency could result in a number of regions in Canada, and at some locations there is sufficient biomass available for utility complexes to generate energy to supply the associated communities (and the power grid) with electricity.

To achieve the objective of doubling, to 7 percent, the contribution of biomass to the national primary energy budget by 1985, the Government of Canada recently put in place four programs involving research and development, prototype demonstrations, and incentives for commercial implementation (Table 2).

Forest industry renewable energy (FIRE) program. The Forest Industry Renewable Energy (FIRE) program provides taxable contributions of up to 20 percent of the approved capital cost of equipment installed by forest industry firms to convert wood or bark residues to energy or a prepared fuel, or to burn sulphite pulp mill liquor to generate energy. In addition to fuel savings, job creation will be substantial; 24,000 person-years of employment are expected by 1984 in the forest industry and forest equipment supply industry.

Biomass energy loan guarantees. With other fuels increasing rapidly in price, reliance on local wood resources as a source of electricity has become attractive in some regions, for example, interior British Columbia, Northern Ontario, and Quebec. Federal loan guarantees will encourage groups of industries, in cooperation with nearby communities and possibly provincial utilities, to establish electrical generating facilities. For each province, two loan guarantees are offered: up to half the capital cost for new or expanded systems based on forest or urban wastes; and up to two-thirds if the high efficiencies associated with joint production of electricity and heat—for industrial processes or district heating—are achieved.

Energy from the forest (ENFOR) program. Much of the basic conversion technology already exists. Combustion of residues in boilers to produce steam and electricity is reasonably well established commercially. Further development and demonstration is, however, required on prepared fuels, including biomass gasification. (The gases produced can be converted to heat by combustion, used as a fuel for gas turbines or used as a chemical feedstock for the synthesis of liquid fuels or other commodities.)

Research is also required regarding the availability of the forest resource for energy production, at given price levels, as well as site-specific environmental impacts. Traditional inventories and production methods have been oriented towards "merchantable timber" for lumber, pulp and paper, and related products; harvesting biomass for energy introduces a new dimension into forestry operations.

To address all of these questions, the ENFOR program sponsors research, development, and small-scale demonstration contracts addressing forest biomass production (inventories; growth and yield; silviculture and harvesting; economic, social, and ecological impacts) and forest biomass conversion (feedstock preparation, prepared fuels conversion, and industrial chemicals conversion technology).

Large-scale prototype demonstrations. Large-scale prototype demonstrations will be assisted under federal-provincial agreements involving cost-sharing with industry; $114 million of federal funds have been allocated, of which about 10 percent is expected to go to forest biomass energy prototype demonstrations.

The Canadian Forestry Service of the Department of the Environment manages the ENFOR program; the other programs are managed by the Department of Energy, Mines, and Resources. These departments also coordinate Canada's involvement in the biomass energy activities of the International Energy Agency.

Replacement of transportation fuels and other petroleum products

In the longer term, the turn of the century and beyond, there is a potential for substitution of as much as 2 EJ of energy annually—up to 20 percent of current primary energy usage. However, questions have been raised about whether this is achievable because of the energy losses involved in conversion to the more useful energy products of methanol and electricity, and because of economic considerations (5). Whatever the exact potential, this would involve extensive harvesting of unused forest stands, including those economically inaccessible for conventional forest products alone, as well as large-scale use of intensive energy forest management concepts, including energy plantations of short and mini-rotation hybrids.

While biomass energy could involve a variety of markets, including electricity and chemicals, use in the transportation sector is the most likely. This sector accounts for about 25 percent of Canadian energy consumption, and this is where the energy crisis is most apparent. Interfuel substitution possibilities are limited, and only liquid fuels presently exhibit the mobility and storability features required. Alcohols, which can be produced from a range of biomass and nonrenewable resources, stand out as versatile and clean-burning alternative liquid fuels that could be brought on stream rapidly in significant quantities. World-wide interest in alcohols has therefore escalated, and several comprehensive government-sponsored studies have recently been undertaken in Canada (1, 3) to consider the feasibility of large-scale alcohol production and use, particularly methanol produced from renewable resources and used in transportation.

While a number of technical questions remain to be resolved, including gasification technologies, distribution of methanol, engine technologies, and emissions and performance in end use, these are expected to be solvable in a relatively straightforward manner. The studies concluded that methanol could be an attractive substitute for gasoline and diesel fuels and would become competitive as world oil prices rise (4). Methanol could have high values in blend uses and could be used in present cars with few modifications. However, because of the relatively low volumes of methanol involved, blend use is seen as a possible transition phase toward use of methanol as a straight transportation fuel. Priority uses of methanol would be in transportation, followed by displacement of middle distillates used in boilers, home furnaces, and process heating. Methanol also might be used for thermal electricity generation, especially peak load shaving; as a fuel for gas turbines or fuel cells; and as a feedstock for the chemical industry. These applications, however, appear less economic. Methanol production, distribution, and use appear to offer various environmental advantages over petroleum products.

Methanol produced by gasification of forest biomass alone as the feedstock, gas stream modification, and synthesis could be economic as a straight transportation fuel when oil prices reach about $25 per barrel and higher (1977 Canadian dollars). This feasibility depends highly on feedstock costs, which are generally expressed in dollars per oven dry ton or metric ton (Table 3).

Moreover, methanol produced from natural gas as the primary feedstock, with forest biomass as the secondary feedstock, would be economic as a straight transportation fuel when oil prices reach about $20 per barrel. If sufficient natural gas were available, large-scale production of methanol could result. And methanol produced from western Canadian coal would be competitive at oil prices of about $22 per barrel. Thus, while it is unlikely that forest biomass alone would initially be used in large-scale methanol production, it could have a major role if world oil prices rise dramatically.

The potential markets for methanol in Canada could be very large. Full penetration of the Canadian road transportation market by methanol as a straight transportation fuel by 2005, displacing gasoline and diesel fuel, would require about 50 billion liters (11 billion imperial gallons) of methanol per year. This volume of methanol contains 0.85 EJ of energy; if made from forest biomass, the primary energy content of the biomass is about 2 EJ. This volume of methanol is equivalent roughly to the displacement of 600,000 barrels of oil per day, the production from five tar sands plants.

While forest biomass represents the major renewable feedstock capable of supporting very large-scale methanol production in Canada, considerable debate is underway regarding the key questions of availability and price

Table 3. Competitiveness of methanol from forest biomass as a straight transportation fuel.

Feedstock Price		Methanol Competitive at Oil Price of ($ per barrel)
$ per ton	$ per metric ton	
10	11	24
20	22	28
30	33	32
40	44	36

of forest biomass. There are also some concerns that a methanol industry might displace traditional sources of wood supply to the forest industry. It is generally felt, however, that this would not occur and that use of residues, residuals, surplus stands, and energy plantations would be highly compatible with the movement towards more intensive management of Canadian forests.

The Canadian forest sector now harvests about 55 million oven dry metric tons (60 million oven dry tons each year), and leaves a similar amount of biomass behind as logging residuals. Moreover, this harvest includes what normally ends up as mill residues. The Canadian forest sector harvest is expected to rise to some 90 million oven dry metric tons (100 million oven dry tons) per year by the end of the century. The volumes of forest biomass that could be involved in large-scale methanol production are significant in comparison with these harvests. For example, production of 50 billion liters of methanol per year from forest biomass would require about 90 million oven dry metric tons of wood feedstock per year. Even using natural gas and biomass as combined feedstocks, 50 billion liters of methanol would require at least 15 million oven oven dry metric tons (16 million oven dry tons) of wood biomass, plus 1 trillion cubic feet of natural gas—about one-half of Canada's current domestic consumption!

The following biomass supplies are forecast to be available after meeting traditional fiber demands. At $22 per oven dry metric ton and below, some 7 million oven dry metric tons of mill residues and logging residuals will be available in 1985, largely in interior British Columbia. At $33 per oven dry metric ton, over 52 million oven dry metric tons of these residues and residuals could be available annually from 1985 to 2025 throughout Canada, although there is likely to be considerable competition for these for forest industry on-site steam and heat generation. At higher prices, up to $44 per oven dry metric ton, volumes of over 92 million oven dry metric tons per year could become available annually from 1985 to 2025 throughout Canada, including significant outputs from energy plantations. Figure 1 shows this biomass availability, and the methanol production that could be associated, at various price levels. It is noteworthy that, for each region in Canada, the forest biomass supply appears adequate to meet regional transportation fuel demands.

While Canadian forest products companies do not presently think of themselves as potential liquid fuel energy producers, and while there are obviously major institutional difficulties that would have to be overcome, development of a large-scale methanol industry could offer significant opportunities: new markets for forest biomass, involving products of high and increasing value; more efficient utilization of the forest resource, with inte-

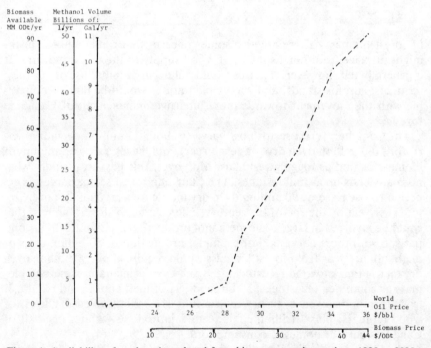

Figure 1. Availability of methanol produced from biomass at various prices, 1985 to 2025.

grated harvesting and mill operations; manufacturing of new harvesting and conversion equipment; and employment of 50,000 to 60,000 person-years annually. This employment generation, falling largely in slow-growth areas across Canada, would be particularly significant.

The possibility of large-scale methanol production and use in Canada raises a number of important energy policy issues. In light of technical and economic questions and the variety of other alternatives open to Canada, there is a clear need to proceed with our investigations on a number of fronts. Thus the Canadian government is also studying the full range of alternatives appropriate for the latter part of this century and beyond.

Conclusion

Canada's forest biomass has the potential to make a major contribution to meeting our energy demand. A number of activities are now underway to promote forest industry energy self-sufficiency and electricity co-generation, with the objective of doubling, to 7 percent, the contribution by forest biomass to Canada's primary energy consumption. Studies of longer-term possibilities have focused on the production of methanol and its use in the transportation sector.

These developments could have major industrial and regional development implications, in addition to the benefits of improved balance of payments and security of energy supply.

Although forest biomass energy initiatives are being spurred by the anticipated petroleum price and supply situation, they also offer an important opportunity for more rational development of Canada's forest industry and complete utilization of the forest resource. Significant advantages could result, including a more diversified product base, increased employment, and improved industry profitability.

REFERENCES

1. Advisory Group on Synthetic Liquid Fuels. 1978. *Liquid fuels in Ontario's future.* Ontario Ministry of Energy, Toronto.
2. Department of Energy, Mines, and Resources. 1977. *Energy—The task ahead.* Report E177-1. Ottawa, Ontario.
3. Intergroup Consulting Economists Ltd. 1978. *Liquid fuels from renewable resources: Feasibility study.* Department of the Environment, Ottawa, Ontario.
4. Keefer, T.A.J. 1979. *Some implications of large-scale methanol production from Canadian forest biomass.* In Proceedings, Third International Symposium on Alcohol Fuels Technology. University of Santa Clara, Santa Clara, California.
5. Nautiyal, J. C. 1979. *The place of forestry in the energy question.* Canadian Journal of Forest Research 9: 68-75.
6. Overend, R. 1978. *Energy and the forest industry.* Renewable Energy Resources Branch Technical Note 5. Department of Energy, Mines and Resources, Ottawa, Ontario.

20
Air storage system energy transfer (ASSET) plants

Z. Stanley Stys

The power generation patterns of society will probably change only slightly in the not-too-distant future. Nuclear and sophisticated, super-critical fossil plants will be the bulk of the base load electric power supply.

Since these plants are costly and efficient, they must be kept loaded to the highest possible level, thus necessitating suitable energy storage facilities.

Such facilities, in order to present advantages over those presently used for this purpose, such as old power plants, gas turbines, cycling units, etc., must operate using much less oil or gas than the present units. They must be less costly than the cycling units. They must be simple to install and operate. Air Storage System Energy Transfer (ASSET) plants fulfill all these requirements. Using only one-third of the oil or gas that gas turbines use, they cost only about half of what a cycling unit costs. They can start in six minutes in an emergency, and no outside power is required to start them. Compared to cycling units, they save on the fuel necessary to keep boilers on fire waiting for the load to come. Partial-load operation is more efficient than a gas turbine and is comparable to steam turbine partial-load efficiency.

ASSET cycle diagram

Figure 1 is a diagram of the ASSET plant. Ambient air is compressed by an axial-flow compressor, intercooled, and boosted up in a high-speed cen-

Z. Stanley Stys is vice-president of Brown Boveri Corporation, North Brunswick, New Jersey.

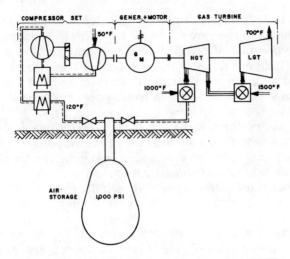

Figure 1. The Air Storage System Energy Transfer (ASSET) plant.

trifugal blower to 70 bar. Aftercooling follows air discharge, before leading to an air storage facility. The generator is used as a motor during the compression cycle.

During the peaking cycle, air is led from the underground storage through a control valve, where the pressure is throttled down to 43 bar at full load before reaching the high-pressure combustion chamber, where it is heated to 550 °C. After passing through a portion of the expander, the gases are reheated in a low-pressure combustion chamber to 830 °C, and upon passing through the end of the expander, the gases are then exhausted to the atmosphere.

The economic foundation of the ASSET plant was the applicability of the high-pressure ratio gas turbine. The standard open-cycle gas turbine operating with a pressure ratio of 1:10 was too low to make this air storage facility economical. A storage pressure of 70 bar greatly reduced the necessary volume of such facility.

To avoid an excessively high pressure drop between the storage cavity and the first expansion stage, several rows of blading were added in the front of the gas turbine, based on experience with a standard steam turbine design. The parameters of the gas entering the first stage of this expander are 43 bar and 550 °C, the parameters of an old-fashioned steam turbine.

Huntorf 290 megawatt ASSET plant

The Nordwestdeutsche Kraftwerke (NWK) of Hamburg, West Germany, ordered the world's first ASSET plant in June 1974. The NWK power system supplies electric power in the coastal area of the Federal Republic of Germany (Figure 2). The company serves a population of some 4.5 million over an area of 34,000 square kilometers, about one-seventh of the entire re-public, and has the highest growth rate of any utility in Germany.

The big proportion of NWK's nuclear capacity requires efficient load management. The NWK supply area is virtually flat and does not permit the installation of a conventional pumped-hydro storage plant which, so far, is the only commercially available load-leveling device at the generating end of an electric power supply system.

The subsoil of northern West Germany, however, contains about 200 salt domes. Most of these domes are well suited and have partly been utilized for underground storage of mineral oil and natural gas. They are also expected to be used for disposal of radioactive wastes.

Two caverns were leached in one of the salt domes to provide for 150,000 cubic meters volume each, sufficient to cover 2 hours full load peak of the NWK system.

The air-storage facility at Huntorf was created by a well-known solution mining or leaching process (Figure 3). Two concentric pipes are introduced in a borehole. Freshwater, pumped through the inner pipe, dissolves the salt and becomes saturated with it. The resulting brine is pumped up the other pipe, and then taken directly to the sea or disposed of in the saltwater aquifer.

The installation is simple (Figure 4). The building has a crane that can service the heaviest piece, with the exception of the generator stator. The whole plant is 40 meters by 20 meters and has a stack 35 meters high. The installation is totally remotely controlled over a 200 kilometer distance. There are no personnel in the plant.

No electric power is necessary to start the unit. This is achieved by leading

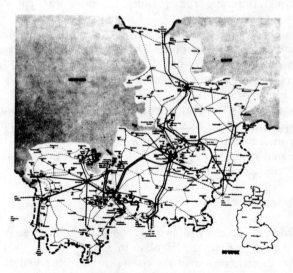

Figure 2. The NWK supply area.

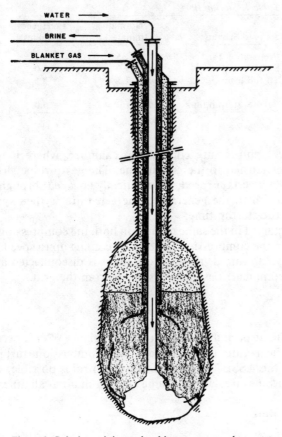

Figure 3. Solution mining or leaching process used to create air storage facility.

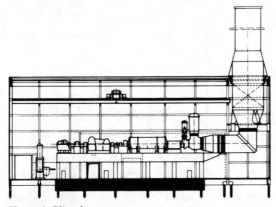

Figure 4. Plant layout.

Table 1. Startup time.

Steps to Startup	Normal (minutes)	Emergency (minutes)
Preparation for start	.5	.5
Synchronize	3.0	3.0
To full load	7.5	2.5
Total startup time	11.0	6.0

the air to the high-pressure combustion chamber, where it is heated to 1,000 °F and exhausted to the gas turbine. The gas turbine shaft starts to rotate and is, at a certain speed, automatically engaged through a synchro-self-shifting clutch to the generator. The generator is then synchronized. Table 1 gives the startup time.

The unit is started in the same manner in both the compression and generation cycles. In the compression cycle, after coming up to speed, the motor-generator is synchronized, then the expander is disconnected and, finally, compression commences as energy is taken from the grid.

Performance

The heat rate at partial load of an ASSET plant (WV) is better than the partial load heat rate of a conventional combustion turbine (WVG) because, with the ASSET plant, mass flow control is possible, whereas the combustion turbine circulates the same amount of air at all times (Figure 5).

Sixty-cycle module

Brown Boveri Corporation was selected as a member of the two teams investigating the feasibility of ASSET plants using two different types of air

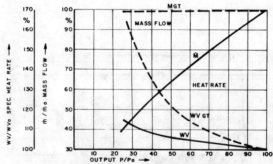

Figure 5. Partial load of the air storage gas turbine and open-cycle gas turbine.

storage facilities. Both studies are sponsored by the Department of Energy and the Electric Power Research Institute (EPRI).

Middle South Services is investigating the feasibility of the installation of ASSET plants in the future generation mix in the system of the Middle South Company's operating companies. Louisiana Power Company or Mississipi Power Company will be chosen to install the first ASSET plant. Both companies have a large number of salt domes in their supply territory where a convenient air storage facility can be established.

Potamac Electric Company, Washington, D.C., selected Acres American

Table 2. Committed new generating plants, fossil and nuclear, per year, 1979-1997.

	Fossil		Nuclear	
Year	Number of Plants	Megawatts	Number of Plants	Megawatts
1979	30	13,250	8	7,917
1980	34	17,139	11	10,959
1981	33	15,113	15	15,987
1982	27	14,042	14	14,241
1983	27	13,702	10	10,472
1984	30	14,813	18	19,483
1985	34	13,962	13	15,010
1986	25	10,559	11	12,645
1987	20	11,130	9	10,033
1988	14	7,668	10	11,136
1989	6	3,635	3	3,740
1990	3	1,375	4	4,226
1991	2	975	3	3,730
1992	1	300	0	0
1993	2	796	2	2,530
1994	0	0	2	2,600
1995	1	625	0	0
1996	1	625	0	0
1997	1	625	0	0
Indef.	16	5,778	7	7,558
Totals	307	146,112	140	152,267

of Buffalo, New York, as the architect-engineer to investigate the feasibility of underground pumped-hydro and ASSET plants using a rock-mined cavern as the air storage facility. Brown Boveri Corporation was selected as the turbomachinery expert investigating different machinery configurations.

General application of ASSET plants to the utility's system

Before adopting energy storage, an electric utility must be assured that favorable economics exist. The obvious economic benefits are the replace-

ment of high-cost fuel with low-cost fuel and better utilization of large base
load units. A less obvious benefit is that even though no energy conservation is attained, scarce fuel conservation can be realized if relatively abundant fuels, nuclear or coal, can be used to replace oil or natural gas. In addition to gaining favorable economics and reducing scarce fuel consumption,
the utility must also be assured that the storage system will mesh properly
with the utility's other capacity on a daily, seasonal, and annual basis.

The main prerequisite of ASSET plants is the availability of off-peak
power from nuclear- and coal-fired plants. Table 2 presents the committed
capacity of this type in the United States.

The basic idea of load management is to improve system efficiency, shift
fuel dependency from limited to more abundant energy resources, reduce
reserve requirements for generaton and transmission capacities, and improve reliability of service to essential loads. The ups and downs in daily
electric power demand can be smoothed by installing an energy storage system that could accomplish the above-mentioned goals.

The availability of salt domes in the Gulf Coast area is shown in figure 6.
Salt mining companies have defunct mines (leached out cavities) in many
areas. These can be easily adapted to create a convenient air storage facility.
The salt deposits, where such facilities can be found, are shown in figure 7.

The porous rock trapped between layers of impermeable strata can also

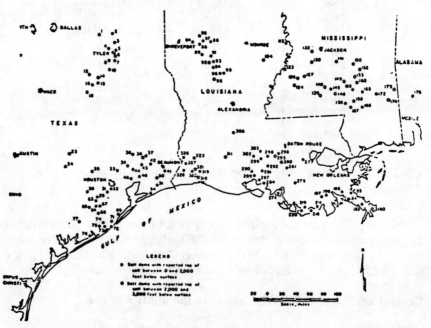

Figure 6. Onshore salt domes that offer good possibilities for salt extraction or underground
storage sites.

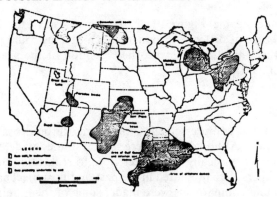

Figure 7. Rock salt deposits in the United States.

☐ FAVORABLE
☐ LESS FAVORABLE
▨ UNFAVORABLE

Figure 8. Aquifer storage facilities.

be used for a potential air storage facility. The technique of storing natural gas in aquifers has been known for decades. Aquifers are available throughout the United States and Katz's book, *Compressed Air Storage,* gives specifics of this type of storage possibility. There are areas within the United States where such aquifer storage facilities can be erected (Figure 8).

The National Science Foundation sponsored a study of the suitability for air storage in New England rock formations with the conclusion that New England's rock formations are suitable for the creation of tight air storage facilities. A hydraulically compensated cavern is probably the most suitable solution for these cases. Figure 9 shows the basic idea of such a constant pressure facility.

Since the earth for millions of years held gas under pressure, there is no reason air could not be stored in this same facility. The same goes for empty oil wells. Defunct iron, potash, and other mines could also be used if proven sound and impermeable. Figure 10 locates numerous caverns that have been mined for storage of different products. Such caverns could also be mined throughout the United States, with the exception of the shaded areas, to create air storage facilities.

Conclusions

The idea of the compressed air storage gas turbine peaking plant is basically not new. Although there were several studies made, some of them still active, there is basically no project close to realization in this country yet. Several papers were presented in the past on this subject and theoretical cost analyses and comparisons were made, some of them quite conclusive.

However, the fact that there is the Huntorf plant in successful operation has resurrected a great interest among utilities and architect-engineers all over the United States. With the availability of salt domes; aquifers; depleted oil and gas wells; defunct salt, potash, iron and other mines, there is a natural potential to build such plants all over the country. Even a man-made cavern, specially excavated for air storage, is not too exhorbitantly high in cost, compared with today's extra additions to fossil and nuclear

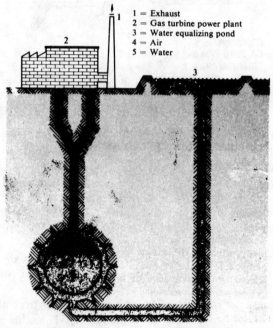

1 = Exhaust
2 = Gas turbine power plant
3 = Water equalizing pond
4 = Air
5 = Water

Figure 9. Hydraulically compensated cavern.

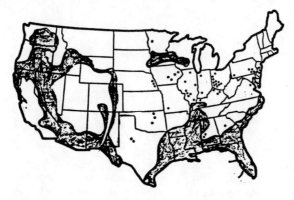

Figure 10. Caverns that have been mined for storage of different products.

plants to comply with environmental and safety requirements only.

With the inevitable growth of nuclear generation, future base load will be generated more and more by this type of plant. Since the peaks grow historically higher and higher, there will be a requirement for finding adequate energy storage, to use energy generated by more efficient and economical base load plants rather than cover them with the inefficient gas turbines that use gas and oil. Air Storage System Energy Transfer plants can accomplish this.

The availability of different possibilities for creating a convenient air-storage facility, such as salt domes, aquifers, mined caverns, defunct mines, depleted oil and gas wells, etc., gives practically every utility in the United States the possibility of building an ASSET plant.

With coming solar and wind energy in the future, such facilities will be almost indispensible due to the intermittent character of these energy sources.

The basic idea to be able to transfer off-peak power to the peaking period, to have a better load factor on the machines, or to defer new capacity investments is appealing to many utilities.

Building an energy storage facility similar to pumped-hydro storage presents a definite advantage from an environmental point of view.

Thus, it is hoped that the Huntorf plant fulfills industry expectations and its example will be followed by other utilities in the United States and around the world.

VIII. ENVIRONMENTAL QUALITY ISSUES IN RESOURCE-CONSTRAINED ECONOMIES

21
Key environmental issues in Canada

Monte Hummel

Once a year in Canada, the auditor general reports to Canadians on how the government is spending our money. This financial audit always brings with it scandalous and sometimes even humorous accounts of waste and inefficiency. I often wonder what the results of an annual biological audit might be. It seems we have carefully honed our tools for measuring all aspects of economic output. Yet we don't have even a crude annual audit of the general welfare of society which all this economic growth is supposed to promote. Nor do we rigorously audit the biological base upon which economic growth depends.

My intention is to give you something of a biological audit, or at least a whirlwind, cross-country tour of environmental quality issues that exist within Canada. The audit is going to be somewhat short and superficial, but let's at least have a look, starting with the Northwest provinces and moving eastward.

Environmental quality issues

In the Yukon Territory mining development is probably a primary concern along with the transportation network that must be put in place to support it. Hydro proposals, in support of both mining and pipeline develop-

---

Monte Hummel is executive director of the World Wildlife Fund, Canada, Toronto, Ontario.

229

ment, threaten many rivers in this part of Canada, especially the Yukon River. Pipelines themselves have been the focus of public and private attention. A particular concern is their impact at river crossings. The Dempster Highway, built to service development in the far north, literally cuts the territory in two. It also bisects the range of migratory caribou herds and has been called a study in how not to proceed when it comes to large-scale development. New wilderness areas and parks have recently been proposed for the Yukon, and already there are conflicts about appropriate uses within them.

In the Northwest Territories exploration and drilling for oil and gas in the High Arctic stand as key environmental issues. This also entails transportation by ice-breaking tankers, with the associated threat of oil spills. The McKenzie Valley pipeline has been quite thoroughly debated and no doubt will be built, though not as originally proposed. There is another proposal for a pipeline from the High Arctic down the west coast of Hudson's Bay. Mining west of Baker Lake has attracted protest on the part of the Inuit Tapirisat. Arsenic from gold smelters is an environmental problem in Yellowknife. Wildlife sanctuaries and new parks have also been proposed for the Northwest Territories. It is here that debate in the future will likely focus around native hunting and fishing rights (and commercial hunting) and the impact they have on wildlife populations, especially on species that are endangered (such as the bowhead whale) or those that are seasonally vulnerable (such as spring bird populations).

Forestry is a key industry in British Columbia, Canada's western, coastal province. Accordingly, logging practices and the rate and method of forest regeneration are constant issues. There are conflicts with wilderness groups, especially those trying to protect the Queen Charlotte Islands; and there are questions surrounding forest spraying practices, as well as spraying in orchard and fruit-growing areas. Herbicides, such as 2-4-D, are being used to control millfoil weed in Okanagan Lake. The damming of salmon rivers, especially the Fraser, is a long-standing issue in British Columbia, which also now faces proposed oil and gas transport by tanker very close to the Canadian coast through areas such as the straits of Juan de Fuca. British Columbia has also been the province where regulation of big game hunting is an issue, as is nonspecific control of predators, such as indiscriminate poisoning programs for wolves.

In Alberta energy is the name of the game. Development of the tar sands presents a sophisticated technological challenge, and entails large capital requirements. In this province are world-renowned western mountain parks, such as Banff and Jasper. Proposals for large developments, such as the one at Lake Louise, or twinning the Trans Canada Highway that passes through both parks, have challenged national parks policy. In cities such as Calgary and Edmonton, which are experienceing tremendous growth with the oil and gas boom, urban sprawl and appropriate planning are now issues. In southeastern Alberta and southwestern Saskatchewan acid rain has arrived as an issue.

Moving east to Saskatchewan, which is Canada's most intensive agricultural province, mention must be made of all the environmental quality issues associated with pesticides, herbicides, fertilizers, and the energetics of agriculture. The loss of prairie habitat to agriculture and drainage of wetlands is of great concern to wildlife biologists. In fact, it has been suggested that the short-grass prairie habitat itself be classified as endangered.

In Manitoba water diversion schemes, such as the Garrison project, are of great concern. The possibility of introducing exotic species and a host of pollution and watershed problems surround this international issue. Cottage development on large but shallow lakes is beginning to loom large in Manitoba. Although the province is principally agricultural, the Whiteshell area in the Southeast, located on the Canadian Shield, has been proposed as a site for deep geological deposit of nuclear wastes.

I could not sufficiently outline the environmental quality issues facing the province of Ontario. Rather than elaborate I will simply list a few: water quality in the Great Lakes, population pressures in urban centers, urban air and water pollution, municipal solid waste disposal versus recycling, loss of prime agricultural land to urbanization, disposal of toxic industrial waste (for example, PCBs), mercury pollution, acid rain, occupational health of workers in the uranium and asbestos industries, floride poisoning on Cornwall Island, and parks policy in the face of a wood shortage for the forest industry. It is also in Ontario where the main focus for nuclear power development exists because Ontario Hydro has by far the most ambitious expansion program in the country. Ontario's prosperity is reflected in the scale of the environmental issues facing it now.

Within Quebec, Montreal still contributes hundreds of gallons of raw sewage every day to the St. Lawrence River. Hull, only a stone's throw away, is another example of a Quebec center where even proper primary sewage treatment is lacking. The James Bay Project, a massive hydroelectric scheme, has gone ahead despite a skimpy joint federal-provincial environmental impact study. The asbestos industry poses problems for workers and is about to be expropriated by the provincial government. Both acid rain and mercury problems are surfacing in different areas of "La Belle Province."

Finally, in the Maritime and Atlantic provinces, key issues are spraying for the spruce bud worm (New Brunswick), nuclear power development (New Brunswick), soil erosion and land ownership (Prince Edward Island), tidal power and siltation on the Bay of Fundy, pollution from a heavy water plant (Nova Scotia), and localized water pollution from sewage and the pulp and paper industry. Oil spills have and continue to be a real concern off Canada's east coast. These concerns are only heightened by the increased tanker traffic associated with the proposed facility at East Port Maine. Perhaps this kind of problem will help Americans better understand why there is some reservation in Canada about a much trumpeted "continental energy pact."

The waters off Newfoundland at one time harbored some of the world's greatest fish stocks. The history of fishing here gives sorry testimony to the inadequacy of the whole theory of management by sustained yield. It just has not worked with marine resources, including seals and whales.

Key issues

I suppose the foregoing is a rather gloomy, distorted national picture, almost a catalogue of ecological horror stories. What key issues emerge?

I am told that Canada's new minister of the environment lists as his national priorities acid rain, toxic wastes, and Great Lakes water quality. My hunch is that the following four issues will emerge as the key ones in Canada over the next five years: (1) the future of nuclear power, as a symbol of the hard versus soft energy path; (2) continued exploitation of oil and gas reserves in the northwestern and High Arctic, with resulting concern expressed by nations other than Canada; (3) the little understood interaction of toxic chemicals found in our water, air, and food; and (4) the impact of native claims for traditional hunting and fishing rights on wildlife populations, especially those species that are officially classed as threatened or endangered.

There was a time when we so-called environmentalists fought like fury to get concern for environmental quality accepted and institutionalized in North America. When you look at the staggering array of current government departments, environmental institutes, university programs, environmental planners, environmental managers, commissioners of public inquiries, special reports, royal commissions, task forces, green papers, white papers, journals, workshops, seminars, and conferences, there can be little doubt about the degree to which this concrn has become institutionalized.

But I wonder. Going back to my original notion of a national biological audit: To what extent has all this talk and institutionalization benefited the environment itself, as opposed to those of us who have made careers out of a concern for it? In other words, perhaps the quality of our concern is one of the most pressing environmental issues facing all of us today.

22
Resource and environmental issues in the Canadian Arctic

A. H. Macpherson and John Mar

The Arctic is a prime example of a resource-constrained economy. Whether we think of the natural biological economy, the traditional human economy that developed there, or the recent technical economy that is currently being injected into or superimposed on the Arctic, the operations of the economy are severely constrained by available resources.

The Canadian Arctic consists roughly of the northern third of Canada. It is the region with the lowest population density in the country, but paradoxically it is the most seriously overpopulated in terms of the land's ability to provide a living.

We have all heard of the wooly mammoths excavated from Siberian permafrost after a cyrogenic entombment of several millenia with flesh still edible (*18*). Such anecdotes emphasize the fact that waste disposal in the Arctic is not a new problem. Indeed, the garbage dumps of arctic explorers with their soldered cans of Bovril pemmican, still edible after a century but of dubious palatability, are distinctive historical monuments north of 60° North latitude.

The earliest human cultures of the Canadian Arctic, of the Paleolithic,

---

A. H. Macpherson is director general for the Western and Northern Region of Environment Canada, Edmonton, Alberta. J. Mar is director of the regional branch of that department's Environmental Protection Service in Edmonton. The authors acknowledge the assistance of E. F. Roots, principal scientific advisor for Environment Canada, in preparation of this manuscript. Photographs were provided by Environment Canada and Peter Bannon of Yellowknife, Northwest Territories.

have left little for us to find other than chips, shards, and tools of stone. The subsequent Thule culture, sea-mammal hunters, left large ground stone tools and a wealth of ivory, antler, and bone implements. Their heavily turfed winter house ruins yielded less durable objects of wood, baleen, and even skin. Burial in collapsed structures was followed quickly by the penetration of permafrost. The mammoths mentioned probably suffered a similar fate, possibly in mud-slips or under collapsing banks.

Ancestors of arctic peoples lived as an integral part of the web of life. Their numbers fluctuated with the numbers and availability of prey animals. Their material possessions were made mostly of biodegradeable, local materials. Their dogs ensured that digestible garbage did not accumulate. The dead were not buried in the permafrost as they are now, but left to re-enter the nutrient cycle through the activities of scavengers and degraders.

The earliest European inhabitants of the Arctic, traders, policemen, and missionaries, also left little evidence of their presence because they were not lavishly equipped by their sponsors, the goods they used were limited by the costs of a long, difficult journey and recycling was undoubtedly prevalent.

It was not until the 1940s and 1950s that the throw-away culture invaded the Arctic in the form of efforts associated with World War II and subsequent distant early warning radar line construction. Mementos of that era mark the North today, such as toppled antenna towers, military equipment and airstrips, dumps of empty fuel drums, and abandoned machinery along the Canol Pipeline route from Norman Wells to Alaska.

The Arctic is as dependent on what happens in other parts of the globe as is any other zone, perhaps more so, because the predicted warming due to carbon dioxide accumulation could have as its most significant effect the diminution of arctic ice, with profound concomitant effects on sea levels, atmospheric circulation, plant zonation, surface water chemistry, and so forth (*10, 13*).

Resource development activity

Natives of the Canadian Arctic exploited and traded certain nonrenewable resources—flints for stone lamps and tools, native copper for arrowheads, etc. Apart from that, and from a more commercial point of view, the first mine in the Canadian Arctic was perhaps that of Martin Frobisher, still to be seen on an island in Frobisher Bay after 400 years (*14*).

However, the issues we wish to address properly start with the post-war prospecting and oil exploration activity. Petroleum exploration came into environmental prominence because it brought seismic survey practices into the permafrost zone with disastrous results initially. The problem was thermokarst erosion resulting from stripping off the active layer (*9*).

Some resulting scars will probably be visible until the next cycle of glacial erosion or marine deposition reshapes the arctic landscapes. As Clarke (*4*) asked, "Who are these people that they should put their mark on the landscape for all time?"

The past decade saw a tremendous acceleration of these activities and, fortunately, a tremendous advance in environmental awareness and know-how by companies participating in resource explorations (*11*), as well as regulatory agencies (*19*). The technology is now highly diversified with drill ships, artificial islands, and strengthened sea-ice platforms all routinely employed in our arctic seas.

The next decade, especially the next few years, will see us well into a new phase of production and transportation of arctic mineral resources. Both tankers and pipelines will undoubtedly be deployed for oil and gas production. The effectiveness of our legislation and regulations and the efficiency of our technologies and management in controlling use of resources from the Arctic while not destroying the land, its productivity, and its people will be put to the test.

Features of the Arctic environment

The arctic environment has been described from one point of view as "unrelenting, harsh, unforgiving, and demanding" and from another as "fragile and tender." These epithets are all valid, but for many reasons (*3, 6*). The arctic environment is a harsh adversary to those who import technology from the subtropical and temperate environments of the southern United States and the Gulf of Mexico. The winter is long, cold, and dark; the navigation season is short and uncertain. For all practical purposes there is no such thing as a growing season. Where the vegetation mat is the essential buffer between thawing summer air temperatures and the frozen mud that underlies much of the arctic tundra for hundreds of meters, and when that vegetation is close to the limits of maintenance and growth, one easily can conceive that its protection and nurture is a difficult, yet essential, task (*1*).

The low ambient temperatures do not encourage chemical weathering, nor do they favor microbial activity. The Siberian mammoth has his modern counterparts in sewage lagoons whose contents tend to retain their distinctive characteristics for a distressingly long period of time. Furthermore, the low ambient temperatures encourage the survival of bacterial pathogens (*2, 5*).

It is interesting to note that arctic animals tend to have correspondingly low production rates. Barren ground caribou, for example, take years longer to mature than temperate zone deer, and their harvestable surpluses are tiny in comparison. Other species, such as lemmings and snow geese, are so close to their environmental limits that the winter snow thickness and its persistence in the spring determines their breeding success on an annual basis (*17*).

Because the ground is generally frozen, water tends to lie on the surface, and little exchange takes place through the groundwater column. Vegetation's chemical composition rather faithfully depicts the nature of materials precipitated on the site from the atmosphere. The possibility that there might be consequent food-chain effects became apparent during the era of atmospheric nuclear bomb testing in the late 1950s when unexpectedly high radionuclide loads were found in northern animals and people. Environmental impact analyses of major future developments will have to take this phenomenon into account.

Another problem is the frequency of inversions that contribute to the prevalence of ice fogs (20) and limit the dispersion of toxic emissions, which tend to accumulate near sources (10).

Circulation of water in the seas and straits between the lands of Arctic Canada is characteristically slow. Because precipitation and runoff contribute more freshwater than is lost by evaporation and because progressive freezing and melting rejects salt to deeper waters, the salinity of surface waters is comparatively low. For much of the year the sea ice forms an extension of the land on which people and land mammals travel. This is hardly surprising in the Central Arctic, but it is noteworthy that the people of Northwest Greenland occasionally cross with dog teams to the shores of Ellesmere Island. Even Hudson Bay has been traversed by Inuit with sleds during these periods.

Ice is a fact of life. The stable ice of winter becomes pack-ice in late summer. Some is swept into permanent polar pack which spirals around, getting lumpier as pressure causes it to pile up and fracture in new places. Old sea ice is easily recognized by its weathered immensity.

Another form of ice, though less common, must also be reckoned with—the iceberg. Icebergs are chunks sloughed off glaciers entering the sea, which track down from Baffin Bay to the Labrador Sea and Newfoundland. A few are carried into the westward channels of the archipelago.

In addition, there are so-called ice islands, which share characteristics of both the permanent polar pack and icebergs (15). Ice islands are large pieces of ice up to 750 square kilometers in area and 30 meters thick that have broken away from the large, floating ice-shelves that lie along the coast of the most northerly island. These generally join the Arctic Ocean gyral, through which they proceed slowly, gradually fragmenting as they travel through the archipelago or into the North Atlantic Ocean.

Ships are impeded and endangered by hazards other than ice. The Beaufort Sea receives vast contributions of silt from the Mackenzie River so that in places of particular interest to oil development the seas are shallow and sandbanks numerous. Some shoals or banks have a core of permafrost beneath the sea bed. The Eastern Arctic, on the other hand, is slowly rebounding from the weight of the last continental ice-sheets; and the rising, rocky coastlines, for example, the Keewatin coast, are rife with shoals and reefs. Detailed charting and installation of navigational aids will take years to complete.

To cope with these hazards, ships for arctic service require ice breaking capability, ice strengthening, and unusually sophisticated navigational and remote-sensing capabilities. In the coming period of year-round navigation in Canadian arctic waters, mariners will have to cope with unprecedented physical problems of darkness, icing, pressure, and wind, as well as with the social and psychological results of isolation and stress.

Marine oil pollution

The potential for serious pollution by oil spills from tankers and terminals operating in the Canadian Arctic is obvious. Industry sources indicate that chronic spillage from marine terminals will be on the order of 0.5 percent of the oil moved. Even this will result in a great deal more spilled oil than anyone wants to see on our seas and shores. Accidents will give us additional problems, accidents ranging from someone leaving a valve open to the wreck of a loaded vessel.

We must admit that we lack the technical capability to deal with oil spills in the arctic seas. The natural processes of evaporation and microbial degradaton are ineffective due to low ambient temperatures. The same difficulty makes burning of spilled oil a possibility only in summer. Oil under ice or incorporated into ice is hard to reach, let alone contain or destroy.

One concern is that spilled oil will migrate to polynia or open leads on which wintering or migrating waterfowl and alcids rely. We could be facing future catastrophic mortality of marine bird populations and perhaps sea mammal populations as well.

Baseline data compilations of environmental information have been made (8), and experiments are underway to evaluate threats and to deal with oil spills. The Canadian Wildlife Service is participating in experiments to determine if polar bears are harmed by spilled crude oil. Under the government/industry Arctic Marine Oil Spill Program (AMOP), numerous experiments are underway on the technical problems of containment and cleanup. No one, however, is optimistic about the chances of coming up with a technological "quick-fix."

Features of Arctic communities

The Inuit are a people in transition. Less than two decades ago, some communities maintained a subsistence economy akin to that which prevailed at the time of the first white establishments. This way of life has virtually disappeared. The Inuit now live in small southern-style communities built around the store, nursing station, school, church, and cooperative.

The workforce is generally underemployed. The above institutions, plus police, airfield, weather station, hotel, and other businesses, provide a few jobs. Town utilities, such as water, sewage, garbage collection, provide others. Migration in and out of the community is high among the whites and low among the Inuit.

Extension of the social infrastructure from southern Canada has progressively insulated the Inuit from health or nourishment limitations imposed by their environment, and populations have burgeoned as a result. The numbers and concentration of people at present make subsistence living impossible. Though "country food" remains important, it is no longer the mainstay of life.

The Inuit have attained a certain political power as the electorate for Northwest Territories' members of the legislative assembly and for a member of Parliament. More such power will fall to them as the government of the Northwest Territories gathers provincial-type responsibilities. They are also on the verge of real economic power, which is expected to come with the conclusion of land rights negotiations.

Social and economic impacts

Industrial developments in the Arctic are burdened by high transport costs and, consequently, are expensive operations. There is emphasis on maximizing production per employee per hour and minimizing investment in infrastructure.

For many enterprises, a self-contained workcamp provides the best solution. Employees are flown in from their homes in the South to work long hours for a period of a few days, after which they return to the South for a respite. Such workcamps can accept indigenous employees if enough can be hired at nearby settlements to make the shuttle service economic. But there is little need for unskilled labor, and the operations are frequently too transient to make on-the-job training economical.

This pattern minimizes the social impacts of development on people in arctic communities. However, the high wages paid workers introduce major disparities in income to settlement life. Predictably, it has also led to a serious problem of alcohol abuse.

The people of the Arctic are also concerned about the impact developments may have on their subsistence resources, such as caribou, marine mammals, polar bears, and fish. As a group, they are not yet ready to rely completely on the larger society for the satisfaction of their social and psychological needs. Subsistence resources give a comforting alternative in the cultural context.

However, some influences of consumerism have already had severe impacts on certain features of environmental quality. Solid waste disposal is difficult in the Arctic where burial requires the excavation of frozen drift, if not solid rock. What goes North from factories in the South stays there. Little disappears unless it is dumped into the lakes or sea. More resistant objects, such as vinyl fragments, plastic bottles and toys, paper boxes, filter tips, and tin cans, litter almost every site of human habitation.

Indeed, if cost-effective delivery of utilities and services were the governing criterion, Canada would not choose to settle her people in the permafrost-underlain northern half of the country. Heating and lighting are demanding and expensive problems. Water and wastewater systems can only be supplied through heated ducts or utilidors. Wastewater treatment is inefficient. Owing to the vast distances, expensive satellites are necessary to handle northern communication systems reliably. Mobility demands heavy investment in equipment and airfields, resulting in high operating costs over vast distances transporting small payloads.

Use and recovery of arctic resources

Renewable resource harvesting, providing it does not exceed harvestable surplus, causes environmental impacts of a local and temporary nature. Fishing, lumbering, trapping, hunting, and tourism generally produce minimal impacts. Certain species have been affected by excessive slaughter, however. The Greenland or bowhead whale populations were severely reduced in the late 1800s, and have not yet recovered to even a fraction of the number that existed a century and a half ago. The polar bear population was severely reduced in the Soviet Union after World War II and its recovery has since been slow. Musk ox populations on the Canadian mainland may not yet have fully recovered from the excessive slaughters of the early decades of this century (4). And some Canadian barren-ground caribou herds and arctic char runs as well continue to decline in the face of excessive annual harvests. Arctic forests grow so slowly that their renewability is little more than a theoretical concept. Indeed, climatic and soil changes may be such that if the present trees were removed, the same species would not regenerate.

Fishing and fish processing can be profitably pursued by communities because the principal arctic food fish, the arctic char, commands premium prices. Trapping and fur clothing manufacture is practiced at several community co-ops, but skins are still shipped to the South for tanning and return.

Tourism is increasing with the establishment of new national parks in the Arctic. Several thriving guest lodges are in operation, the attraction being the opportunity to catch trophy fish.

Nonrenewable resource activities, on the other hand, are carried out as heavily capitalized mechanized ventures and can result in rather major impacts (7). Mining is nonetheless an important contributor to the northern economy because it generates new wealth from within the Arctic and offers steady jobs. Since the 1940s, this industry contributed some 90 percent of the combined value of production in the Northwest Territories. Gold and uranium were the first minerals sought in the Northwest Territories. Arsenic, a by-product of the roasting of gold ores, has presented containment problems and been a major concern of regulatory agencies. Containment is satisfactory at present, but long-term storage of the waste depends on the maintenance of the permafrost that holds the material.

Oil and the Arctic environment

The oil and gas industry began production in the Northwest Territories at Norman Wells in 1936 (11). Exploration for oil began in the Mackenzie Delta in the 1960s, but major expansions occurred after the Prudhoe Bay,

Alaska, strike in 1968 and the Atkinson Point discovery in 1970. The quest is now largely offshore in the Beaufort Sea and the High Arctic. Artificial islands have been built to drill in the shallow waters off the mouth of the Mackenzie River. These have obvious advantages, particularly for production wells, but they pose problems by disturbing the sea bed and near-shore breeding grounds in biologically critical areas. Drilling from specially strengthened areas of sea ice was pioneered by Panarctic; so far over two dozen holes have been drilled. The first hole spudded by a drillship in ice-covered waters in the Canadian Arctic was in 1958 in Hudson Bay. The major current program is in the Beaufort Sea but a number of companies have drilling programs planned for eastern Arctic waters. Two, in fact, are already drilling off the coast of Baffin Island.

Arctic marine drilling requires vast logistic support operation and presumably an imposing financial support operation as well. It is highly transient as well as seasonal. Staging, vehicular support, weather and ice formation systems, positioning systems, operationally ready blow-out prevention, oil spill tracking, and clean-up procedures and machinery must all be managed in concert with the drilling project. Environmental concern has focused on the risk of accidental oil spills, but any such massive intrusion entrains many more prosaic potential impacts that planning and monitoring must control. The drilling operation itself is significant because of the amount of material that is discharged into the sea. Composition of drilling mud is very important in this connection.

The concern over chronic oil spills in the production phase has already been mentioned. However, immediate concern focuses on the potential for blow-out, particularly in the light of the recent episode in the Gulf of Mexico, which spewed 30,000 barrels a day into a comparatively pristine marine ecosystem. Such a spill in the Beaufort Sea would degrade the area for decades.

Operating conditions under which Arctic exploratory drilling projects take place have the strictest regulations applied anywhere. Particular restrictions are applied to minimize the risk of blow-out late in the year when a relief well can no longer be drilled. No one, however, can completely guard against the risk of equipment failure or human error, and the stakes are great.

Impacts of community development

The development of communities has local effects that bring about impacts directly on the lives of the inhabitants. Much can be done to adapt communities to the North, to control the distribution of snow drifts, to protect people from the weather, to trap sunlight, and so on. Community water supplies must be protected from contamination, for example, from fuel supplies, and refuse disposal grounds should be downwind and hidden.

But what of power needs? Today most small northern communities still depend on local diesel electric plants. Only a few use hydropower. Major power-using developments, for example, gas plants and pipelines, could change this picture radically for many communities. The impacts of hydro-electric dams are well-known. The drowning of productive river valleys by the filling of head-ponds and the effects of the reversed hydrograph downstream are phenomena that have been studied extensively. Such effects can be severe in the Arctic, where valley floors play a critical role in the ecosystem, where the biological cycle is delicately balanced on changes in timing of the hydrological cycle. The alternative to blocking lake outlets and raising their levels to improve storage capacity has another set of impacts: flooding of the permafrost can lead to thermokarst effects and solifluction, which may degrade the productive capacity of aquatic ecosystems. In view of these serious consequences, alternative power technologies, such as small nuclear power plants, might be competitive.

Transport systems, particularly railways, roads, and pipelines, each have a train of environmental consequences. Some of these are controllable, given effort and financing. For example, if forcing a stream through culverts makes it too swift for fish to ascend, a bridge could be an appropriate, if expensive, alternative. Some problems are not so easily overcome. One in particular that looks at first to be trivial is a consequence of snowplowing. Roads and railbeds become traps for roving mammals, and the mammals are often forced to run in panic along the track from an approaching vehicle. With the slim margin of energy possessed by arctic animals in winter, any animal forced to flee in panic, even if it is not hit, is likely to die soon after it escapes.

Road building in the North requires attention to preserving the permafrost and natural drainage. Winter trails also require precautionary work to ensure the terrain is not damaged. Scraping loose snow into trails to ensure that vehicles can run on this pad is a common practice. Successful regeneration of cuts requires careful preplanning (12).

Pipelines present special problems. The construction of the Alyeska line was a major breakthrough for innovative technology, both in the elevated sections and in constructing the berm that contains the buried portions. A gas line through this terrain will present quite different problems because gas, unlike oil, can be chilled. An unresolved problem is the best temperature for gas passing through discontinuous permafrost—too warm and the ice will melt, too cold and groundwater will freeze to it.

Socioeconomic considerations

A 1972 federal policy statement, "Northern Development in the Seventies," gave the government's priorities as people first, environment second, and nonrenewable resource development third. In practice, resource development decisions for the North are taking into account the environment implications through the current federal "Environmental Assessment and Review Process." If and when all possible protective and mitigatory measures are implemented, certain irreducible impacts to the environment and the northern communities will remain. The ultimate decision will necessarily involve trade-offs. These, as in the case of energy resource developments, will often be to the advantage of the southern society and to the disadvantage, temporarily at least, of the North.

Reconciling all affected interests will become increasingly difficult if each application is treated as a separate problem. Perhaps a longer term resource development plan that recognizes the compatible and the competitive needs of the northern communities will become a necessary focus for participatory social planning in the future. As Hemstock (*11*) suggested, "There must be a master plan for orderly arctic development."

Conclusion

We described representative examples of environmental issues within the context of a summary review of industrial and social development in the Canadian Arctic. We attempted to treat these with some sense of proportion. The socioeconomic aspects of environmental quality issues are acknowledged as dominant, but no simple solutions have been proposed to the problems identified. Indeed, the rationalization of northern environmental and social risks resulting from resource use and recovery is being justified at present only in terms of prolonging present lifestyles in the South.

As one thoughtful commentator reacted to the recent pipeline enquiries by Justice Berger and Mr. Kenneth Lysyk, "Both reports fail to deal with the most important question in the North today: the development of some sort of moral and ethical basis for action there. To do this will require close scrutiny and understanding of the motives and assumptions of decision-making in southern Canada. Their territory is less known, and more perilous, than the Canadian North has ever been" (*16*).

A restatement of government policy that addresses the issues of the eighties and makes a new commitment to forward planning for Canada, for the Inuit, for industry, and for the environment are among today's challenges. They are as formidable as any arctic challenge of the past. We must find ways of both protecting and making full and responsible use of the land and its resources while ensuring freedom to its people.

REFERENCES

1. Barnett, D. M., S. A. Edlund, and D. A. Hodgson. 1975. *Sensitivity of surface materials and vegetation to disturbance in the Queen Elizabeth Islands.* Arctic 28(1): 74-76.
2. Bell, J. B., J.F.J. Zaal, and J. M. Vanderpost. 1976. *The bacterial quality of lake waters at Yellowknife, Northwest Territories.* Arctic 29(3): 138-146.
3. Bliss, L. C. 1970. *Oil and ecology in the Arctic.* In F. K. Hare [ed.] *The Tundra Environment.* University of Toronto Press, Toronto, Ontario.
4. Clarke, C.H.D. 1973. *Terrestrial wildlife and northern development.* In Arctic Alternatives. Canadian Arctic Resources Committee, Ottawa, Ontario.
5. DiGiovanni, C., et al. 1962. *Some microbiological and sanitary aspects of military operations in Greenland.* Arctic 15(2): 155-159.

6. Dunbar, M. J. 1973. *Stability and fragility in arctic ecosystems.* Arctic 26(3): 179-185.
7. Eedy, Wilson. 1974. *Environmental cause/effect phenomena relating to technological development in the Canadian Arctic.* NRCC No. 13688. National Research Council, Ottawa, Ontario.
8. Fenco Consultants Ltd., and F. F. Slaney and Co. Ltd. 1978. *An arctic atlas: Background information for developing marine oil spill countermeasures.* EPS-9-EC-78-1. Environment Canada, Ottawa, Ontario.
9. Haag, R. W., and L. C. Bliss. 1974. *Energy budget changes following surface disturbance to replant tundra.* Journal Applied Ecology 11: 355-374.
10. Hare, F. K. 1968. *The tundra climate.* The Arctic Quarterly Journal 94(402): 439-459. University of Toronto Press, Toronto, Ontario.
11. Hemstock, A. 1970. *Industry and the arctic environment.* In F. K. Hare [ed.] *The Tundra Environment.* University of Toronto Press, Toronto, Ontario.
12. Jackman, A. H. 1973. *The impact of new highways upon wilderness areas.* Arctic 26(1): 68-73.
13. Kellogg, W. W. 1978. *Effects of human activities on global climate—part II.* World Meteorological Organization Bulletin 27(1): 3-9.
14. Kenyon, N. 1975. *All is not golde that shineth.* Beaver 306(1): 40-46.
15. Koenig, L. S., K. R. Greenaway, Moira Dunbar, and G. Hattersley-Smith. 1952. *Arctic ice island.* Arctic 5(2): 67-103.
16. Lotz, Jim. 1977. *Northern pipelines and southern assumptions.* Arctic 30(4): 199-204.
17. Mackay, G. A. 1970. *Climate: A critical factor on the tundra.* In F. K. Hare [ed.] *The Tundra Environment.* University of Toronto Press, Toronto, Ontario.
18. Nordenskiold, A. E. 1881. *The voyage of the Vega round Asia and Europe.* McMillan and Co. London, England.
19. Riddick, J. 1974. *Conservation of tundra.* In J. S. Maini and A. Carlisle [eds.] *Conservation in Canada, a Conspectus.* Publication No. 1340. Environment Canada, Canadian Forestry Service, Ottawa, Ontario.
20. Robinson, E., W. C. Thurman, and E. J. Wiggins. 1957. *Ice fog as a problem of air pollution in the Arctic.* Arctic 10(2): 89-104.

23
Constraints imposed on agriculture by water quality management planning

Melville W. Gray and Gerald A. Stoltenberg

Change is said to be constant. Over the years we have seen continual change in the shift of population from rural to urban development. The urbanization of America was accompanied by the development of a technological society and, in most states, a shift in political structure from rural to urban areas. Technological advances enabled the farmer-rancher to operate more efficiently on an ever-increasing scale to provide the food and fiber to support society. These changing conditions resulted in larger farms and ranches, but fewer farmers and ranchers, thus contributing further to the change in the political influence structure from rural to urban.

Today, the nation and the U.S. Department of Agriculture (USDA) are having difficulty in defining what constitutes the family farm. Size of the farm in terms of acreage has distinct problems for definition purposes, as does gross income or percent of individual income. The situation is further complicated as more and more individual farm families seek supplemental income by employment within the urban areas on a full- or part-time basis.

Throughout the years, urban growth and development has been accompanied by increased environmental stress. Society, within an urban setting, that we believe is an inherently unnatural setting for man, rebelled at the continued environmental insults and demanded clean water, clean air, safe

Melville W. Gray is director and Gerald A. Stoltenberg is deputy director of the Division of Environment, Kansas Department of Health and Environment, Topeka.

drinking water, control of toxic materials, restrictions on pesticides, general refuse control, improved environmental working conditions, and, in general, a preservation of nature and natural considerations for the benefit of all.

To further the demands of society, comprehensive and complicated laws have been enacted. Massive control programs with severe penalties of $25,000 to $50,000 per day have been authorized and may be imposed for violations of these environmental requirements. Under law, authorities have been granted to agencies at the state and federal levels to not only stipulate and establish environmental standards, but also to specify specific types of treatment for control of environmental insults, as evidenced in the Safe Drinking Water Act of 1975 and the Clean Water Act of 1977.

Restraints on farmers

Some segments of society in the United States look upon the American farmer as the last of the independents, a sort of free spirit with a minimum of constraints, who can work the land at his will. Without enumerating or considering marketing and other financial constraints, the average American farmer has been constrainted by an ever-increasing number of environmental requirements. The use of pesticides is carefully controlled. Many pesticides require licensed commercial applicators or training and certification of the farmer. Farmers are required to control noxious weeds under penalty of law, and, in the event of over zealous application or drift of the pesticide causing damage to off-site silvaculture or fisheries, the farmer is subject to penalties under water quality statutes and/or punitive damages. The value of death of migratory waterfowl has been established at $500 each by the controlling federal agency and the courts. Irrigation return flow must be carefully controlled and, in most cases, reapplied because of the organic content and increased mineralization to comply with water quality law. Under water quality law, feedlots are carefully controlled to prevent pollution of both surface and groundwaters. Feedlots and dairy farms are not only subject to controls for prevention of pollution to both surface and groundwaters, but also are subject to general sanitation requirements for prevention of significant insect and rodent problems. In the case of Grade A dairy farms, the farmer must provide for acceptable sanitary considerations in the construction of his water supply well and domestic sewerage system for his residence.

The farmer now is subject to installation of back-flow prevention devices on irrigation wells where fertilizers or other chemicals are added to the water system prior to application. He must also properly plug abandoned water wells to prevent surface contamination to the groundwater aquifer.

The air quality control program is relatively new to the farmer, although general soil conservation practices have long been an important but unheralded aspect of particulate pollution control. Statutory authority for control of wind erosion by emergency tillage has been in effect for many years. The control of particulates from feedmills are within the jurisdiction of statewide air quality control programs or are activated on a complaint basis. Odor control or the prevention of odor, particularly related to animal feedlots and dairy farms, is a problem facing the farmer, with additional court precedents being established each year either under general nuisance statutes or through formal air quality control programs. In Kansas, odor is listed specifically as an air pollutant; and it is the state's responsibility, through the air quality control statutes, to abate odor pollution where it is determined to be significant to the extent that it interferes with enjoyment of life and property.

A relatively new constraint within the environmental field is ambient noise. While we know of no formal regulatory programs for imposing noise standards in the agricultural community, recourse is available through the courts under general nuisance statutes, particularly where noise interferes with the sleep of nearby residents. Our agency has been involved with complaints of noise with animal-feeding floors and even the installation of irrigation wells adjacent to or across the road from farm residences.

The matter of water rights has long been with the farmer. Aside from the principal objective to obtain and maintain a quantity of water, he is further constrained by legal requirements relating to any changes in a drainage course where it leaves his property. Additional statutory requirements may be imposed relating to both water rights and to structural safety where surface impoundments are constructed.

In this quick review of environmental constraints, it would appear that the farmer is not the free spirit that some have contended. It is the prudent farmer who looks both to the left and right, up and down, and all around before undertaking a new operation or making significant changes in an existing operation.

"The" Act

On October 18, 1972, the Federal Water Pollution Control Act (P.L. 92-500) became a reality. There can be no question that this water law is the most comprehensive and complete environmental statute enacted. It is also perhaps one of the most cussed and discussed statutes ever enacted. Within this book-length document, Congress originally established six goals and six significant policies. These were amended in 1977 to include two additional policies, one of which is pertinent to the subject at hand. It is also desirable to set the stage by reiterating certain of these goals and policies as they relate to the agricultural community.

Within the goals, Congress states "(1) It is the national goal that the discharge of pollutants into navigable waters be eliminated by 1985...(5) It is a national policy that areawide waste treatment management planning processes be developed and implemented to assure adequate control of sources of pollutants in each state...."

Among the pertinent policies as established by Congress, the first is "(b) It is the policy of the Congress to recognize, preserve, and protect the primary responsibilities and rights of states to prevent, reduce, and eliminate pollution, to plan the development and use (including restoration, preservation, and enhancement) of land and water resources...."

Originally the final policy was as follows: "(f) *It is the national policy that to the maximum extent possible the procedures utilized for implementing this act shall encourage the drastic minimization of paperwork and the interagency decision procedures, and the best use of available manpower and funds, so as to prevent needless duplication and unnecessary delays at all levels of government"* (emphasis added). The new policy, much to the relief of most states and of significance to agriculture, is as follows, "(g) It is the policy of Congress that the authority of each state to allocate quantities of water within its jurisdiction shall not be superceded, abrogated, or otherwise impaired by this Act. It is the further policy of Congress that nothing in this Act shall be construed to supercede or abrogate rights to quantities of water which have been established by any state, federal agencies shall cooperate with the state and local agencies to develop comprehensive solutions to prevent, reduce, and eliminate pollution in concert with programs for managing water resources."

Water quality management

To provide for areawide waste treatment management, Section 208 of P.L. 92-500 required the governors of each state to establish an agency or agencies to develop a statewide management plan to restore and maintain water quality and otherwise achieve the goals of the act. These statewide plans, among other things, were required to identify measures necessary to carry out the plan, the time necessary, the cost of carrying out the plan, and the economic, social, and environmental impact of carrying out the plan. Section F required "a process to (i) identify, if appropriate, agriculturally and silvaculturally related nonpoint sources of pollution, including return flows from irrigated agriculture, and their cumulative effects, runoff from manure disposal areas and from land used for livestock and crop production, and (ii) set forth procedures and methods (including land use requirements) to control to the extent feasible such sources...." Within numerous other paragraphs of Section 208, reference was made to agriculture, irrigation, and land controls and protection.

Congress adopted significant new amendments to Section 208 in 1977. These amendments authorized the secretary of agriculture, with the concurrence of the administrator, to provide cost-share monies, through contracts with rural landowners, to incorporate best management practices to control nonpoint source pollution for improvement of water quality. Various restrictions have been imposed for entering into these contracts, including the requirement to maintain the best management practices throughout the life of the contract. Failure to maintain such practices could require the landowner to reimburse the federal government for cost-share funds. The transfer of title or interest in the rural land, having participated in cost-share monies, requires that the new owner-operator agree to fulfill the conditions of the contract or the original owner must reimburse any cost-share funds received. The whole intent and purpose of this new language is to provide a mechanism of management and cost-share funds to institute best management practices for nonpoint source pollution control that specifically will benefit and improve water quality. This new program and the cost-share funds are not intended to supplant the soil conservation cost-share programs, which are designed to protect soil resources.

Are federal agencies serious in their attempts to achieve the national goals for water quality through the restoration of the nation's water system? The answer to this question should be apparent. Over the past seven years Congress allocated billions of dollars annually to provide for upgraded treatment of municipal wastes and to require and enforce regulations and standards over industrial sources, prevention of detrimental discharges from mine lands, and the restoration of such lands.

Congress is aware that the original estimate for restoring the nation's waters, with total control of all municipal effluents, was $18 billion. In a short two years after enactment of P.L. 92-500, National Water Quality Commission studies indicated that the cost of total implementation of statutory requirements and achievement of the goals would exceed $350 billion. Through the intervening years Congress has become aware that even though municipal waste treatment and industrial waste treatment facilities rapidly were approaching completion, in most instances and certainly in agricultural states, significant overall improvement in the quality of water was not approaching the national goals. Throughout the years, the funding priorities of the Environmental Protection Agency (EPA) tended to restrict grants for other than sewage treatment, and the recent amendments to the Water Pollution Control Act have further restricted grant eligibility for municipalities. The Congress however has not reduced or eliminated requirements for control of all sources of water pollution.

The Kansas water quality management plan

Kansas' governor appointed the Department of Health and Environment, through the Division of Environment, to be the lead agency responsible for developing a statewide water quality management plan under the requirements of Section 208 of P.L. 92-500. After establishing an outline for planning and technical elements, a technical planning committee was established, consisting of thirteen water-related state agencies and the Soil Conservation Service (SCS). This committee was responsible for developing technical solutions and preparation of detailed technical reports that form the basis for the water quality plan.

A planning and policy advisory committee was also established, consisting of two units: the state and federal agency unit, consisting of 24 agencies, and a local government unit, consisting of 36 representatives from cities, counties, conservation districts, watershed districts, and others. The com-

Table 1. Kansas 208 planning alternative analysis process. *

Management Category	BMP or Technical Capability	Environmental Benefit or Quantif.	Economic Impact (+) or (−)	Political Accept- ability	Recommended Control Program†	Priority	
Agricultural runoff	Alt. 1	%	$	−		#	
	2	%	$	+	Best mandatory	#	Yield attainable water quality standards
	3	%	$	−		#	
	4	%	$	+	Best voluntary	#	
Municipal waste treatment	Alt. 1	%	$	+		#	
	2	%	$	+	Best mandatory	#	
	3	%	$	−		#	
Mineral intrusion	Alt. 1	%	$	+	Best mandatory	#	
	2	%	$	−		#	
	3	%	$	+		#	

*Alternative solutions developed by the major planning agencies will be analyzed considering factors of environmental benefit, economic impact, and political or social acceptability.
†The total of control programs chosen must be within projected available resources in two categories: (1) federal construction grant money; (2) state, local, and private money. The total commitment of resources for control programs chosen must be within that which the state economy will bear. This will be a legislative determination based on plan recommendations and national input factors such as artificial pricing systems and subsidies.

mittee was to review and comment on a continuous basis throughout the development of the plan.

The foundation for the Kansas water quality management plan is the application of an alternative analysis process (Table 1). This process involves the consideration of alternate levels of treatment within each of the fourteen categories contributing significant pollutants, such as agricultural runoff, industrial wastes, etc. For each level of technical control capability or treatment within each category quantification of results were determined as follows:

• The environmental benefit relating to water quality.

• The economic impact, including both capital costs and overall state monetary benefits. In agricultural runoff considerations, this also included a separate determination for economic benefits to agriculture.

• The political and social acceptability for each alternate level of treatment.

• A recommended mandatory or voluntary control program for each alternate level of control.

• Prioritization and time schedules for implementation of statewide control programs by category.

From the beginning, it was recognized that implementation of the statewide plan would depend on continued availability of federal construction grants, and cost-share monies and programs must be within the means of the state, local, and private sector. Additionally, cost effectiveness of many portions of the plan could be influenced significantly by artificial pricing systems and subsidies. Consequently, the completed water quality management plan was submitted to the 1979 Kansas Legislature for consideration, modification, and endorsement. After studying the plan, the legislators endorsed the plan and enacted five new statutes for early implementation of the plan. They now are considering other actions for subsequent sessions.

Perhaps one of the unusual factors relating to the water quality management plan is that, through endorsement or adoption by the legislature, the alternative level of treatment or control endorsed in the plan has become best management practices for the state of Kansas. Additionally, the Department of Health and Enviroment, as the water quality agency, has been instructed to adopt state water quality standards that can be met through implementation of the plan. This might be considered contrary to EPA's policy of adopting water quality standards and then developing an implementation plan that will meet these predetermined water quality standards.

Table 2. Statewide water quality index (WQI)*—incremental increases in WQI resulting from implementation of each pollution source category.

Source and Treatment Level		High Flow Less than 10% of Time		Low Flow More than 90% of Time	
		Increment of WQI	Resulting WQI†	Increment of WQI	Resulting WQI†
Municipal	Level I		49		82
	Level II	1.2	50.2	1.4	83.4
	Level III	0.4	50.6	0.9	84.3
Stormwater†	Level I		49		
	Level II	0.1	49.1	No contribution	
	Level III	0.2	49.3	at low flow	
Agriculture runoff†	Level I		49		
	Level II	7.6	56.6	No contribution	
	Level III	9.6	66.2	at low flow	
Industrial	Level I		49		82
	Level II	0.5	49.5	0.8	82.8
	Level III	0.0	49.5	0.0	82.8
Construction†	Level I		49		
	Level II	0.1	49.1	No contribution	
	Level III	0.1	49.2	at low flow	
Mine drainage	Level I		49		82
	Level II	0.1	49.1	0.2	82.2
	Level III	0.1	49.2	0.3	82.5
Mineral inflow	Level I		49		82
	Level II	0.4	49.4	0.6	82.6
	Level III	0.6	50.0	0.8	83.4
Total state-wide WQI	Level I		49		82
	Level II		59		85
	Level III		70		87

*Those waters with indexes above 60 or 70 will generally meet requirements of the Kansas Water Quality Standards.

†Resulting WQI represents the improvement from implementation of each individual source category proposal.

To provide for evaluation of cost benefits and environmental benefits, alternative levels of treatment were predetermined for each of the categories of investigaton. Three such alternative levels were determined.

• Level I, existing level. This level corresponds to existing treatment practices and infers that there will be no additional cost over and above those already incurred.

• Level II, intermediate treatment level. This level of treatment essentially is equivalent to the first proposed level above existing treatment practices corresponding to a minimum increase in treatment practices above existing levels and requires an increase in cost over and above those already incurred.

• Level III, full treatment level. This level roughly corresponds to the concept of zero discharge of pollutants insofar as this concept appears to be technically feasible in Kansas.

Sources contributing significant quantities of pollutants in Kansas were analyzed within fourteen categories as follows: (1) municipal sewage systems, (2) industrial waste, (3) feedlot waste, (4) residual waste, (5) petroleum activities, (6) salt mining, (7) coal mining, (8) mineral resources, (9) agricultural runoff, (10) urban stormwater, (11) construction erosion, (12) combined sewers, (13) irrigation, and (14) mineral intrusion.

Each source category then was analyzed for each of the three levels of treatment and their contributions and impact upon environmental quality compared through the use of a water quality index adapted from the procedures developed by the National Sanitation Foundation. The water quality index approach was previously applied and validated by the National Sanitation Foundation in the Kansas River Basin.

Agricultural analysis, soil loss. Specifically for agriculture and the relationship of soil conservation to water quality, treatment levels were defined as follows.

• Level I. The present conservation land treatment program to protect the soil base projected by increments to the year 2000.

• Level II. This treatment level assumes that all land areas involving agricultural runoff are adequately protected from erosion to protect the soil base. Presently 50 to 60 percent of the approximately 53 million acres of agricultural land are considered to be adequately protected for preservation of the soil resource.

• Level III. It is assumed that all land areas involving agricultural runoff are treated to level II and additional treatment is provided necessary to reduce the discharge rate of sediment to streams to that estimated to have existed before the effects of man's land use activities.

Table 2 shows the results of this analysis. It can be concluded that agricultural nonpoint source runoff is the most significant influencing factor during periods of rainfall runoff and increased stream flows. It must also be recognized that effects of agricultural runoff can be more significant within a given stream segment as opposed to statewide considerations. The effect on segments can be more significant because of attenuating factors that are directly proportional to increasing areas of tributary watersheds.

Of the approximately 53 million acres of land in the state of Kansas, USDA's Kansas Conservation Needs Inventory evaluated approximately 49.5 million acres of land and determined that ± 30 million acres consisted of cropland and 18 million acres of pasture and rangeland. In Kansas, Midwest Research Institute studies indicate that sediment yield from cropland is 87 percent and from range and pastureland 12 percent. The Water Quality Management Plan concluded that sediment loads delivered to streams for level I range over the state from 0.5 to 3.3 tons per acre per year; level II, 0.5 to 1.3 tons per acre per year; and level III, 0.1 to 0.6 tons per acre per year.

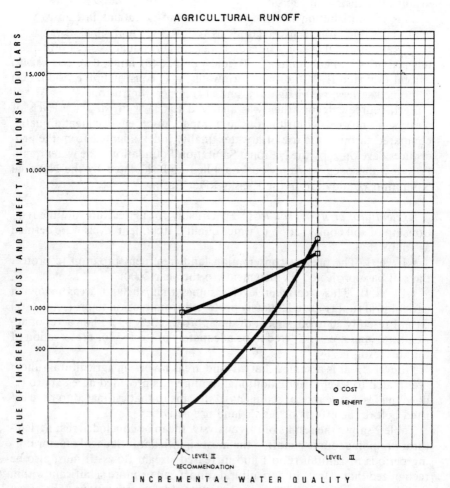

Figure 1. Comparison of cost and benefits at alternative water quality conditions.

The cost to reach level II is estimated at $508 million, with an annual maintenance cost of $11 million. The cost to reach level III is estimated at $3.6 billion, with an annual maintenance cost of $26 million. Within the present annual funding rate for soil conservation practices, it would require 30 years to reach level II. If level II were to be reached within a 20-year period, which is the consideration for the water quality management plan, certain additional benefits from an economic standpoint could accrue to both the landowner and state water resources. Figure 1 depicts the cost-benefit relationships of this incremental program acceleration. In comparison with figure 2, the incremental water quality benefits indicate a benefit-cost relationship for agricultural runoff of about 5.5, while the final statewide

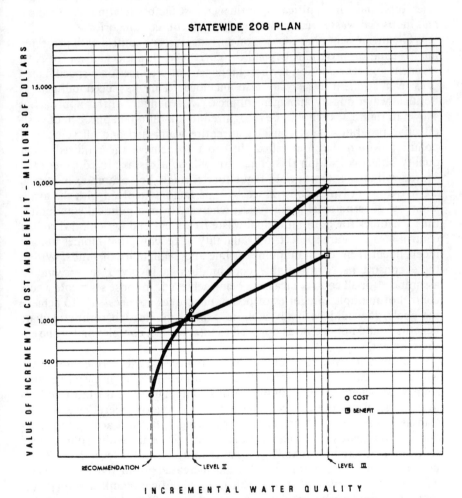

Figure 2. Comparison of cost and benefits at alternative water quality conditions.

water quality management plan, at the recommendation level of implementation and financing, provides a benefit-cost ratio of about three.

The continuing planning process

As provided for in federal law and as dictated by common sense, the continuing planning process for water quality control is essential if the objectives are to be achieved within an acceptable economic framework. New factors relating to control programs will continually surface and must be considered. Of particular importance is the current energy crisis. Energy trends were not reflected in the economic analysis of the Kansas Water Quality Management Plan. This will have considerable impact on recreational benefits resulting from use patterns on state and federal lakes and reservoirs, and will significantly influence cost factors relating to municipal and industrial waste treatment as well as all source categories.

While the present plan is based on current levels of control with projected implementation programs beyond the current level, a mechanism for reassessment and reevaluation for best management practices on a specific area or stream-segment basis was also included. This has been defined as "critical water quality management area." A schematic of this approach is shown in figure 3. It should be recognized that a rational approach of cost-effective programs must consider an entire watershed and all sources of pollution within that watershed. In order to achieve the required water quality objectives within this concept it will be necessary to consider each source within the appropriate regulatory format. For example, industrial waste treatment is not constrained by time factors involved with the availability of governmental grant funds; whereas, from a political standpoint, time schedules for both municipal waste treatment and agricultural runoff control measures are subject to availability of federal grant monies but are independent from the standpoint of time and availability of funds. Within these constraints, considerable coordination is involved in arriving at assurances for all control measures being achieved. In those segments where control of multiple categories of pollutant sources are necessary to achieve the goals, it would be inadvisable to expend monies where intermediate benefits would not accrue as opposed to total project completion for the entire segment.

Additional investigation and planning are necessary to define those areas where "excessive" pollution control measures will result in negative environmental benefits. For example, in providing agricultural runoff control to level III, it has been shown that 9 of the 19 major federal reservoirs in Kansas will not have water quality improvement, but will actually have reduced water quality resulting from increased light penetration from reduced sediment loads and the inability to reduce nutrients to the level that will not produce significant aquatic growths. The increased productivity of the lakes will bring about accelerated eutrophication. Significant bank erosion is currently taking place below clarified releases from federal reservoirs. Small

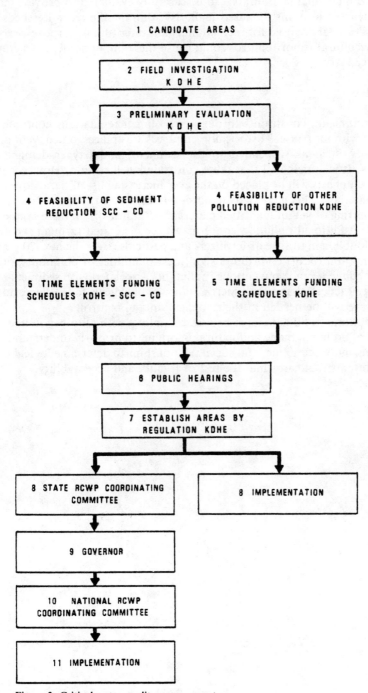

Figure 3. Critical water quality management areas.

state and municipal lakes must also be carefully evaluated to provide maximum benefits in terms of water quality. Within the limited watersheds of these lakes, that are used for recreational and water supply purposes, excessive agricultural runoff control could cause these impoundment structures to be dry lakes.

Summary

Environmental constraints through government regulations continue to increase without pause. Historically, emphasis was placed on conventional pollutants, such as suspended solids, sediment, and oxygen-demanding organics. It is anticipated that these constraints will remain. However, increased emphasis will be placed on the ever-increasing list of hazardous and toxic materials. This increased emphasis will affect agriculture through future reporting of yet unquantified materials with their origin from nonpoint sources. Additional pollution concerns will be generated through the projected doubling in the use of fertilizers and pesticides over the next 20 years.

Agricultural runoff contributes significant quantities of pollutants, principally sediment, and conventional pollutants associated with sediment. As farming practices change and increased use of chemicals takes place, additional care will be needed in their application and control.

Agricultural pollutants must be assessed, along with all other sources of pollution, both manmade and natural in origin, to properly understand the environmental, economic, and social relationships to determine logical program formats that can stand the test of legality and acceptability.

24
Maintaining environmental quality and resource productivity through intelligent watershed management

J. K. Koelliker and J. M. Steichen

A watershed is defined as "all land area and water within the confines of a drainage divide" (3). This straightforward definition is satisfying from a scientific or academic point of view. Watershed management means "use, regulation, and treatment of water and land resources of a watershed to accomplish stated objectives" (3). Watershed management clearly involves social, political, and economic factors. A technically feasible plan can fail if these factors are not fully appreciated. Political and hydrologic boundaries rarely coincide. Several competing units of government may be involved. A watershed can also involve several different ecosystems. This is easily observed in large river systems but can also be true for smaller watersheds.

Intelligent management of natural resources is one of the major challenges facing our society today. Whether the discussion is about energy resources or watershed management, the term "intelligent management" can have different meanings for different people. Decisions are made on the basis of values and beliefs as well as facts. We professional managers of soil and water resources have a responsibility to define the issues involved better. We must be clear in stating observed facts and correcting erroneous beliefs. We must then trust the public and its representatives to evaluate these facts with their own value systems and reach rational decisions.

J. K. Koelliker is associate professor of civil engineering and J. M. Steichen is assistant professor of agricultural engineering, Kansas State University, Manhattan, Kansas.

Clearly stating facts about processes within a watershed is not easy. A watershed is a complex interactive system that is difficult to conceptualize completely. Engineers and scientists have worked for years to define various aspects of hydrologic system within a watershed. We have resorted to models that, although parts are physically based, still rely on empirical or lumped parameters to define complex processes not fully understood. A watershed's reaction to a planned or unplanned change in land use, flood control, or other manipulation depends on many factors.

A watershed management plan is analogous to an environmental impact statement. Even though the plan may appear to be single-functioned on the surface, proposed action may bring about unplanned or unexpected changes. Therefore, an assessment of proposed action should be made, alternatives considered, and comments from others received.

Our nation is developing areawide water quality management plans under Section 208 of the Federal Water Pollution Control Act of 1972 (P.L. 92-500). For agricultural areas we have generally recognized and included soil erosion control with structural measures, particularly terraces. Reduced tillage systems that use crop residue to protect the soil surface from direct rainfall impact and use of cover crops are also effective in erosion reduction. These practices are examples of best management practices. Best management practices are selected to improve instream water quality. However, no strong documentation exists as to their effectiveness in improving water quality. Some correlation probably exists.

Just as with any watershed management plan, each watershed must be considered individually in developing intelligent management plans to meet Section 208 requirements.

Water quality and quantity tradeoffs

Kansas has a resource-constrained economy because there is not enough water to allow optimum crop production per unit area. Irrigation development is an answer to increased production where sufficient water is available. Surface water resources are especially scarce in western Kansas. Surface water yield there is low and sporadic. Since average annual precipitation increases nearly linearly from 410 to 1,060 millimeters (16 to 42 inches) from west to east across the state, surface water yield also increases.

The U.S. Army Corps of Engineers built several multipurpose reservoirs in northwest and north central Kansas and the Bureau of Reclamation distributes water from these reservoirs to organized irrigation districts. One of these reservoirs, Webster in Rooks County, provides an example of what might and will happen to surface water resources in this area when 208-type best management practices are applied.

Webster Reservoir is located on the upper end of the South Fork Solomon River in the Solomon River Basin (Figure 1). While the practices employed in this watershed are not aimed specifically at improving water quality, they have been adopted to reduce wind erosion and improve utilization of the rangeland resources under the Great Plains Conservation Program of the Soil Conservation Service (SCS) and Agricultural Stabilization and Conservation Service (ASCS) following the drought of the mid-1950s. However, these same practices are best management practices or similar enough to those proposed to illustrate this point.

The 2,690-square-kilometer (1,040-square-mile) South Fork Solomon River watershed is flat with a poorly defined drainage network in the western half. Stream channels lie above the water table and contain flowing water only during and after runoff events, which are few and far between. Soils in this area are deep silt loams. The eastern half of the watershed is characterized by regular branching tributary streams that give the land a rolling topography. Soils here are deep and moderately deep silt loams and clays. Annual precipitation increases from 480 to 580 millimeters (19 to 23 inches) from west to east. Annual lake evaporation is 1,500 to 1,550 millimeters (60-62 inches). Annual water yield increases from 5 millimeters (0.2 inches) at the west end to 25 millimeters (1.0 inches) at Webster Reservoir. Nearly all water yield results from surface runoff and subsequent drainout as base flow from flood waters stored in the alluvium along the stream.

The climate is characterized by dry, cold winters and warm summers. Most of the annual precipitation occurs from thunderstorms during the 170-day growing season, April to October. Rainfall is frequently quite variable over the watershed both from year to year and from a single storm.

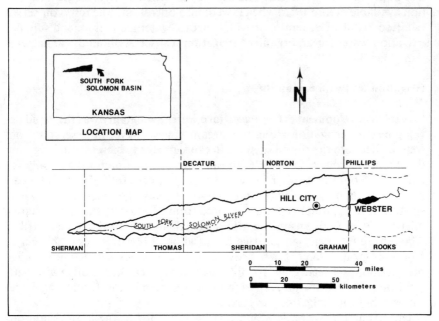

Figure 1. Location of South Fork Solomon River basin above Webster Reservoir.

Interactions of climate and crop production practices result in the need for water erosion control on sloping lands and provisions for wind erosion control on almost all cropland.

Nearly all the land in the basin is used for agriculture. Uses have remained relatively constant during 1948 to 1975, with about 10 percent in grain sorghum and corn. The remainder is evenly divided with 45 percent in cover crops of pasture, tame hay, and alfalfa and 45 percent in winter wheat-fallow (*10*). Soil conservation practices, especially terraces and stock water ponds, increased linearly during the period. About 20 to 25 percent of the land in the entire basin is terraced. About 20 to 25 percent of the entire basin is also included in the drainage area above stock water ponds. Stubble mulching on wheat-fallow increased rapidly since 1957. Today, stubble mulching is practiced on about two-thirds of the wheat-fallow acreage in the watershed.

Rapid adoption of soil and water conservation practices have helped maintain the land's productivity in the watershed. These practices have likely reduced water erosion by at least 50 percent. Stock water ponds improved pasture and rangeland utilization and management in the watershed. In many areas, water supply availability was the limiting factor in utilization of this important resource. Stubble mulching is a time-proven practice for decreasing wind and water erosion and increasing soil moisture availability for subsequent wheat production.

The U.S. Army Corps of Engineers and Bureau of Reclamation designed and built Webster Reservoir. The design was based on hydrologic information available before 1956, when it went into operation. The reservoir serves as a flood control structure, provides surface water recreation, and supplies irrigation water for an organized irrigation district of about 3,440 hectares (8,500 acres).

Irrigation and water quantity

A third development affecting surface water availability was the rapid development of irrigation along the stream valley above the reservoir from wells drilled into the river alluvium. Because of steady increases in irrigation development from 1955 to 1976, the amount of water pumped annually for irrigation from this aquifer increased more than fivefold (*7*). Withdrawals now equal about 20 percent of the long-term total water yield of the watershed. In Kansas, water rights are secured from the state by the appropriative doctrine. Prospective users file with the chief engineer of the State Board of Agriculture for such rights. Irrigation of about 2,000 hectares (5,000 acres) from this groundwater source provides increased crop productivity, forage production, and feed grain for livestock in an area that is otherwise deficient of such feed stuffs. Apparent improved resource utilization again resulted from this irrigation development.

Unfortunately, these developments have not led to the ideal conditions that were envisioned. The amount of total annual water yield and the base flow portion of that yield have decreased, especially since 1965. During the period from 1957 to 1965, the amount of total annual water yields to Webster was about as anticipated from the design calculations. During this same period precipitation was 12 percent above average. However, during 1966 to 1975, total water yield to Webster has been only about 35 percent of the amount anticipated while precipitation was only 3 percent below average. As a result, the irrigation district has had little water. Historically, total flow from the watershed equaled or exceeded the long-term average about one year in three. Since 1965, the same flows have been equaled or exceeded only once in ten years.

As a result of water yield decreases in the watershed, the Bureau of Reclamation began the Solomon River Water Management Study (1). It will evaluate possible causes for the decrease of flow into Webster. Preliminary results show that changes in soil and water conservation practices, precipitation, and groundwater withdrawal are contributing to the decrease (9).

Conservation practices are probably the main cause of the long-term decrease in flow. We used a continuous water budget model (8) to estimate the precipitation excess for Thiessen daily precipitation amounts over the South Fork Solomon River for 1948 to 1975. The annual precipitation excess (an estimate of the ability of precipitation to become runoff) correlates better with annual flows than annual precipitation does. The precipitation excess was calculated from the SCS curve number method (4) with land and cover conditions that represented conditions in the South Fork Solomon River for the period 1948 to 1956. The model held the curve numbers constant throughout the period of study and we calculated the precipitation excess for each daily precipitation amount from 1948 to 1956. The effects of precipitation differences from conservation practices effects were then separated. We compared annual precipitation excess to adjusted total flow. This included the amount measured at the gauging station plus groundwater withdrawal for irrigation upstream (7). The withdrawal was included because it has been demonstrated there is good hydraulic connection between the stream and the alluvial aquifer.

On figure 2, the lines represent best fits of the annual precipitation excess versus adjusted total annual flow for three periods. Correlation coefficients are 0.95, 0.87, and 0.71 for the periods 1948 to 1956, 1957 to 1965, and 1966 to 1975, respectively. The lines may curve upward above annual precipitation excess of 80 millimeters. Since a precipitation excess above 80 millimeters occurs only about once in ten years, those values are relatively unimportant considering the long-term water yield for the watershed. The decreasing slope of the lines for later periods can be attributed primarily to the changes brought about by adoption of soil and water conservation practices. Considering the 28-year average annual precipitation excess value of 39 millimeters (1.54 inches), we estimate that adjusted total annual flow for an average year during 1966 to 1975 would be only 40 percent of what would have been expected during the 1948 to 1956 period.

Soil and water conservation practices (best management practices) clearly reduced instream water quantity. It is questionable whether such practices should be required in areas where water quantity is already a major concern. The quantity issue overshadows the concern for quality improvement. Any watershed management plan in this type of climatic region must recognize that effects on instream water supply are foremost in importance. A water quality management plan that leaves little or no water for instream uses makes little sense.

The problem of soil erosion

The dryland wheat production region of north central Oregon has severe soil erosion problems. Parts of it are priority areas under the 208 program in Oregon. The Willow Creek watershed represents conditions in this area. Its headwaters rise on the north slopes of the northern Rocky Mountains land resource area, flow through a portion of the Palouse and Nez Perce Prairies onward across the Columbia Plateau, and finally flow through the Columbia Basin to the Columbia River on the north (5). A general map of the area is shown in figure 3.

The climate of the watershed is characterized by hot, dry summers and cold winters. Precipitation varies from less than 190 millimeters (7.5 inches) at the outlet to over 510 millimeters (20 inches) in the headwaters. Most precipitation occurs during the November to March period. Summers may have periods of more than a month with no shower activity. However, intense summer storms with rainfall rates of up to 100 millimeters (4 inches)

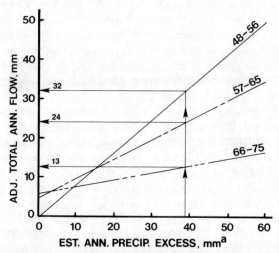

Figure 2. Adjusted total annual flow for South Fork Solomon River above Webster Reservoir for three periods 1948 to 1975, as influenced by estimated annual precipitation excess. [a]Assumes land use and cover conditions for 1948 to 1956 constant throughout 1948 to 1975.

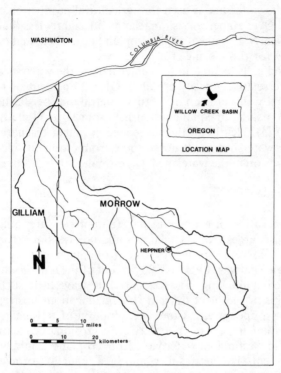

Figure 3. Location of Willow Creek basin, Oregon.

per hour can occur and occasionally cause severe flood damage but usually cover localized areas. Most of the winter precipitation at higher altitudes occurs as snow that provides for stream flows during late spring and early summer. Annual snowfall varies from over 2,500 millimeters (100 inches) in the headwaters to less than 250 millimeters (10 inches) at the lower elevations near the Columbia River.

The topography of the watershed is characterized by steep, forested mountains in the upper regions, sloping into a grassland-foothill range, changing into rolling hills, and finally undulating flats. Because the main stream and tributaries are deeply incised, relief is generally great. Landslopes are generally from 3 to 50 percent. Average landslope is about 8 percent.

Soils in the watershed are mainly of loessial origin and typically grade to finer textures with increasing distance from the Columbia River. In many locations, the underlying material has been exposed either by erosion or by lack of original deposition of soil. Finer-textured soils are used primarily for cropland unless they are too steep or shallow, in which case they are rangeland. In the upper region of the basin the elevation is too high for crop production; therefore, the lands are primarily rangeland and forest.

Nearly all the watershed is used for agricultural production as rangeland and cropland. Over 50 percent is rangeland and slightly less than 40 percent is cropland. Nearly 45 percent of the cropland is in wheat and barley and 45 percent fallow for those same crops.

The cropland soils located in the center half of the watershed have steep slopes and are relatively easily erodible. Over 30 percent of the cropland area has annual water erosion of 22 to 45 metric tons per hectare (10 to 20 tons per acre), nearly an equal amount has from 11 to 33 metric tons (5-15 tons per acre) (5). Nearly all the suspended sediment discharges from the Willow Creek watershed are believed to be from cropland since 94 percent of the gross erosion in the watershed was estimated to be from cropland (1).

Section 208 tradeoffs

At first observation, it is obvious that, to improve water quality, control of sediment discharges from cropland would be essential. From the standpoint of soil conservation measures to control upland erosion, there appear to be several alternatives. Less than 20 percent of the land needing to be terraced is treated. Fallowing practices currently leave little surface residue. Sediment basins or sediment traps at strategic locations upstream could be placed below cropped areas. Complete adoption of terracing, mulch-type fallow, and sediment traps might reduce gross erosion by at least 75 percent. At the same time, estimated water yield from cropland would be reduced by at least 35 percent. The net result would be a reduction of average annual water yield of about 11 percent from the total watershed due to the adoption of conservation practices. That decrease would not be significant since downstream use of water from cropland is not critical.

An 11 percent decrease in runoff would result in an estimated 22 percent decrease in total sediment delivered to the outlet of the watershed. Net result and major benefit to improved water quality would be about 80,000 metric tons (90,000 tons) less sediment annually added to the Columbia River system. That much less sediment would have little impact on water quality in the Columbia. The amount of sediment dischargd would be reduced much less than the amount of soil erosion prevented upstream. This can be attributed to conditions in the watershed. The stream channel in its lower reach appears to have been filling with sediment since crop production began. It is somewhat choked with sediments deposited as flood flows passed through. A decrease in the annual total flows would slightly decrease the sediment-carrying capacity of the stream.

However, even though water leaving cropland areas might not have its sediment-carrying capacity satisfied or exceeded, it would pick up sediment from the stream channel until the sediment transport capacity was satisfied. The sediment transport capacity of a stream is a direct function of its discharge and the availability of material from overland flow or from the stream channel. Sediment in the stream channel is available. After long periods of time when the stream cuts to more erosion-resistant materials, the amount of sediment discharged from the watershed might decrease more than indicated by the current sediment-discharge curve. Establishment of those conditions would take years.

Establishing priorities

Water quality considerations appear to be of low priority in the Willow Creek watershed. Soil resource maintenance is more important for the continued maintenance of environmental quality in this watershed. Best management practices are definitely needed. However, adopting them for reasons outlined in Section 208 would be clear deception. The estimated annual cost of $1.5 to $3 million to reduce erosion on cropland must be weighed against the average annual reduction of 80,000 metric tons (90,000 tons) of sediment delivered to the outlet of the watershed. Adotion of structural measures to control erosion, especially terracing of cropland, is open to debate. Since a portion of erosion occurs as a consequence of rain and snowmelt together, the functioning of terracing as a water-handling structure is not always assured. Snow may block the channel and accumulated runoff will flow over the terrace ridge.

Additionally, erosion occurs infrequently. When conditions that do cause severe erosion occur, they create runoff that may be of a magnitude too large to justify economically terrace-type structures to control them. Over a six-year record of suspended sediment measurements from this watershed, 97 percent of the sediment was delivered during only 1 percent of the total time in 30 percent of the total water discharge. Mulch-type systems on long, steep slopes are not effective once runoff begins since water velocities become high enough to create rills and gullies. Sediment-trapping structures must be considered temporary measures to treat symptoms of a long-term problem.

Conversion of highly erodible cropland to pasture or grassland appears to be the only approach to reduce soil erosion to allowable levels. This would necessitate a change in production on portions of the watershed from grain to livestock, primarily beef. Such a program at first appears economically unfeasible. However, our current agricultural programs are subsidizing wheat production. In this case, continued soil erosion is being subsidized by allowing otherwise marginal wheat production to remain unprofitable.

In this particular watershed, highly erodible cropland produces about 10 to 20 kilograms (22 to 44 pounds) of sediment per kilogram (2.2 pounds) of wheat produced. If the subsidy payments to wheat plus the annual cost of structural measures and cropping practices to control erosion on the erosive cropland at a level similar to grassland were instead put into subsidies for beef production, a system of agricultural production could result that would be no more costly to society. Current federal agricultural programs do not provide direct subsidy for beef production for land use changes from cropland to grassland as an alternative. However, for critical and unusual situations such as this watershed, it appears to be a workable alternative.

Regardless of the watershed management plan developed, if best management practices are required it appears that soil resource base protection will benefit more than improvement of instream water quality.

Priority planning in Missouri

The development of the Missouri 208 plan (*2*) dealing with agricultural nonpoint sources is an example of the decision-making process in watershed management. Selection of high-priority areas for funding by the Rural Clean Water Program was required.

An extensive public involvement program provided Missouri citizens with a chance to participate in this process in their home counties. They recognized that soil erosion and stream sedimentation from cropland are major problems in northern Missouri. Of course, attention was focused on the area known to have the highest soil erosion rates, the loess hills area of northwestern Missouri where steep slopes and deep soils are continuously planted to row crops, often without terracing. Annual sheet erosion of tilled cropland (about 47 percent of the total area) averages about 65 metric tons per hectare (29 tons per acre).

Priority of subbasins was made using four criteria (listed in order of importance): (1) public reservoirs—number, size, and severity of water quality and quantity problems caused by agricultural erosion; (2) potential stream habitat recovery—percentage of stream channel that has not been channelized, also capable of maintaining habitat because of channel stability; (3)

Figure 4. Statewide 208 priority areas based on potential water quality benefits from erosion control (*3*).

208 regional priority; (4) sediment delivery to streams.

Northeast Missouri had the top regional priority by this analysis. In this region the Salt River, which drains into Clarence Cannon Reservoir (Figure 4), was selected as first priority. At first, this selection surprised many. The basin was chosen because of the need to protect Cannon Reservoir and several smaller public water supplies. The streams also had greater potential for improvement. Nearly all of the streams had not been channelized, and the natural stream beds have more stone and gravel than other north Missouri streams. Streams in the loess hills of northwest Missouri are heavily channelized and flow directly to the Missouri River. Conditions similar to Willow Creek prevail.

Tilled cropland (44 percent of the area) in the Salt River basin has an average soil loss of about 47 metric tons per hectare (21 tons per acre) per year. From the standpoint of soil resource protection, this soil loss is more critical than the loss in the loess hills. Most of northeast Missouri has a claypan soil with about 25 to 30 centimeters (10 to 12 inches) of topsoil above a claypan. During the past 100 years it is estimated that about one-half of the original topsoil was lost to erosion. Unlike Willow Creek, the 208 program will have a twofold effect. Also, unlike the South Fork Solomon, water quantity will probably be affected very little by best management practices.

Conclusion

The South Fork Solomon situation vividly points out what might happen in a watershed when there is incomplete knowledge of programs and efforts being developed for a watershed by the various managers involved. While each manager may have a well-conceived plan for his portion of the watershed or for the entire watershed for a particular purpose, the sum result of applications of all programs can result in undesirable effects. In no instance is any one manager at fault. However, in the end someone or all may suffer.

Willow Creek points out that solving some of our environmental problems and maintaining resource productivity may take new and innovative planning. Those plans might not require technical innovations but instead involve political and social innovations in order that the plan become effective. In no case, however, should a program needed to bring about soil erosion control be disguised as a plan to improve water quality. In a situation such as Willow Creek, where little water quality improvement can be accomplished, such a program would decrease the credibility of those in charge of watershed management.

The planning program in Missouri emphasizes an important point to technical people. Engineers, scientists, and others working in the technical areas are often accused of misunderstanding the political process. We expect decisions to be made based on fact. We assume that by explaining the facts of a problem to another, he will come to the same decision. We must understand that decisions are based on beliefs and values as well as facts. We must rely on educational and informational programs put forth to the people, who can then make a rational conclusion and choice based on that information. At that point we may lose control. The public must be informed at an early state in the planning process. If it is involved in the identification of objectives, it will likely support the means to achieve them. This is different than holding a public hearing and announcing "this is how it's going to be." Finally, we must remember that personal values are highly regarded in our society. The right to own, use, and enjoy private property is such a value.

REFERENCES

1. Koelliker, J. K. 1979. *Evaluation of suspended sediment discharges from the Willow Creek basin.* WRRI-60. Water Resources Research Institute, Oregon State University, Corvallis, Oregon.
2. Missouri Department of Natural Resources. 1979. *Missouri water quality management plan.* Jefferson City, Missouri.
3. Soil Conservation Society of America. 1976. *Resource conservation glossary.* Ankeny, Iowa.
4. U.S. Department of Agriculture, Soil Conservation Service. 1972. *National engineering handbook, section 4—hydrology.* Washington, D.C.
5. U.S. Department of Agriculture, Soil Conservation Service. 1974. *Columbia-Blue Mountain resource conservation and development project.* Portland, Oregon.
6. U.S. Department of the Interior, Bureau of Reclamation. 1978. *Solomon River basin water management study.* Kansas Reclamation Office, Topeka, Kansas.
7. Weston, L. K. 1979. *Groundwater reconnaissance of the South Fork Solomon River basin above Webster Reservoir northwest Kansas.* Bureau of Reclamation, Denver, Colorado.
8. Zovne, J. J., and J. K. Koelliker. 1979. *Application of continuous watershed modelling to feedlot runoff management and control.* Environmental Protection Agency, Washington, D.C.
9. Zovne, J. J., and J. K. Koelliker. 1978. *Soil and water conservation practices effect on the water budget of the Solomon River basin, Kansas—Part II—effect on runoff and water yield.* Bureau of Reclamation, Denver, Colorado.
10. Zovne, J. J., H. L. Manges, J. A. Hobbs, J. A. Anschutz, and J. K. Koelliker. 1979. *Soil and water conservation practices effect on the water budget of the Solomon River basin, Kansas—Part I—A literature survey.* Bureau of Reclamation, Denver, Colorado.

IX. EDUCATING PEOPLE TO ADJUST TO ISSUES IN RESOURCE-CONSTRAINED ECONOMIES

25
Educating people to adjust to resource-constrained economies: An overview

Robert F. Keith and George R. Francis

In discussing the nature of education in resource-scarce societies, it is helpful to consider first the notion of scarcity. For most involved in conservation, the resources in question are soils, water, forests, energy, minerals, and food. The argument generally proceeds along the lines that as population expands, technology changes, and global trading patterns grow, the availability of these resources, at least on a per capita basis, will diminish—they will become scarce. Ours is not a world of equitable distribution. Scarcity has always plagued people somewhere and some more than others. What concerns many North Americans is the view that our highly consumptive lifestyles cannot be maintained at their present levels much longer and that changes are imminent. The question is, "What kinds of change?"

Though the spectre of absolute limits is significant such as in the case of petroleum, a more prevalent issue, at least in the short term, is that of relative scarcity, that is, we may not be as well off as we were previously and others may be either better or worse off than we will be. These are not inconsequential issues. As such they beg the question, "Why are important resources in scarce supply?" Is it simply that they exist in finite quantities that approach exhaustion? Is it that what we thought of as renewable, and

Robert F. Keith and George R. Francis are professors of the Department of Man-Environment Studies, University of Waterloo, Waterloo, Ontario, Canada.

271

thus infinitely available resources, are now better thought of as being finite? Is it that we perceive major ecosystems, and the vital resources of which they are composed, on the verge of destruction?

Specifically, if soils are truly a key resource for society, why are we faced with such major problems as the salinization of Canadian prairie soils and the widespread conversion of prime agricultural lands to other uses? Why is the incidence of highly toxic chemicals and acid rains threatening the viability of such an important system as the Great Lakes? Why are the wood industries of North America faced with declining supplies and the need to exploit more remote, costlier, timber stands? And why do we seem to be so vulnerable to the vagaries of energy supply and demand?

Forces shaping resource use

We are clearly faced with much more than simply a question of resource supply and demand. To understand the nature of a resource-constrained economy it is essential to recognize and deal explicitly with the political, economic, social, and ethical forces that shape and animate contemporary patterns of resource use. We are not simply confronted with physical limits. The constraints are as much ones of political, social, and institutional conditions. The control and management of resources and the distribution of benefits and costs are central questions in the resource-constraint dilemma. In casting the problem in such a framework, several issues become apparent:

• The limitations of the market place as the prime determinant of resource development and use.

• Centralized and entrenched centers of economic and political power.

• A lack of consideration of alternative futures and policies. Often, the options among which we choose do not fairly reflect the widest possible set of alternatives.

• The tendency to assume that marginal modifications to the status quo will suffice, that is, a quick technical fix buys some time.

• Our apparent inability, at least in a sustained fashion, to develop a sense of overview, a larger sense of purpose and direction in which one can juxtapose a variety of possible courses of action and recognize some of the important interdependencies.

• The failure of our institutions and organizations to forge effective linkages and develop more coordinated approaches to issues, alternatives, and opportunities.

• Growing concern for the increasing scale of economic activities and such associated issues as human alienation and powerlessness.

• A continuing belief in the validity of the growth ethic.

• A feeling on the part of many that individuals, organizations, even societies are in a state of drift and that our political and economic systems are being called upon to react to various forces, including resource scarcities, on an ad hoc basis.

Of particular concern is the nature of the human response to these issues, or as a colleague has termed it, "behavior in the crunch" (2). What follows are general observations on society and on educational responses to the "crunch" or resource-constrained societies.

Perspectives on society

To speak of education for resource-constrained economies poses several questions about the nature of our society. In particular, a sense of the future and what is fundamental and desirable for society are important considerations in any attempt to fashion educational strategies and opportunities. Our opinion is that the task confronting all of us is something more than simply adapting to or easing into a resource-constrained economy. Rather, it is a task of recognizing and designing actions towards a number of fundamental shifts in the nature of our society. While the attributes of society on which such shifts might be based are self-evident to many people, the fact remains that we have yet to embark on such a course in a systematic and sustained manner.

Clearly a central feature of the future is the notion of sustainable and high quality environments. One does not need to dwell at length on the necessity of healthy ecological and resource systems for human well-being. In part, society's concerns must shift from resource exploitation and human well-being based on consumption of capital stocks to that of conservation, preservation, rehabilitation, and sustainable human systems based upon income stocks.

Of importance too, is a greater emphasis upon social equity. Global and regional disparities persist, even increase, despite efforts to the contrary. Social harmony in the future will depend in part upon redressing current imbalances both within and between societies.

In the quest for sustainable environments and social equity some degree of decentralization and the emergence of new institutions and organizations is likely, particularly should the notions of self-reliance and self-regulation gain acceptance. This is not to suggest policies of isolation. Rather, based upon local and regional needs and resources, individuals and communities can begin to exert more influence over their own affairs. Nor does such an approach suggest peoples working at cross-purposes with others. Clearly there is a need for some over-arching sense of direction and socially acceptable goals.

Beyond this, a greater degree of autonomy for opportunity can be fostered. The educational implications of this notion are particularly important. Narrow approaches must give way to more comprehensive and integrated approaches. Disciplinary and professional specialization in education has its parallel in institutional and organizational specialization and fragmentation. Our inability to link a multitude of constituencies in an evolving design and development process constitutes one of the major barriers to the design of alternatives.

In summary, a number of shifts in society seem desirable (4):

From	To
environmental exploitation	sustainable quality environments
social inequalities and disparities	social equity
highly centralized, control systems	decentralized, self-regulating systems
vulnerable dependencies	self-reliance
the technological fix as a starting point	socio-cultural design and appropriate technology
narrow, sectoral perspectives	holism and comprehensiveness
reductionism	integration and synthesis

Perspectives on education

The social and intellectual turmoil of the 1960s and early 1970s paid particular attention to the significance of environment and resources. The degradation of ecosystems and exploitation of resources became popular issues for organized study and action. The need for broad perspectives that linked environment, society, technology, and economy was recognized and pursued. Some, but by no means all, saw the environmental education movement as a means to address fundamental questions of ecology, society, development, and futures. For those attempting such a broad mission, the purposes, the content, and the pedagogy of education were to be seriously examined and more often than not recast and redirected. The intent was to transcend traditional disciplinary and professional boundaries and to integrate particular kinds of knowledge in wider normative frameworks.

Moreover, the need to design alternative futures became an important element of such approaches to environmental education. This in turn required alternative approaches to learning, ones that emphasized evolving and flexible processes, a greater emphasis on problem-solving situations, a tolerance for uncertainty and ambiguity, and a sense of ingenuity and innovativeness. In essence, the "way we learn" became a substantive focus for environmental education.

Whether one wishes to speak of environmental education or educating people for resource-constrained economies, many of the same considerations apply. In spite of a number of efforts to redesign and redirect educational opportunities, we have changed very little overall.

Specialization, reductionism, and the consequent fragmentation of ideas and organizations laying claim to those ideas persist in spite of claims to the contrary and pleas for change. Rivalry among disciplines and professions at universities for intellectual territoriality attests to the absurd levels to which the problem has escalated. Such debates underscore our collective inability to address societal issues, such as resource-constrained economies, in broadly conceived frameworks that are explicitly normative and futures oriented.

Contemporary education also reflects the interests of such major institutions as government and business and thus the political economy of a region or country. Concern for the job-work-training functions of education, particularly at the universities and colleges, is a manifestation of this reflection. Thus, the structural attributes of the North American society and economy can be viewed as significant constraints to efforts at redesigning redirecting society.

Moreover, there is reason to question the long term capacity of both governments and business to create enough employment opportunities for our youth. Governments are retreating from the job market. Balanced budgets and cutbacks do not augur well for the employability of future graduates. The preoccupation of our economy with massive capital intensive projects likewise does not bode well for job futures. While it might be argued that by maintaining an ever-growing number of such projects and programs a continuous supply of jobs will be available, the concern here and elsewhere for resource-constrained economic futures and environmental sustainability would suggest that such a view is dubious at best.

Little attention has emerged in educational circles for alternative futures including the resource-constrained society. To some extent even environmental education has backed off this issue. The preoccupation with environmental impact assessment is a case in point. In focusing on this area of study, we risk being trapped in a situation where our work is essentially geared to mitigating the worst possible effects of development and enhancing the best. Environmental impact assessments are not used, at this time, as a method or approach to fundamental questions of society and environment. Those choices are made, then assessments conducted. There are few mechanisms in society and few opportunities in education to question seriously the underlying purposes and directions in which society is moving.

In an article on science education Locke (3) argues that the educational system has not resolved the problems that resulted in the crises of the 1960s. He suggests: "...science educators have so concentrated on professional training that they have neglected to look ahead for the majority of students and in so doing have missed a responsibility to use their immense power to shape the future....The continued increase in the rate of change to everything about us creates a need for education to become a lifelong process. Graduating no longer prepares someone for a lifetime's work. The focus of education must now be more upon how to adapt, how to predict and keep up with change." While adaptability and a lifelong approach to education ought to be central aspects of educational thinking, it should be clear that the task is more than keeping up with change. To try to keep up is to always be behind—to be reacting to something or someone else's initiatives. What is called for now is the need to conceive, design, and direct change in purposeful ways, that is, we must design futures. Whether in the fields of science, environment, or resources, our educational efforts to date are wanting.

Educational principles for the future

We are not trying to articulate yet another curriculum or set of course offerings. Rather, it is an attempt to set out a few principles upon which education for alternative resource futures might be based. The manifestation of these principles in real terms. will, and should, vary according to interests, locale, experience, issues, and opportunities.

• There is a need for more explicit approaches to the normative aspect of education for the future. Too often norms and ethics are ignored or dealt with implicitly. The concepts of environmental sustainability, social equity, and self-reliance qualify, in our view, as significant normative dimensions upon which learning experiences should be based.

• Greater emphasis in education upon conceiving, designing, and articulating alternative futures is important. The array of options needs to be expanded. Traditional approaches that emphasize extrapolations of present trends, marginal adjustments, and technical fixes will not suffice. In addition to notions of futures themselves is the need for the study of strategic and operational planning, that would move us from where we are towards preferred futures.

• The complexity of educational undertakings requires a loosening up to permit a greater degree of scope and balance to learning situations, both of which are necessary prerequisites for integration and synthesis. This is not to suggest that each of us are responsible for all things. Instead, in a vibrant, evolving learning context, the sharing and accumulation of experiences will engender wider perspectives.

• Education for alternative futures must encourage, not just tolerate, diversity. A premium must be placed upon that which is unique and creative. Traditional pedagogical approaches must not act as barriers to novel, educational pursuits. Given the current constraint situation, at least in universities and colleges, the task of educational innovation will most likely, and unfortunately, be more difficult. Instead of capitalizing upon the constraints to rethink the purposes, content, and style of education, we will probably tend to some traditional interpretations of the slogan "more scholar for the dollar."

• In keeping with the need for diversity, it will be important to view education as an evolving and flexible process. This suggests that both content (information) and process (learning, teaching styles, and contexts) should be seen as open-ended, branching, and linking systems. That which is novel, rather than proven, and general, rather than specific, should be fostered. Rough-edged activism, intellectual speculation, educational entrepreneurship, and alternative lifestyles should all find support in approaches to educating people for resource-constrained societies and alternative futures. "Order through fluctuation" (*1*) might best describe the process.

• In terms of lifelong education, the problem-solving pedagogy has distinct merit. Issue identification and clarification, the design of alternative courses of action, the evaluation of the same, the implementation and management of options, and reevaluation and redesign are basic to education for evolving alternative futures. This is not to suggest one should, or even could, ignore accumulated knowledge. On the contrary, what is required and to be fostered under such approaches is a more sensitive view of the nature of information and ways of using it. Rather than knowledge for its own sake, knowledge in support of some purpose or objectives becomes essential. Such a redirection of the knowledge-making industry is necessary.

• Very much related to the problem-solving approach is the need to invest ourselves in what are often referred to as real world issues. Whether one is concerned with local, national, or global issues working in conjunction with the diverse interests and capabilities that resource and environmental issues attract is an important feature of educating people for the future. Academic isolation can only render such institutions less relevant to the task at hand. In the real world context we can find the necessary juxtaposition of self-directed learning and other-directed learning that derives from involvement with many actors, thus creating an interdependent process.

It may well be the case that we will come to define the future not as resource scarce but as resource rich. Much will depend, of course, on how we define resources and their use. What are currently seen as constraints or limits may well be turned into opportunities and benefits. Succeeding generations may perceive the "Conserver Society" as one that is well endowed to meet basic human needs in the biophysical, social, and cultural domains.

The contribution of education to such a future at this time is in doubt. An educational system that is faced with constraints and tends toward retrenchment and self-serving traditions, will in all likelihood contribute little. An educational system that becomes increasingly innovative, flexible, and capable of fostering alternatives within itself will more likely contribute to an evolutionary perspective on alternative futures. Should the educational process adopt a broader sense of mission and a wider view of alternative approaches, the likelihood that society will reflect those views is greater. Should the educational process fail at such a task, society will in all likelihood be truly constrained.

REFERENCES

1. Jantsch, Erich. 1975. *Design for evolution.* George Braziller, New York, New York.
2. Lerner, Sally C. 1979. *Behaviour in the crunch.* Alternatives: Perspectives on Society and Environment, 8(2): 5-11.
3. Locke, Michael. 1979. *Teaching for survival in the 21st century.* Canadian Association of University Teachers Bulletin, 26(1).
4. Robertson, James 1978. *The sane alternative: Signposts to a self-fulfilling future.* James Robertson, London, England.

26
Conservation education through the planning process: The Land Between the Lakes experience

Richard L. Cottrell

Once upon a time there was an environmental movement. "We're ruining our resources" rang the hue and cry from Oakland to Atlanta. Radical youngsters found themselves fighting side by side with grandmothers of all ages to save the baby seals, stop construction of several power plants, halt the Alaskan pipeline, and "protect" Yellowstone and other parks from the tourists.

And, much of it was good, for the time was right to bring to big government and big business the restraining influence provided by a socially and environmentally conscious public.

College students across the land provided most of the leadership and much of the environmental enthusiasm. However, most college students and graduates have little or no formal education in management of natural resources. Wildlife harvest, timber cutting, stream channelization, dam and lake building, and any form of outdoor recreation not associated with wilderness were and still are bad!

Resource managers found themselves under fire for carrying on or prescribing resource activities that had evolved in the realm of so-called professionalism. Most of these well-meaning managers viewed themselves as conservationists and good stewards. Thus, they found the attacks on their prac-

Richard L. Cottrell is senior recreation specialist with the Tennessee Valley Authority, and formerly served as chief of outdoor recreation at TVA's Land Between the Lakes.

tices shocking, frightening, and bewildering.

The sciences and procedures involved in most forms of resource management are quite advanced. We know, for instance, how to handle water movement on both agrarian and wild lands. We can compute the carrying capacity of a given piece of land for domestic livestock and various species of wild animals. We also understand how to maximize timber production and even know how to manage lands for multiple uses, all without negative impact on our finite resource base.

However, as a result of the ubiquitous environmentalist, resource specialists have in recent years tended to hide their light under the proverbial basket. They often try to keep timber harvests (even selective cuts) out of sight and out of mind. They bury wildlife watering ponds deep in the woods, and woe be unto the manager who allows the public a view of bulldozer tracks in a pristine meadow.

The environmental movement has also had considerable impact on the realm of recreation services. Partly as a result of pressure from environmentalists and partly due to the strong resource orientation of the majority of today's recreation managers, the major emphasis in outdoor recreation by many federal agencies in recent years has been on the twin W's, wilderness and winter sports.

Park managers have been commended for these efforts by environmental groups, hardly surprising when you give it some thought. Most of the voices raised in defense of limited development and dispersed recreation use are the voices of the young, the well-educated, and the well-to-do.

Generally speaking, these are groups with the time, the money, the physical ability, and the inclination to take part in cross-country skiing, whitewater boating, back-country camping, long-distance hiking, all justifiable forms of recreation and all requiring wilderness of some degree for a worthwhile experience.

This emphasis on wilderness is relatively comfortable for most management types trained to deal with trees, soils, and wildlife rather than people. Wilderness users, once their resource needs are met, are generally inclined to "do their own thing" and not "bother" managers.

Intensive use—people-oriented recreation—on the other hand, requires working face-to-face with users on a continuing basis. Many resource-trained managers and planners are seemingly uncomfortable with this role.

Student reaction to recreation management challenges

Each year, a host of college students majoring in outdoor recreation visit the Tennessee Valley Authority's Land Between the Lakes to learn first-hand about on-site recreation management. During tours of TVA's developed family campgrounds, these students learn about planning and building reinforced, environmentally sound campsites (the universal campsite concept). These sites consist of a chat-covered gravel camping pad and parking spur bordered (and thus defined) by railroad ties.

Invariably, some students in every tour group challenge their tour leaders on these campsites: "I wouldn't pitch a tent on a gravel pad; nobody else would want to either."

Fact is, research indicates 69 percent of tent campers in our developed family campgrounds prefer this reinforced surface over any other surfacing material, including natural ground and grass (1). Obviously these tent campers aren't the back-packing crowd, but they are the users of family campgrounds.

Students, and others for whom environmental preservation and wilderness use are key concerns, tend to generalize their personal feelings to the public as a whole.

The young backpacker might scoff at a campsite complete with electrical hook-up and a visitor with a 22-foot travel trailer, but what about the 65-year-old grandfather whose heart condition requires refrigerated medicine? Should he be denied an outdoor experience because of a physical problem?

How many wheelchair-bound children do you see on the Appalachian Trail? Is it because these folks aren't interested in experiencing the out-of-doors? Or is it because many resource-based recreation professionals haven't considered the needs of all the people? Challenges to some are barriers to others.

Where is all this leading? Today's college student is tomorrow's manager. Their personal preferences cannot be allowed to set the direction for future recreation management. Nor can most of the nation's resources be devoted to anything less than the entire spectrum of types of users.

A national demonstration project

Professionals can share these philosophies with today's students in the hope of planting the seed of a social conscience in them. Which brings me to TVA's Land Between the Lakes, the nation's only federal demonstration in recreation, environmental education, and resource management.

In terms of recreation alone, Land Between the Lakes provides camping opportunities for families, hunters and fishermen, horseback and off-road enthusiasts, wilderness users, and organized groups; trails for the long-distance hiker, day-hiker, bicyclist, motorcyclist, four-wheeler, the handicapped, and the nature enthusiast; special programs for a host of clientele groups; day camps for the underprivileged; and consumptive and nonconsumptive recreation concerning wildlife.

The list of recreation opportunities is already quite lengthy and, most assuredly, is not static. Fulfilling the role as a national demonstration provides the forum for trying new ideas constantly.

Goals at Land Between the Lakes include managing this 170,000-acre block of public land for multiple use, providing recreation opportunities for all types of users, and sharing our findings, successes, and failures with recreation professionals and students nationwide, indeed, internationally.

The Land Between the Lakes staff has also found at least one key to imparting a bit of resource knowledge to 450 to 500 college students per year who have little or no academic inclinations toward resource management. Over the years college students majoring in outdoor recreation and resource management began to visit Land Between the Lakes in ever-increasing numbers. The impact on staff of these single visits by 10 to 15 schools each year became quite a challenge. Since TVA wanted even more schools and professionals to visit the national demonstration area, another more effective way had to be developed.

The Land Between the Lakes consortium

TVA staff also knew they had to have a part in helping resource and non-resource students learn that conservation means wise use rather than lock up, nonuse, or use for only those who are young and physically fit. One answer, after some evaluation, is the Land Between the Lakes consortium process. What is it? How does it work? What are the tangible and intangible benefits? Does it take the edge off student environmental emotionalism?

A consortium is defined as a gathering of groups with similar interests. Land Between the Lakes now has 20 universities involved in four of these consortia. Three of these include students from 15 curricula involving outdoor recreation. The fourth consortium includes students involved in the outdoor recreation option of five prominent forestry schools. Some of the schools involved include North Carolina State, Michigan State University, University of Georgia, University of Illinois, University of Missouri, University of Tennessee, and Western Kentucky University.

Objectives vary for the four consortia, but a review indicates basic similarities. Here are the objectives from the oldest of the four consortia:

1. To provide an educational environment in which students can gain proficiencies and knowledge they would not be able to acquire in the normal university classroom.

2. To develop a knowledge of the design, operation, and administration of outdoor recreational facilities.

3. To enrich the students' recreation curriculum by association with students from other universities, new instructional emphasis, specialized instructional proficiencies, and governmental agency professionals.

4. To generate a familiarity with Land Between the Lakes as a national recreation and demonstration area as a resource for post-graduation, on the job, use.

Each of the five universities may bring a maximum of 20 junior, senior, or graduate students, meaning 100 students is a full consortium. Usually at least two faculty members from each school come with these students. Land Between the Lakes provides the housing and food service as inexpensively as possible. All students and faculty are housed at Brandon Spring Group Camp.

Interestingly, the four consortia come (for most of the schools involved) at a vacation period for students. One begins on January 2; the March consortium hits the Easter break; the one in May ties into the week after semester system schools begin their summer vacation; and the September consortium comes just before quarter system schools begin their fall term.

The students come for a week or 10 days of learning and sharing together when most others are on vacation.

Curricula for the consortia

Curriculum for each consortium is designed by the faculty, including TVA, six months or so before the particular gathering. Since each consortium is given serious critique by the students, the faculty uses the ratings as a guide to next year's program.

Typical curriculum for a recreation consortium includes tours of the demonstration facilities at Land Between the Lakes and other recreational topics, such as research, visitor protection, national issues, mistakes, and programming. The faculty also brings in outside speakers from the United States Army Corps of Engineers, American Motorcyclist Association, National Park Service, Coleman Company, United States Army, and so forth.

A day of team recreation or resource problem-solving adds togetherness flavor to the process.

Each consortium includes at least one session on each of the Land Between the Lakes forestry, wildlife, and fisheries programs. Often this is the first and perhaps only exposure many recreation students ever get to the serious technical management of base resources.

They find that proper timber thinning and "crop" selection are important parts of park planning. They also learn to question "plunking" camp and picnic areas into stands of large old growth trees. They are surprised that timber management is critical to the management of wildlife, from songbirds to fallow deer.

Land Between the Lakes contains the first federally designated off-road vehicle area in the nation, and the monitoring, research, and actual use patterns are explained to most consortium groups. This is done by TVA staff and the American Motorcyclist Association. Many students are shocked to hear what has and hasn't happened to wildlife, soils, and vegetation. They also find this form of outdoor recreation can be quite rewarding if it's positively managed. Perhaps the most important findings are that users are family groups with interests similar to other trail users, that wildlife hasn't been eliminated, that many of their opinions had been formed from unfounded environmental emotionalism, that this is a form of outdoor recreation worthy of adding to the planning process.

Faculty and students alike learn that teens will camp with their families if the family campgrounds include big doses of fun programming for everyone. They also learn teens have been turned off by the no programming at all or the interpretive only practices of most agencies. We hope, too, the lesson is learned by all recreation students that park professionals should not be involved in the family alienation process, but rather in one of uniting, strengthening, and healing.

Over 1,000 students from the 20 universities have graduated from a Land Between the Lakes consortium. It is a demanding, rewarding process that is now being successfully copied by other agencies in the Midwest and South.

The "once upon a time there was an environmental movement" is still with us. Hopefully it always will be this way. The consortium process is one way to guide and channel at least a few students toward making better, less emotion-filled decisions.

Two rewards

Two rewards come to mind, both experienced in 1979. In one case, a student, who was quite belligerent during the early parts of a consortium, shook hands with me after graduation saying, "You and the other staff folks have really helped me get it all together. I was against all sorts of things before this week, but now will look beyond my likes and dislikes to research, reason, and learn how to (if possible) provide activities for everyone." Perhaps an even greater reward for the long consortium hours put in by the staff came when the American Motorcyclist Association representative said, "We are really beginning to see positive results of your consortium process. We're finding young professionals all over America who have attended one of your consortia in past years. Their minds aren't closed to working with us in providing a positive enjoyable experience for ORV users."

Hand wringing and foot stomping won't help resource managers enlighten an environmentalist. Education is the answer, and the consortium process is one good pathway to follow.

REFERENCE

1. Hultsman, John T. 1976. *Site selection criteria employed by users of impact-resistant campsites.* Master's Thesis. University of Missouri, Columbia. 98 pp.

27
Managing resource professionals to operate in an interdisciplinary process

Wayne Greenall

The following suggestions are for managers, particularly middle-level managers in the public service, who may be considering the merits and drawbacks of initiating an interdisciplinary approach to the study of a particular problem. I assume that they will be necessarily sceptical of techniques such as the interdisciplinary approach. Most probably they have witnessed or participated in the implementation of other organizational and managerial innovations in recent years. As such, they have seen one technique follow another, each heralded by great promises and each subsequently acknowledged to be inappropriate to many situations.

Thus, I expect that managers will be sceptical. I expect them to want to know if the interdisciplinary approach is appropriate to their situation and, if it is, how it can be made to work. For them, I offer the following suggestions.

Keep the big picture in mind

My first suggestion stems from the fact that I basically agree with sceptical managers. An interdisciplinary approach is often inappropriate. One way to find out if an interdisciplinary approach is called for is to think

Wayne Greenall is president of EAL—Externality Associates Ltd., Consulting Geographers, Economists and Planners, Toronto, Ontario.

about it in a broad context. However, let's first make sure that we share the same definition. An interdisciplinary approach is one that stresses interactions among the people tackling a problem. By necessity, it is a time-consuming approach.

Now, let's look at the merits and drawbacks of using this type of approach. A broad overview is required. Managers often fall into the trap of viewing the interdisciplinary approach too narrowly. As shown in figure 1, they focus on the approach itself and view it simply as a method of bringing a variety of human resources together to focus on a problem.

I believe that a broader view is required if one is to avoid launching an interdisciplinary endeavor on an inappropriate sea. Problems do not exist in a vacuum. They occur in several contexts, such as administrative, managerial,

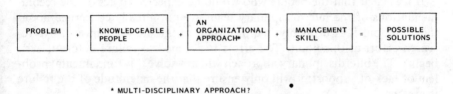

Figure 1. The narrow context for thinking about the suitability of the interdisciplinary approach.

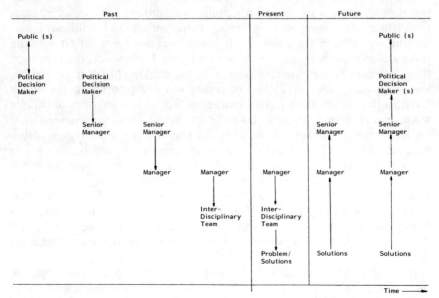

Figure 2. A broader context for thinking about the suitability of the interdisciplinary approach.

or political. Someone must define them, someone must decide that they warrant attention, and someone must decide what, if any, solutions are to be implemented to solve or partially solve them. This wider context is depicted in figure 2.

A manager faced with a problem that seems suited to the interdisciplinary approach may find it useful to evaluate the overall appropriateness of the approach by referring to figure 2. Let us assume that you are such a manager. Think for a moment. Go back in time. Who identified the problem? Was it you, your superior, his political master, or a public interest group? Then, try to look forward in time. Try to identify the types of measures that may be required to solve the problem. Are the most important ones likely to be minor administrative changes or will they involve major administrative and political changes? Are the people who would have to make such changes the same people who defined the problem?

If it is clear that the people who would be expected to act on the recommendations of the interdisciplinary team are not already concerned about the situation, it is probably inappropriate to initiate a comprehensive research effort at this point. The effort is doomed to failure before it even begins. The interdisciplinary approach will not solve this fundamental problem of lack of support; it will only ensure that the magnitude of the failure is greater.

Evaluating the time factor

The time dimension should also be taken into consideration in evaluating the appropriateness of the interdisciplinary approach. The many interactions that take place between senior management and politicians and various segments of the public while lower level managers get on with the tasks assigned to them are not shown on figure 2. However, the results of these interactions are important factors in the working life of most middle-level managers. New perceptions of reality and new priorities at the senior levels in the organization have a marked effect on the activities of middle managers. High-priority projects can be downgraded and new ones initiated on short notice. The work initiated in response to one crisis is often superseded by work to respond to a newer, more urgent crisis.

Such changes are a fact of organizational life. There is never as much time as one would like to get the job done. If one plans a lengthy study program, one runs a high risk of not being able to complete it. The answers that everyone was waiting to hear 18 months ago may be of little interest to anyone when an organization shifts gears in response to a new crisis, and the financial and manpower resources available for the study suddenly diminish.

It is important in considering the interdisciplinary approach to recognize that it is a time-consuming one and to try to assess how much time is really likely to be available for the team's work. If the problem is complex and seems to require a lengthy research program, consideration should be given to the possibility of breaking it down into a number of simpler, less time-consuming subproblems. Many of these subproblems are likely to be less demanding in terms of the amount of interdisciplinary activity required. In many cases, the simpler multidisciplinary approach, with several professionals working in parallel on a less-complex subproblem, may produce useful results in a fairly short period of time.

Meeting expectations

Another important factor to take into account in considering the advisability of using the interdisciplinary approach is that of morale. This type of approach, to be successful, has to pull people together and make them focus on superordinate goals, that is, goals that transcend their own goals. In analyzing a problem and in developing and evaluating potential solutions, a very strong team spirit is likely to develop within the interdisciplinary group. Morale will be high.

However, the high level of morale will also be accompanied by high expectations. The team will expect that many, if not all, of its recommendations will be implemented. If the team's report to senior management is not followed by action, serious morale problems will develop. Some members of the now-defunct team will resign in protest, others will stay on to fight the battle another day, copies of the team's report may be leaked to the press, and efforts to mount other interdisciplinary studies within the organization will receive reduced support. All in all, the organization will pay a high price in terms of morale.

In considering an interdisciplinary approach, therefore, it is important to clearly establish the expectations of senior management. Are they responding to a political desire to decrease public interest in the matter by referring it to a long-term study group? Do they want recommendations for actions now, particularly ones that are in agreement with decisions already taken?

In trying to decide what degree of support the team's work is likely to receive and the extent to which its recommendations are likely to be seriously considered for implementation, a manager may find it useful to establish where the problem lies on the issue-attention cycle (Figure 3). As a manager, it is important to understand this cycle. Most problems can be related to it. Consider where the pollution, energy, and inflation problems of the past decade lie at different points on the curve.

Now consider your problem. Has interest in it already peaked? Does the public no longer want to hear about sacrifices that will be required for the problem to be solved? Are politicians and senior managers, aware that this is the general public mood, only attempting to further reduce interest in the matter by assigning a matter raised by a narrow, special-interest group to a "long-term interdisciplinary study"? Is the issue nearing the peak of public interest? Is there a chance to strike while the iron is hot, provided some good policy measures can be developed quickly? Will the time that seems to be available be sufficient to carry out an interdisciplinary study? Or would a less time-consuming multidisciplinary approach be more appropriate?

These are questions that every manager should ask himself or herself before initiating an interdisciplinary approach. If you ask yourself these questions, you may well decide that the interdisciplinary approach is not warranted. However, if you decide that it is appropriate, the following additional suggestions may be of interest.

Think before you leap

Interdisciplinary groups work best as a team rather than as a loose collection of individuals. To be effective, a team needs a leader, someone in overall command of the group and with clear links to senior management.

You may well believe that any manager should be capable of running an interdisciplnary group. In principle, you may be right. However, a certain type of manager is particularly effective when put in charge of an interdisciplinary group. This is the manager who is more politician than administrator. Most middle-level managers are a bit of both. However managers who, on balance, are more politically oriented, that is they are

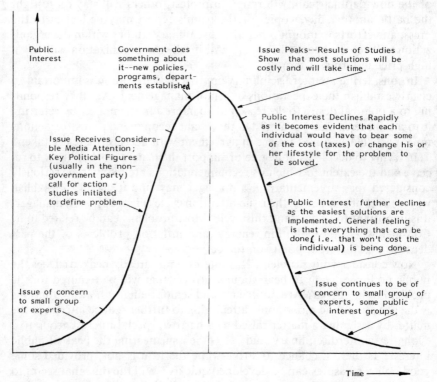

Figure 3. The issue-attention cycle.

capable of working with people to reconcile impossible demands with limited resources, are likely to be most effective at the head of an interdisciplinary team.

Such a manager will give direction to the team's work through a combination of continuing consultation and, where necessary, firm decision-making. He or she will also have the ability to establish the belief that a certain reciprocity of influence exists within the team.

This last characteristic is critical. In order for an interdisciplinary team to work effectively there must be a reciprocity of influence between the leader of the team and each member of the team. The leader can develop this by being open to the ideas and suggestions of team members, making it clear to them why their ideas and suggestions are being accepted or rejected, and, having agreed to their proposal, being willing to defend it before senior management. If a team leader is capable of doing these things, he or she will find that team members will be willing to take directions and to accept the fact that for the overall good of the team someone has to make hard decisions, particularly decisions that mean that individuals will have to channel their work along lines they would not have chosen to pursue.

Not every manager is enough of a politician to establish this reciprocity of influence within the team. You may not be such a manager. If you are not, it will undermine the team's performance. You will probably be viewed as a roadblock, somebody who does not want to rock the boat.

If you are not the political type, you should appoint someone else to lead the team. If administrative matters are more your strong point, you will be more effective and less of a roadblock if you act as the secretary to whatever high-level group is to receive the results of the team's work.

Establish a real team, not a paper team

Establish a real team. It is easier to establish a paper team, one composed of people working on the problem on a part-time basis and in their own offices. But paper teams do not work. They fail because they hinder rather than facilitate the day-to-day, informal interactions that are critical to the interdisciplinary approach. If anything, paper teams enable team members to do their own thing and provide members with ready excuses ("something else came up in our department") for not meeting deadlines.

I am not saying that one large team should be established and based in one common office. This is not necessary. Everyone need not be on hand all the time; part-time participation may be appropriate for some team members. However, the core of the group must occupy the same suite of offices and, as far as possible, spend most of their time focusing on the problem.

The members of the core group should probably be generalists rather than specialists. They should act as a managerial group, assisting the manager to take a broad overview of the problem, helping support and coordinate the manager to identify research priorities, fostering interactions among other professionals on the team, and, wherever possible, highlighting the interlinkages among the various factors associated with the problem.

Build a management core group into the structure of the team

The structure of the interdisciplinary team is an important consideration. Groups of people are like an oil and water mix. If left alone for long enough, they will stratify. This stratification should be planned rather than accidental.

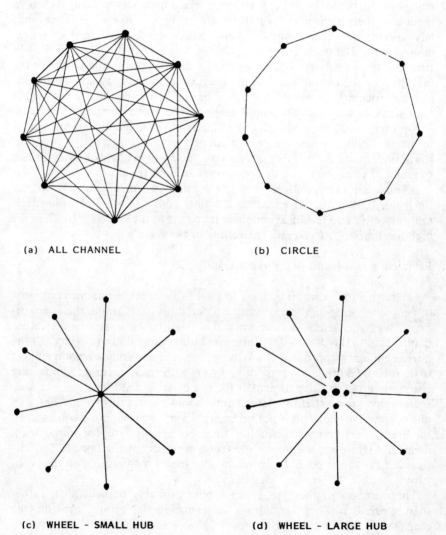

(a) ALL CHANNEL   (b) CIRCLE

(c) WHEEL - SMALL HUB   (d) WHEEL - LARGE HUB

Figure 4. Organizational alternatives for an interdisciplinary team.

Figure 4 shows the several possible ways that an interdisciplinary team could be structured. These structural alternatives have been labeled all-channel, circular, and wagon wheel. The all-channel alternative is one that involves little formal structure. It is most effective in thoroughly exploring every aspect of a problem. It is also the most time consuming. Much time is wasted and, as such, is unlikely to yield useful results in the limited time available to most teams. The circular structure imposes a certain discipline on the interactions and, thus, takes less time. However, it tends to promote individual rather than group efforts. The wagon wheel structural alternatives are perhaps the quickest to reach decisions and the best for fostering an overall sense of direction. Small interdisciplinary groups can usually be managed by one person; large groups will usually require a manager and core group at the center of the wheel.

Pay attention to the choice and use of people

Management and people are the keys to the interdisciplinary approach. To be successful, one has to have the right type of manager, the right type of people in the managerial core group, and the right people as full-time or part-time staff members. It is no simple matter to get these people. Good people are the last people that most other managers want to part with. Thus, it is easy for temporary groups, such as an interdisciplinary team, to become a dumping place for deadwood from other parts of the organization.

This tendency must be vigorously resisted. It is critical that the right people be obtained for the team. The core group should be composed of people with a technical background and sufficient experience to have broad outlooks. They should be generalists rather than specialists. It may be necessary to contract outsiders to fill some of these core group positions.

Some deadwood will inevitably creep into the team, perhaps as a result of a deal made with another manager for the use of one of his more valued staff members. One often has to take a bit of deadwood to get a key person for the team. However, one can usually move deadwood off to the side, assigning them to an administrative support role. However, no progress can be made if one does not have first-class people in key staff positions.

In selecting people for the interdisciplinary team, care should be taken to make sure that the team is sufficiently broad in terms of the disciplines represented. Research on most resource and resource-related problems will usually require the interaction of individuals from a fairly wide range of disciplines. It is important in selecting these disciplines to make sure that people trained in the soft sciences as well as people trained in the hard sciences are included on the team.

To work effectively the team must evolve

Someone once said that in any moderate-sized group of people working on a problem there will be least one benevolent despot who knows all, sees little, and from a distance keeps the peace; one peerless leader who, with self-sacrifice noticeable to all, takes on numerous responsibilities; one gloom and doom fellow who is convinced that the whole venture is headed for failure; one workaholic who keeps the whole effort going; one utopian who brings dreams, goals, and imagination to the group's work; and one blunt fellow who calls things as he or she sees them.

In a more serious vein, it is apparent that over time something happens to the individuals who come together as a group. The group itself takes on its own personality, generally one characterized by an image of success or failure. In other words, eventually the attitude of the gloom and doom fellow or the utopian comes to dominate the group.

In a well-managed team, the development of this group personality can be fostered by careful development of the core group. Most core groups will undergo several stages of development. They will evolve. Handy (*1*) identified four such changes:

• Forming. Soon after the group comes together it will discuss its purposes and objectives. Most individuals will be concerned with establishing their identify within the group through reference to their training and previous experience.

• Storming. Most core groups go through a rough period when their initial loose consensus as to purpose, approach, and individual roles is challenged, debated, and re-established. Personal agendas usually surface at this time, and a considerable amount of interpersonal hostility occurs. Some people even leave the core group.

• Norming. If the storming period has been successful and the core group has been able to reach a consensus on more realistic set of objectives, procedures, and roles, it will re-form through reference to these revised norms. Some additional storms may occur as the core group reorientates the rest of the team to these norms. At this stage, agreement will be reached within the team on matters such as to how decisions are to be taken, the levels of interpersonal trust and openness that are appropriate, and the degree of commitment to the team's superordinate goals that is required.

• Performing. Once the first three stages of group development have been completed successfully, a mature core group and, eventually, a mature interdisciplinary team will emerge. As a team, it will be capable of performing well under pressure for lengthy periods.

This evolution seldom occurs naturally. There is a tendency for groups to avoid conflict, to never get into the storming stage. Instead of confronting one another, people resign from the core group or from other positions on the team. Those who remain engage in minor debates, usually without reaching any firm agreement. Hidden agendas are common at most meetings. In general, the core group fails to evolve and thus does not reach a level of performance.

This evolution can only be fostered by one person—the man or woman at the center of the group. The manager of the interdisciplinary team has to precipitate a certain amount of conflict by forcing debates on key questions early in the life of the team. Most managers tend to avoid this sort of situation because it looks messy to outsiders. However, it is vital to the ultimate success of the team and should not be avoided.

Communicating with senior management

Do not fall into the trap of thinking that the result of the team's work will be a report. Too many reports are sitting on shelves gathering dust and much of the work that went into them has been wasted.

Think instead of the various audiences that will, or could, be interested in the team's recommendations. Ask yourself what sort of language they are most comfortable with and what kinds of analogies and concrete examples they are likely to find helpful. If you have these things in mind in the early stages of the team's work, you can plan to package the results in ways that will be attractive to each of its potential audiences.

A report is probably the last thing that most audiences will want to receive. It will only be another piece of reading material. Most will want an oral presentation. My preference in making presentations to senior management is to use a dual approach. I prefer to give an oral summary of the team's findings and at the same time to show a series of slides providing concrete examples of the magnitude of the problem, the possibilities for action, and the consequences of various actions. Most of my effort goes to the development of this presentation. I play down the actual report. The report itself is usually just a series of working papers bound in a nondescript cover.

Undoubtedly, you are in the best position to know who your audiences are and what types of presentation format they will most likely want. Think about this matter early in the team's work and do not fall into the trap of putting all your effort into producing a glossy report that few decision-makers will ever read.

REFERENCE

1. Handy, C. 1976. *Understanding organizations.* Penguin Books, London, England.

X. RESOURCE-CONSTRAINED ECONOMIES: A DISCUSSION

28
Resource-constrained economies: Problems and answers

Jeff Carroll and Lee B. Shields

Within the last decade, the gap between the future availability of natural resources in North America and the demand for their use has become apparent to many people. Futurists predict that in the next decade our social, economic, and political systems may be radically altered as we adapt to serious constraints.

What will be the most critical problems we will face in natural resource management and allocation during the next 10 years? How should these problems or priorities be ranked? What can individuals, private organizations, or governmental agencies do to find solutions to these problems?

These questions were addressed during a unique roundtable discussion at the 34th annual meeting of the Soil Conservation Society of America in Ottawa. In two separate sessions, lasting most of the afternoon, more than 80 groups of 10 people each—people from all over North America—discussed these questions, then agreed on two separate lists of issues as being the most critical for the 1980s.

Instructions for the discussion

Following a brief introduction, the two groups of participants were given the following instructions:

Jeff Carroll is coordinator of environmental education programs with the Forest Service, U.S. Department of Agriculture, Washington, D.C. Lee Shields is assistant director of the Information Division with the Soil Conservation Service, U.S. Department of Agriculture, Washington, D.C.

"*Task 1*: Your first task is to select a leader for your table to: (a) aid the discussion at your table; (b) make sure you stay on schedule and finish your tasks; and (c) meet from 3:00-3:30 p.m. with leaders from other tables, present your points of view, and help develop a combined report for presentation at the plenary session and for publication in the proceedings.

"*Task 2*: You may want to select a recorder for your table to help the leader by taking notes. This is optional.

"*Task 3*: As a group, discuss and try to reach a consensus on these questions: (a) Based on your personal understanding and the presentations by the morning speakers, what resource constraints, if any, do you see in North America for the next 10 years? Why? (b) Considering social, economic, and natural resource impacts, time frame or urgency, and long-range effects, what are the six most critical constraints? How would you rank them in order of priority? (c) To address any one of these critical constraints (choose one): (i) What could an individual do? (ii) What could an organization such as SCSA do? (iii) What could a federal, provincial, state, or local government do?"

From the questions received during the discussion period, it was soon obvious that although the primary topic for the annual meeting was "Resource-Constrained Economies: The North American Dilemma" there was little agreement on exactly what constituted a resource constraint and whether or not some constraints were bad. At many tables, the discussion centered on the fact that constraints on one person's resource base or actions often mean protection of rights or property or increased profits for someone else. The realization that there were many different viewpoints and that people were affected differently by resource constraints was a valuable product of the exercise.

The critical issues

After the discussion, representatives from each table met (in each room) to develop and rank a list of the five most critical issues in a resource-constrained economy. Those issues specified by one group were as follows:

1. Poor human attitudes toward politics and changing social conditions.
2. Limited resources and the lack of recycling.
3. Declining economic conditions, including inflation and the unstable cost-benefit ratios of intensive resource management.
4. Unwise land allocation, use, treatment, and legislation.
5. Limited technology in resource management.

These are general since they represent a consensus of over 400 people. Some tables addressed physical resources, such as fuel, water, agricultural land, or air; others focused on social issues reflected in resource use, such as population growth, inflation, uhbanization, or the equalization of standards of life for all social groups.

The greatest variety of responses came from the discussions of what could or should be done. Suggested solutions ranged from strict government control of all resource uses to a return to locally self-sufficient economies. The majority of responses favored a middle-line approach for individuals, organizations, and governments, emphasizing education and the involvement of an educated public in setting policy and managing resources.

Education at all levels was considered to be of paramount importance, "to bring about change in people's expectations," so that everyone will "understand resource limitations," and so that "no one rocks the boat with 'me first' social and political action" but will all "work together."

Throughout the reports there was general optimism that North America could successfully solve its resource problems. Yet several added words of caution concerning "bureaucratic inflation," manipulation by the media and the advertising industry, and the feeling that "we don't get the true facts from government or industry."

Critical issues identified by the second group were as follows:

1. Loss or mismanagement of productive cropland.

2. Limited availability of all forms of energy.

3. Poor public attitudes reflected in a lack of personal responsibility, a lack of public support, and a lack of informed leadership.

4. Depletion of quality water supplies.

5. Declining economic conditions.

This group chose to work together on recommendations for facing the energy crisis. Many of their decisions, however, would apply to facing other constraints as well.

For individual action, their first priority was to take personal action "to conserve current energy supplies." The second and third actions were to "become personally more responsive to and involved in all environmental issues" and "to dare to try new systems and update old ones." The fourth step was to "let others know—to inform, advocate and implement," which reflected the group's sixth-ranking constraint, noted as "lack of education." As the final personal step, people should "support legislators who are concerned and active regarding energy solutions."

For organizational action, the second group recommended the following:

1. Invite lawmakers and decision-makers to informational meetings and pressure them to take informed action on energy issues.

2. Educate the public through policy statements and by speaking out on critical issues in the media.

3. Involve the public in discussions and in actually doing specific things.

4. Encourage zoning and the location of productive lands to optimize transportation and energy use.

5. Be positive; tell people what they can do.

6. Encourage low-energy farming methods.

7. Unite with other groups concerned with similar issues.

The second group also recommended that governmental agencies at all levels:

1. Provide financial incentives and positive regulation for energy problems.

2. Produce more facts and communicate them to the public.

3. Get their own programs in order and coordinate better with other agencies.

4. Provide for longer term conservation funding, and seek legislation that is flexible to meet changing situations.

5. Clarify existing legislation; do away with laws that no longer meet current needs; provide new thinking on such issues as farmland retention; set national priorities; and, most of all, provide positive leadership.

Some consensus

Both discussion groups agreed on three of the top five constraints: Loss or mismanagement of the land resource base, poor attitudes of the general public, and declining economic conditions. If the water and energy concerns of the second group were expanded, they also would fit the concern for limited resources voiced by the first group. Thus "limited technology" was the only concern not emphasized in both groups.

The recommended actions by both groups emphasized personal commitment and the education of others so that they too could become involved.

In modern society it is difficult to gain consensus on even simple problems in small groups. That more than 800 people reached this level of agreement may indicate the universality of the recognized constraints and may suggest that when united by common interest and understanding, all North Americans can work together toward a common goal.

If we commit ourselves to this end, "the North American dilemma" in the 1980s may not be as critical as predicted.

Index

Acreage, 165, 205
Acreage Reserve Program, 136
Acres American of Buffalo, N.Y., 221
Adequacy of Conservation Systems in Cropland, 160
Agricultural Stabilization and Conservation Service, 65, 259
Agriculture, 8, 26, 42-45, 59, 79, 99, 105, 123, 127, 131, 137, 140-142, 164, 177, 195, 205, 231, 247; Peri-urban, 41-42
Air, 4, 49, 51, 103, 209, 232, 244-246
Air storage facility, 218, 221-225
Air Storage System Energy Transfer (ASSET), 216-217, 220, 222, 225
Alcohol, 146-148, 212, 238
American Mining Congress, 186
American Motorcycle Association, 282-283
Animals, 127, 241, 246; bears, 237-239; deer, 235; dog teams, 236; koala, 32; lemmings, 235; mammoths, 234; musk ox, 239; wolves, 30, 31, 230
Aquifers, 223-225
Arctic Marine Oil Spill Program, 237
Argonne National Laboratory, 189
Assessments, 75-77, 85, 87-89, 93
Atmosphere, 10, 13, 234

Balance of payments, 5, 40, 133, 208, 215
Baleen, 234
Barnett, Harold, 152
Beef, 195-196
Berger, Justice, 242
Bergland, Bob, 65, 68-69, 170, 173
Berm, 241
Biomass, 110-111, 208-213, 215
Birds, 21, 230, 237

Boulding, Kenneth, 152
Boundary Waters Treaty, 50, 61
British Columbia Land Commission, 197
British North American Act of 1867, 59
Brown Boveri Corp., 220-221

Canada, 10, 14-15, 38-39, 41, 50, 55, 58, 96-97, 99-101, 119, 123-124, 126, 133, 159, 163, 172, 179, 193-197, 199-200, 207-210, 212-215, 229, 232; Alberta, 9, 230; Atkinson Point, 240; Atlantic Province, 231; Banff, 230; British Columbia, 193-198, 200, 210, 214, 230; Calgary, 230; Canada Arctic, 236; Canadian Arch, 240; Canadian prairie soils, 272; Canadian Shield, 193, 231; Cornwall Island, 231; Edmonton, 230; Ellesmere Island, 236; Fraser Valley, 197, 230; Frobisher Bay, 234; Gardiner Dam, 97; Garrison Project, 231; High Arctic, 230, 232; Hudson Bay, 236, 240; Inuit, 230, 236-238, 242; James Bay Project, 231; Jasper, 230; Keewatin Coast, 236; La Belle Province, 231; Lake Diefenbaker, 97-98; Lake Louise, 230; Labrador Sea, 236; Mckenzie, 230, 236, 239-240; Manitoba, 98, 231; Montreal, 231; Maritimes, 193-194, 231; New Brunswick, 231; Newfoundland, 231, 236; Northwest Territories, 230, 232, 238-239; Nova Scotia, 231; Okanagan Lake, 230; Okanagan Valley, 197; Ontario, 53-54, 175-177, 181, 183, 195, 210, 231; Peace River, 193; Prince Edward Island, 231; Saskatchewan, 98, 198-199, 231; Trans Canadian Highway, 230; Vancouver Island, 197; Victoria, 197; Whiteshell